Voter Backlash and Elite Misperception

Existing theories of election-related violence often assume that if elites instigate violence, they must benefit electorally from doing so. With a focus on Kenya, this book employs a wide array of data and empirical methods to demonstrate that – contrary to conventional wisdom – violence can be a costly strategy resulting in significant voter backlash. The book argues that politicians often fail to perceive these costs and thus employ violence as an electoral tactic even when its efficacy is doubtful. Election-related violence can therefore be explained not solely by the electoral benefits it provides but by politicians' misperceptions about its effectiveness as an electoral tactic. The book also shows that violence in founding elections – the first elections held under a new multiparty regime – has long-lasting effects on politicians' (mis)perceptions about its usefulness, explaining why some countries' elections suffer from recurrent bouts of violence while others do not.

Steven C. Rosenzweig is Assistant Professor in Political Science at Boston University. His research focuses on electoral violence and democratic accountability.

Voter Backlash and Elite Misperception

The Logic of Violence in Electoral Competition

STEVEN C. ROSENZWEIG

Boston University

Shaftesbury Road, Cambridge CB2 8EA, United Kingdom

One Liberty Plaza, 20th Floor, New York, NY 10006, USA

477 Williamstown Road, Port Melbourne, VIC 3207, Australia

314–321, 3rd Floor, Plot 3, Splendor Forum, Jasola District Centre, New Delhi – 110025, India

103 Penang Road, #05–06/07, Visioncrest Commercial, Singapore 238467

Cambridge University Press is part of Cambridge University Press & Assessment, a department of the University of Cambridge.

We share the University's mission to contribute to society through the pursuit of education, learning and research at the highest international levels of excellence.

www.cambridge.org
Information on this title: www.cambridge.org/9781009354899
DOI: 10.1017/9781009354905

© Steven C. Rosenzweig 2023

This publication is in copyright. Subject to statutory exception and to the provisions of relevant collective licensing agreements, no reproduction of any part may take place without the written permission of Cambridge University Press & Assessment.

First published 2023
First paperback edition 2025

A catalogue record for this publication is available from the British Library

Library of Congress Cataloging-in-Publication data
NAMES: Rosenzweig, Steven C., 1985– author.
TITLE: Voter backlash and elite misperception : the logic of violence in electoral competition / Steven C. Rosenzweig.
DESCRIPTION: Cambridge, United Kingdom ; New York, NY : Cambridge University Press, 2023. | Includes bibliographical references and index.
IDENTIFIERS: LCCN 2022062006 | ISBN 9781009354882 (hardback) | ISBN 9781009354905 (ebook)
SUBJECTS: LCSH: Voter intimidation – Kenya – Case studies. | Political violence – Kenya – Case studies. | Political crimes and offenses – Kenya – Case studies. | Presidents – Kenya – Election – Case studies.
CLASSIFICATION: LCC JC328.6 .R68 2023 | DDC 362.88/931096762–dc23/eng/20230315
LC record available at https://lccn.loc.gov/2022062006

ISBN 978-1-009-35488-2 Hardback
ISBN 978-1-009-35489-9 Paperback

Cambridge University Press & Assessment has no responsibility for the persistence or accuracy of URLs for external or third-party internet websites referred to in this publication and does not guarantee that any content on such websites is, or will remain, accurate or appropriate.

To Jen, for your unconditional love and partnership over all these years.

Contents

List of Figures	*page* xi
List of Tables	xiii
Preface	xv
Acknowledgments	xvii

1 Introduction   1
    1.1 Election-Related Violence   3
    1.2 Existing Explanations   8
    1.3 Violence as a Result of Elite Misperception   11
    1.4 Empirical Strategy   14
    1.5 Plan of the Book   18

2 Election-Related Violence in Kenya and around the World   21
    2.1 Election-Related Violence around the World   22
       2.1.1 Varieties of Violence in Electoral Competition   23
       2.1.2 Motivations for Violence in Electoral Competition   28
    2.2 Election-Related Violence in Kenya   30
       2.2.1 A History of Election-Related Violence   31
       2.2.2 Colonial and Early Independence Kenya and the Roots of Ethnic Conflict   33
       2.2.3 Elections and Violence in the Multiparty Era   35
       2.2.4 The Central Role of Political Elites   38
       2.2.5 The Case of Kenya in Comparative Context   40
    2.3 The Special Role of Ethnicity in Political Violence   41

3 Theorizing Election-Related Violence: Toward a Theory of Elite Misperception   44
    3.1 Structural Explanations   46

	3.2		Strategic, Microlevel Explanations	50
		3.2.1	Violence as Coercion	50
		3.2.2	Violence as Persuasion	56
	3.3		Violence as a Result of Elite Misperception	58
4	Violence and Election Outcomes			75
	4.1		Violence and Election Outcomes in Kenya in the 1990s	76
	4.2		The 2007/08 Post-election Violence and 2013 Election Outcomes	80
	4.3		Summary of Findings	84
5	How Violence Affects Voting: Coercion, Persuasion, and Backlash			86
	5.1		Violence as Coercion	87
	5.2		Violence, Persuasion, and Voter Backlash	91
		5.2.1	The Effect of Violence on Vote Choice	93
		5.2.2	Testing Potential Mechanisms of Persuasion	105
		5.2.3	The Effects of Ethnic Rhetoric on Voting and Violence	109
		5.2.4	Implications for Voting and Elections in the Real World	113
	5.3		Summary of Findings	114
6	Elite Misperception and Election-Related Violence			115
	6.1		Politicians' (Mis)Perceptions about the Effects of Violence and Ethnic Rhetoric on Vote Choice	115
		6.1.1	Politicians' Perceptions about the Effect of Violence on Vote Choice	117
		6.1.2	Politicians' Perceptions about the Effect of Ethnic Rhetoric on Vote Choice	119
	6.2		Is It Actually "Misperception?" Addressing Alternative Explanations	121
	6.3		Are Politicians' Misperceptions due to Lack of Information?	124
	6.4		Summary of Findings	128
7	Voter Backlash, Elite Misperception, and Violence beyond Kenya			130
	7.1		Elite Misperception, Founding Elections, and Cross-National Variation in Election-Related Violence	132
	7.2		Case Studies of Elections and Violence beyond Kenya	135
		7.2.1	Indonesia	137
		7.2.2	Pakistan	140
		7.2.3	Ghana	143
		7.2.4	Nigeria	147
		7.2.5	Brazil	151
8	Conclusion			156

Appendix A Sampling Strategy for the Survey in Nakuru, Kisumu, and Narok	165
Appendix B Supplementary Analyses	167
Appendix C Candidate Vignettes and Outcome Questions	175
Appendix D Politician Information Experiment Memo and Contact Scripts	181
References	185
Index	199

Figures

4.1	Map of violence in Kenyan parliamentary constituencies, 1992–1997	page 78
5.1	Effect of violence on vote choice	97
5.2	Effect of violence and ethnic rhetoric on support for candidate-endorsed policies	99
5.3	Attributed responsibility for violence described in the vignettes	102
5.4	Effect of violence and ethnic rhetoric on support for candidate-endorsed policies, violence affected vs. unaffected respondents, coethnics only	104
5.5	Effect of violence on voter perceptions of candidates' private goods provision	106
5.6	Effect of violence on voter perceptions of candidates' ability and effectiveness	108
5.7	Effect of violence on voter perceptions of candidates' ability and effectiveness (coethnics only)	109
5.8	Effect of violence on the salience of ethnicity and security	110
5.9	Effect of ethnic rhetoric on vote choice and violence	112
6.1	Politicians' perceptions of the effect of violence and ethnic rhetoric on vote choice	117
6.2	Politician perceptions vs. voter preferences over violence and ethnic rhetoric	121
6.3	Difference in politician perceptions vs. voter preferences over violence and ethnic rhetoric	122
6.4	Effects of providing information to MP candidates on preelection violence	127
7.1	Sankey diagram of violence in founding and subsequent elections	134
B.1	Balance on attributed violence treatment (main voter survey)	167

B.2	Balance on coethnic vs. non-coethnic treatment (main voter survey)	168
B.3	Balance on ethnic rhetoric treatment (main voter survey)	168
B.4	Balance on violence and ethnic rhetoric treatments (politician survey)	169
B.5	Effect of defensive violence on vote choice	170
B.6	Effect of violence on support for candidate-endorsed policies among young, less educated men	172
B.7	Politicians' perceptions of the effect of violence and ethnic rhetoric on vote choice	173

Tables

1.1	Summary of empirical analysis: research questions, methods, and data	*page* 16
4.1	Violence and KANU election outcomes, 1992–1997	80
4.2	Alleged perpetrators of 07/08 election violence and 2013 electoral performance	82
5.1	Effect of violence on voter turnout in Kenyan elections, 1992–1997	89
5.2	Descriptive statistics for Kenyan voter survey, $N = 483$	95
5.3	Experimental design	96
5.4	Conjoint experiment design	101
7.1	Founding election violence and violence in subsequent elections	135
B.1	Pretreatment covariate balance for violence and ethnic rhetoric treatments, policy endorsement experiments	169
B.2	Effect of violence on KANU election outcomes, 1992–1997	171
B.3	Effect of any prior violence on KANU election outcomes, 1992–1997	171
B.4	Effect of any prior violence on voter turnout in Kenyan elections, 1992–1997	172
B.5	Mean likelihood of supporting candidates across treatment groups, with 95 percent confidence intervals	173

Preface

This is not the book I expected to write when I embarked on field work for my dissertation in the fall of 2013. At the time, Uhuru Kenyatta and William Ruto – both of whom had been indicted by the ICC for their alleged involvement in the large-scale outbreak of violence in the aftermath of the 2007 general election – had recently been elected president and deputy president of Kenya. Given their electoral victory, and the apparent lack of electoral consequences for the violence, I formulated a theory of election-related violence positing that, especially in a highly polarized political environment with substantial animosity between competing groups, violence may increase candidates' support among a segment of the population by signaling certain traits – strength, commitment to the in-group, or an ability to provide protection or to get things done – that voters may seek in a candidate for office. I laid out this theory in my dissertation prospectus and designed a series of experiments meant to test its observable implications.

As the data came in, it became increasingly clear that my initial thinking was not at all in line with reality. Rather than increasing support among some segment of the population, or signaling certain traits that voters might find attractive, allegations of violence appeared to significantly undermine support for candidates for office, even among their coethnic base. Furthermore, violent candidates were viewed as less likely to deliver on the sorts of outcomes that voters most desired. In short, rather than providing some advantage, violence appeared associated with a significant electoral cost, the benefits of direct coercion aside. Given that most voters are not subject to direct coercion from violence themselves, the effects of violence on public opinion seemed substantial enough to constitute a cost that would militate against the effectiveness of violence as an electoral tactic.

Thus began my quest to understand why – despite the questionable efficacy of violence as an electoral tactic – it remained such a common tool employed by politicians seeking office in Kenya, and my attention turned to the beliefs of the candidates themselves. Were they aware of the potential for voter backlash against violence, or did they fail to perceive this and therefore overestimate its potential benefits relative to its costs? As is clear from the foregoing, I found the latter to be the case, and I found a new direction that, over the years, eventually led to the completion of this book.

Thankfully, by simply following the data, I ended up coming to a much more hopeful conclusion than my initial theorizing suggested. My hope is that the findings in this book provide – in addition to shedding light on the causes and consequences of election-related violence – some useful food for thought on potentially new, innovative approaches to combating such violence in places where it is endemic or on the rise.

Acknowledgments

I owe a debt of gratitude to numerous people in my professional and personal life for helping me to complete this book.

First and foremost, I must thank my exceptional dissertation committee: Thad Dunning, Kate Baldwin, Sue Stokes, and Steven Wilkinson, for their generous advice and support over the years. From its inception, they have offered incredibly valuable and incisive feedback that has vastly improved the project, as well as encouragement when the going got tough. Special thanks go to Thad for taking such a deep interest in my work and development as a scholar, and for acting as a tireless advocate on my behalf.

Other current or former Yale faculty who provided advice and assistance during my time as a graduate student include Ana de la O, Susan Hyde, Ken Scheve, Tariq Thachil, and Libby Wood. Thank you to all.

I had the great fortune and pleasure of going through the Ph.D. program at Yale with incredibly talented and genial colleagues. Particular thanks go to Lionel Beehner, Rob Blair, Natália Bueno, Dan Feder, Germán Feierherd, Nikhar Gaikwad, Malte Lierl, Tumi Makgetla, Constantine Manda, Lucy Martin, Gareth Nellis, Pia Raffler, Niloufer Siddiqui, Rory Truex, Guadalupe Tuñon, Mike Weaver, and Beth Wellman for their feedback, support, and friendship over the years.

The political science department at Boston University (BU) has provided an excellent intellectual home for me since the fall of 2017. Thank you to all my colleagues for creating such a warm and welcoming environment, and especially to Taylor Boas, Neta Crawford, Katie Einstein, Tim Longman, Cathie Martin, Max Palmer, and Spencer Piston for their advice along the way.

I've benefited from many valuable discussions about this project with scholars outside of Yale and BU, especially Leo Arriola, Danny Choi, Kim Yi Dionne, Jean Ensminger, Andy Harris, Mai Hassan, Jeremy Horowitz, Nahomi Ichino, Kathleen Klaus, Eric Kramon, Adrienne LeBas, Aila Matanock, Eoin McGuirk, Ken Opalo, Lily Tsai, and Lauren Young. Sarah Birch, Jeremy Horowitz, Adrienne LeBas, Gabrielle Lynch, Ken Opalo, and my BU colleagues Taylor Boas and Tim Longman participated in a terrific book conference (held virtually due to the COVID-19 pandemic) in November 2020. Thank you for taking the time to provide such detailed and useful feedback.

For my field research in Kenya, I am indebted to Faizan Diwan for his invaluable advice on survey implementation, as well as to my excellent teams of research assistants and survey enumerators: Christine Auguste, Anthony Kigera, Joshua Kubutha, James Mwangi, Carolyne Ngenyura, and Elyvalet Yegon in Nakuru; Moses Nyabola, Nicholas Otieno Moi, Sam Ouma, and Denish Owiti in Kisumu; Alex Kosen, Stanley Nkoitiko, Daniel Saidimu, and Bob Turasha in Narok; and Cecil Abungu, Imani Jaoko, and Amina Mohamed in Nairobi. Luis Francheschi at Strathmore University was instrumental in helping me find my Nairobi-based research team. Nicholas Mwenda and Tom Wolf at Ipsos Kenya were helpful partners in implementing my survey questions on their quarterly, nationally representative survey. Financial support for the research was provided by Yale's MacMillan Center for International and Area Studies, the Leitner Program in Political Economy, and the Council on African Studies, as well as Boston University through a faculty start-up grant.

Thanks go as well to Rachel Blaifeder, who served as an excellent editor at Cambridge University Press, for her helpful advice and enthusiasm for the manuscript, and to Jadyn Fauconier-Herry for supporting the publication process there. I'm also grateful to Rachel's predecessor Sara Doskow for expressing interest in the initial proposal.

Finally, and most importantly, I must thank my family. Thank you to my in-laws and the entire Breckheimer clan for their unwavering support during this very long process; to Steve Blitz, for his constant encouragement; to my brothers, Kenny and David Rosenzweig, for always making me laugh and ensuring I never take myself too seriously; to my late father, Jeffrey Rosenzweig, for stoking my interest in the world beyond our borders; and to my mother, Lizanne Rosenzweig, for instilling in me the empathy for others that I hope always guides my work. As for my three boys, Jeremy came into the world as my dissertation was nearing its completion, Asher while I worked to transition the dissertation into a book, and Dylan just as I completed final revisions with the book under contract. All have brought indescribable joy and perspective into my life. The greatest thanks by far goes to my wife and partner, Jen, who has demonstrated superhuman patience and selflessness while I pursued the Ph.D. and completed the book. From New Haven to Nairobi, to Boston and beyond, and over the many years in which I've pursued this project, I never would have made it here without you.

1

Introduction

> He protects their interests and from their enemies by giving them pangas [machetes].
> —Kenyan County Assembly Member

> I need a leader who can preach peace, not provide pangas to the youth.
> —Kenyan voter, Narok County

Violence is frequently viewed as an unfortunate yet unsurprising by-product of electoral competition in divided societies in the developing world, an unsavory but effective tactic for the politicians that use it. Wilkinson and Haid (2009, 2), for example, describe politically motivated ethnic riots as "a particularly brutal and effective form of campaign expenditure," while Klopp (2001, 503) refers to the "raw, Machiavellian success" of instigating ethnic clashes as "an effective short-term strategy for 'winning' multi-party elections." If politicians choose to employ violence, the argument goes, it is because they benefit electorally from doing so. Yet the efficacy of violence as an electoral tactic is far from certain, as is the ability of politicians to accurately infer its relative costs and benefits. As one review of the literature on election-related violence noted, existing research "seek[s] to explain when and where electoral violence happens" without adequately addressing "whether the use of violence actually advances the goals of those who deploy it" (Staniland, 2014, 113). Answers to the former question are incomplete, however, without satisfactory answers to the latter.

This book focuses on the question of how violence affects election outcomes and whether these effects are in line with how politicians – and, by extension, scholars – perceive them. In doing so, it demonstrates that – contrary to the conventional wisdom – violence is a costly electoral strategy, triggering significant voter backlash that undermines its effectiveness. Politicians fail to fully perceive these costs, and this misperception leads them to employ violence as an electoral tactic even when its efficacy is in doubt. Election-related violence can therefore be explained not solely by the electoral benefits it provides, but by politicians' misperceptions about its effectiveness as an electoral tactic.

A theory of violence resulting from elite misperception, as I describe below, can explain the incidence and persistence of election-related violence, even where its efficacy as an electoral tactic is questionable. It can also explain cross-national variation by focusing our attention on how and why misperceptions about the effects of violence emerge and persist over time, with particular attention to the outsized role of founding elections – the first elections held after a transition to multiparty competition – in shaping the likelihood of violence in elections for years to come. The findings presented in this book suggest that political elites' misperceptions about voter preferences can play an important role in determining why some countries suffer from recurrent bouts of election-related violence while others do not.

The empirical focus of the book is on Kenya, a prominent case in the literature. But the insights generated here likely apply to a wide range of cases where election-related violence is prevalent, particularly those where (1) elites are central actors in initiating violence and (2) elections are competitive enough to offer voters a real choice at the polls. In such contexts, politicians must negotiate a trade-off between the potential benefits of violent coercion and the costs of voter backlash against their use of violence, since voters are free to select alternative candidates when casting their ballots. While the literature has focused its attention on the electoral *benefits* of violence, the findings presented here suggest we must more carefully analyze its *costs*. We should also reevaluate the extent to which political elites are able to accurately assess the relative costs and benefits of violence and other electoral tactics, a task that the evidence indicates is much more challenging than commonly assumed. Encouragingly, the findings of this book suggest that violence need not be inherent to hotly contested elections in divided societies. If violence is more costly than politicians tend to believe, then efforts to combat it need not counter but rather *appeal* to politicians' electoral self-interest; simply bringing their beliefs about voter preferences in line with the reality should reduce the chances that they choose a violent approach.

1.1 ELECTION-RELATED VIOLENCE

Election-related violence is common throughout the world (Human Rights Watch, 1995a; Fischer, 2002; Bekoe, 2012; Staniland, 2014; Birch, 2020; Birch, Daxecker, and Höglund, 2020). Not just a feature of authoritarian regimes, such violence is common in places that hold competitive elections – the focus of this book – as well. It occurs in countries as diverse as Kenya, Sri Lanka, Colombia, Nigeria, Bangladesh, Jamaica, Indonesia, Côte d'Ivoire, and India, the world's largest democracy. In fact, as multiparty elections – however imperfect – have spread around the world, election-related violence is becoming an ever more prominent form of political violence.[1] With the ballot box being the primary means to power in most countries, violence is particularly likely to arise from electoral conflict rather than direct contests for power or over the nature of the regime. In a reflection of the increasing importance of election violence as a form of political violence in recent years, the number of intrastate wars (and deaths associated with them) has gone down steadily since the end of the Cold War (Gleditsch et al., 2002), whereas incidents of election-related violence increased markedly from 1989 to 2007 before reducing slightly thereafter (Daxecker and Jung, 2018). In fact, 50 percent of elections between 1990 and 2012 saw at least three incidents of violence, with deadly violence occurring in just under a third (Birch, Daxecker, and Höglund, 2020).[2] In short, while elections are meant to be a peaceful means of determining who rules, they frequently fail to meet that ideal, and election-related violence has become an increasingly important phenomenon to study and better understand (Birch, Daxecker, and Höglund, 2020).

Electoral (or election-related) violence has been defined as "violent or coercive acts carried out for the purpose of affecting the process or results of an election" (Söderberg Kovacs, 2018, 5) or "a subtype of political violence that either aims to influence electoral processes in the run-up to election day or takes place as a violent response to elections because of concerns over electoral conduct" (Daxecker and Jung, 2018, 54),

---

[1] V-Dem data from 2020 shows that all but a handful of countries hold elections – imperfect as they may be – to select national leaders, and the modal country is one that holds competitive (if flawed) elections of the type that are the focus of this book (Coppedge et al., 2021).
[2] The figures cited by Birch et al. come from the Electoral Contention and Violence (ECAV) dataset (Daxecker, Amicarelli, and Jung, 2019).

and I largely follow these definitions in this book. In practice, of course, it is often impossible to definitively ascribe motives to, or understand the specific role played by, the political actors allegedly involved in strategically fomenting violence (Horowitz, 2001, 236–238; Birch, Daxecker, and Höglund, 2020). Thus, what constitutes violence that "aims to influence electoral processes" and can therefore be characterized as election related is not always clear cut; it implies making choices about how to categorize particular violent incidents that invariably result in some Type I or Type II error.

Inherent to a motive-based definition is the idea that the violence at question is targeted at *elections themselves* – rather than, say, a regime that happens to be holding an election. In other words, violence specifically meant to influence voting would constitute electoral violence, but insurgent attacks on government institutions not tasked with administering or adjudicating elections or armed criminal groups battling the security forces – even if they occur around election time – would not.[3] Similarly, as per Paul Staniland's typology (Staniland, 2014), intra-systemic violence (i.e., violence used to influence election outcomes) would count, whereas anti-systemic violence (i.e., violence aimed at replacing the political system at large) – even if timed around elections – would not.

Leaving the issue of what constitutes *election-related* violence aside, there is also the question of what we categorize as violence in the first place. Birch, Daxecker, and Höglund (2020) define it as "coercive acts against humans, property, and infrastructure" that are "levied by political actors to purposefully influence the process and outcome of elections" (4). Yet, this leaves open the question of what constitutes a "coercive act." Furthermore, some actions that might be considered coercive – such as verbal threats or a display of weaponry – are not necessarily acts of *violence* in and of themselves. Given the greater ambiguity around what constitutes coercion – as well as the fact that the logic of making (perhaps empty) violent threats versus carrying out actual violence may differ – I narrow the concept of violence in this book to physical acts of violence against people and property. This includes murder, maiming, and rape of groups and individuals such as opposition politicians,

---

[3] Harish and Toha (2019) distinguish between voter-, candidate-, and government agency-targeted violence. But while the focus in this book is on how voters respond to violence, the violence they respond to could be targeted at any of these potential targets.

supporters, and government officials. It also includes property destruction (for instance via arson) of homes, businesses, places of worship, or political party and/or candidate offices.

An additional consideration that scholars have often cited in defining what constitutes election-related violence is its timing (e.g., Höglund, 2009; Straus and Taylor, 2012). Notably, the definitions cited above do *not* cite timing as a defining factor. In reality, violence intending to affect election outcomes – for instance by changing local electoral demography for future elections (Steele, 2011; Harris, 2013; Kasara, 2016) – can occur at any time, including years in advance of an election, or in the aftermath of a recent election as politicians look to shape the electorate for the future.[4] Voters may also consider violence perpetrated years earlier – including in the aftermath of previous elections – when making their decision about who to vote for in a given electoral cycle. Söderberg Kovacs (2018) argues that

> [w]hile we agree that electoral violence can take place at all stages of the electoral process – notably before, during and after an election – it is close to impossible to pin down the exact time period this includes (and excludes) in the context of new and emerging democracies in developing states.... The strategic electoral game is an ongoing process and an integral part of party politics itself. (6)

I concur, and I therefore follow Söderberg Kovacs and others in choosing not to narrow the focus to violence that occurs within a specific timeframe around an election.

Like Söderberg Kovacs (2018), Daxecker and Jung (2018), and others, I define election-related violence primarily by its strategic purpose rather than its timing (while acknowledging the difficulties associated with attributing motives to particular acts of violence in practice). I deviate somewhat from common definitions of the concept, however, by homing in on physical acts of violence to the exclusion of the more ambiguous (and possibly distinct) concept of "coercion." Election-related violence, for the purposes of this book, may therefore be defined as *physical acts of violence carried out for the purpose of affecting the results of an election*.

---

[4] Patterns of postelection violence in Kenya in 2007/08, for instance, looked similar in many ways to previous bouts of *pre*-election violence in terms of its targeting and geographic focus, suggesting a similar logic in which politicians sought to take advantage of the postelection chaos to shape the electoral environment for the future.

Related to the question of timing is the fact that the logic of elite misperception described in this book – whereby violence triggers voter backlash against the politicians who use it, but, failing to perceive this, they continue to employ it despite its costs – applies most straightforwardly to what has been called "pre-election" violence, that is, violence in the run-up to voting. As noted, however, (1) even postelection violence is often geared toward shaping future elections and (2) voters may take into account the participation of politicians in previous bouts of violence when deciding for whom to vote, including postelection violence that may have occurred in previous electoral cycles. The theory should therefore apply to election-related violence carried out at any point in time.

As described in greater detail in Chapter 2, election-related violence can take a number of different forms. In more authoritarian regimes, violence may be perpetrated by the state itself through the use of the police and other security forces. In cases of genuine (if imperfect) electoral competition that are the focus of this book, however, violence usually takes one of three forms. First, violence may be perpetrated by militias directly affiliated with political parties or individual candidates for office, as in Bangladesh (Husain, 2002), Sri Lanka (Höglund and Piyarathne, 2009), Pakistan (Siddiqui, 2022), or Indonesia (Wilson, 2010). Second, violence may be perpetrated by criminal gangs or armed groups allied with particular parties and candidates, as with gangs in Nigeria (Human Rights Watch, 2007; Reno, 2011), Kenya (Klopp and Kamungi, 2008; Waki Commission, 2008; Mueller, 2011; Dercon and Gutiérrez-Romero, 2012), and Jamaica (Sives, 2010), and paramilitaries in Colombia (Acemoglu, Robinson, and Santos, 2013). Finally, civilian riots may be instigated by politicians for political gain, either directly or through the use of inflammatory rhetoric, as in India (Brass, 2003; Wilkinson, 2004; Berenschot, 2012), Bangladesh (Datta, 2004), Sri Lanka (Kearney, 1985), and Indonesia (van Klinken, 2007). Violence may be more coordinated or spontaneous, more grassroots or hierarchical in its organization. Still, the most significant outbreaks of election-related violence tend to result from the maneuverings of political elites (Human Rights Watch, 1995b; Wilkinson, 2004), and it is such violence that is the focus of this book.

In Kenya, the primary case that I analyze, violence has taken all of these forms and has been a feature of politics since the reintroduction of multiparty elections in the early 1990s. In all, approximately 2,000 people were killed and 400,000 displaced in politically motivated ethnic violence throughout the 1990s (Human Rights Watch, 2002), with numerous reports indicating that the violence was largely instigated and organized by both senior and local politicians from the ruling Kenya African National Union (KANU) seeking to maintain their hold on power (Human Rights Watch, 1995a, 2002; Akiwumi, Bosire, and Ondeyo, 1999b; Klopp, 2001). Large-scale violence reoccurred around the contested 2007 election, most dramatically in its aftermath, resulting in more than 1,100 deaths and more than 650,000 people displaced (Waki Commission, 2008; Lynch, 2009). Despite being more limited in scale and less highly publicized than earlier outbreaks, communal violence killed 500 and displaced 118,000 in the run-up to elections in 2013 (Human Rights Watch, 2013). In elections in 2017, violent incidents occurred in multiple parts of the country, including in its aftermath stemming from conflict over contested results (KNCHR, 2017a,b).

Substantial evidence suggests that local and national politicians have been directly complicit in organizing, financing, directing, or inciting the violence of the last 30 years. Much of the violence from 1991 to 1998 was carried out by organized ethnic militias that had specifically trained for their missions and were allegedly paid by KANU politicians for each person they killed or home they destroyed (Human Rights Watch, 1995a; Akiwumi, Bosire, and Ondeyo, 1999b; Laakso, 2007). In addition to their direct (though behind-the-scenes) involvement in the clashes, KANU politicians laid the groundwork for conflict with the use of violent, ethnicized rhetoric (Klopp, 2001). Politicians played a similar role in more recent outbreaks of violence, including in 2007, with leaders on both sides of the contest allegedly holding meetings, providing financing, forming alliances with criminal gangs, and inciting their supporters to attack perceived supporters of the opposing party (KNCHR, 2008; Waki Commission, 2008; Mutui, 2011). Importantly, the violence in Kenya is not a purely local phenomenon outside the control of political leaders. Interviews with politicians at various levels of government revealed a widespread acknowledgment that top party officials have the ability to tamp down on local conflict should they so choose.[5]

Why is violence a common feature of elections in Kenya and other parts of the world? Why do politicians employ violence as an electoral tactic, and how does it affect voting?

---

[5] Interviews with more than five dozen Kenyan politicians, conducted from July 2014 to June 2015.

1.2 EXISTING EXPLANATIONS

In seeking to answer these questions, the literature has focused on the structural conditions that make violence a possible and potentially attractive tactic, as well as on how it may be strategically used to help parties and candidates win elections. In other words, structural theories have posited the social, economic, and political conditions that make election-related violence more likely in some places than others, while more microlevel, strategic explanations focus on why parties and candidates choose to employ violence when structural conditions make it a viable option.[6]

Structural theories have identified numerous conditions that increase the likelihood of election-related violence, usually by raising the stakes of election outcomes (Mueller, 2008; Boone, 2011; Fjelde and Höglund, 2015; Birch, 2020; Klaus, 2020) or hampering the effectiveness and impartiality of electoral administration and enforcement of the law (Mueller, 2008; Burchard, 2015; Claes, 2016). Work in this vein has argued, for example, that the likelihood of election-related violence depends on the strength of democratic institutions and levels of corruption (Mueller, 2008; Burchard, 2015; Kanyinga, 2018; Birch, 2020); electoral rules and institutional design (Burchard, 2015; Fjelde and Höglund, 2015; Claes, 2016; Daxecker, 2020); rule of law and legal accountability (Mueller, 2008; Hafner-Burton, Hyde, and Jablonski, 2013; Burchard, 2015; Kanyinga, 2018); the nature of the party system (Wilkinson, 2004; Fjelde, 2020; Wahman and Goldring, 2020); international election observation (Daxecker, 2012; Smidt, 2016; von Borzyskowski, 2019); and systems and patterns of land tenure and ownership (Kanyinga, 2009; Boone, 2011; Klaus and Mitchell, 2015; Klaus, 2020).

Other theories – including the theory of elite misperception I posit in this book – assume a context in which structural conditions make violence possible, but seek to explain why office-seeking parties and candidates choose violence in place of, or in addition to, nonviolent tactics. In doing so, existing research on the strategic use of violence by parties and

---

[6] Politicians may also, in some circumstances, strategically instigate violence with nonelectoral goals in mind, for instance, to allow themselves or their allies to seize land, or for other forms of financial gain. However, for the purposes of evaluating the theory of elite misperception put forward in this book, (1) it makes sense to focus on the *hard* cases for the theory, that is, those where winning elections *does* appear to be the primary aim and (2) even if politicians' primary aim is nonelectoral, they still must contend with the electoral effects from employing violence (at least in the competitive electoral contexts the theory applies to), so insights on those electoral effects are still relevant.

candidates has focused on how violence may help them win elections.[7] Such explanations can be categorized into two overarching mechanisms by which it might: *coercion* and *persuasion*.

Most straightforwardly, violence may be used to *coerce* voters, preventing them from voting or forcing them to vote against their preferences.[8] As a purely coercive tool, politicians may use violence to reduce voter turnout, especially among supporters of the opposition (Chaturvedi, 2005; Bratton, 2008; Collier and Vicente, 2012, 2014; Condra et al., 2018; von Borzyskowski, Daxecker, and Kuhn, 2021). They may also use it to persuade voters to change their vote for fear of reprisals (Wantchekon, 1999; Ellman and Wantchekon, 2000; Acemoglu, Robinson, and Santos, 2013), or to displace voters in order to produce a more favorable electorate in a given locality (Steele, 2011; Harris, 2013; Kasara, 2016). Importantly, while the number of voters directly affected by violent coercion is likely to be, in most cases, relatively small,[9] violence can also shape election outcomes by influencing the voting calculus of a much larger – and therefore more electorally relevant – group of voters: those that are aware of, but not directly affected by, the violence. It is therefore crucial to understand how violence influences this pivotal group of voters.

Several theories of election-related violence look beyond direct coercion to posit that violence may be used not just to coerce but to *persuade* voters to support them at the polls, for example, by shaping voter preferences or demonstrating candidates' willingness and ability to provide what voters want. For instance, in contexts where group identities are highly salient and intergroup animosity is exceptionally high, members of a particular group might obtain some expressive benefit from violence committed against a hated out-group. Thus, a politician responsible for such violence might benefit from increased support among members of the in-group to which he provided the "good" of out-group violence

---

[7] As per the above discussion of what constitutes election-related violence, the focus here is on intra-systemic (not anti-systemic) violence (Staniland, 2014).

[8] Note that while the focus here is on violence targeting voters, violence may be targeted at rival politicians or government institutions as well (Harish and Toha, 2019). As long as such attacks are aimed at influencing election outcomes – and they affect voters' decision-making calculus – they are relevant to the analysis in this book. To be sure, even when targeting politicians or government officials, those who employ violence must contend with its consequences for their standing with voters.

[9] Bratton (2008), for example, finds that just 4 percent of voters overall, and 13 percent in the most affected region, experienced instances of intimidation in the quite violent 2007 elections in Nigeria.

(Horowitz, 1985; Petersen, 2002). Violence may also be used to signal certain candidate traits that particular segments of the electorate value (Vaishnav, 2017). Politicians might use violence to signal, for example, that they are willing and able to defend their coethnics against security threats from other groups, or to signal their toughness or ability to get things done. In addition, many studies have argued that politicians in ethnically diverse societies instigate intergroup violence in an attempt to shore up their support among coethnic voters by polarizing the electorate along ethnic lines, particularly when such voters may lean toward other parties on the basis of policy preferences or cross-cutting identities (Fearon and Laitin, 2000; Horowitz, 2001; Klopp, 2001; Brass, 2003; Wilkinson, 2004).

Alternatively, violence could be an indirect by-product of other tactics that politicians find useful, such as the use of heated ethnic rhetoric. Even if violence per se is not an explicit strategy of politicians seeking to rally their coethnic base, the heated ethnic rhetoric such candidates employ in their appeals to the in-group may increase intergroup animosity and the likelihood that violence breaks out (Rabushka and Shepsle, 1972; Horowitz, 1985; Benesch, 2011).

Existing explanations for election-related violence share two untested assumptions, however, that this book seeks to address. First, in search of a rationale for why elites choose violence, existing theories assume that if elites instigate violence, that they must benefit electorally from doing so. They therefore focus almost exclusively on the benefits of violence without seriously considering its costs, thereby providing an incomplete picture of the effects of violence on election outcomes. This focus remains despite limited evidence that violence is in fact an effective tactic for winning elections, as well as the real possibility that voters may use the ballot box to reject violent candidates at the polls. Existing explanations also turn on the assumption that political elites accurately assess the relative costs and benefits of violence and act accordingly, that is, that they have adequate information about its efficacy as an electoral tactic and objectively assess that information when deciding what strategy to pursue. Such accounts discount the possibility that politicians misperceive voter preferences and the efficacy of various campaign tactics, which a growing body of research suggests is more common than the literature has tended to assume. In contrast, this book posits a theory of violence that takes seriously the possibility that violence may generate voter backlash that undermines its effectiveness as a means of winning elections, but that political elites – failing to perceive this – overestimate its ability to help them win elections and employ violence as an electoral tactic anyway.

1.3 VIOLENCE AS A RESULT OF ELITE MISPERCEPTION

I propose a theory of violence as a result of elite misperception that relies on two observations that complicate the assumptions upon which existing theories of the strategic use of electoral violence rest. The first is that, despite the focus in the literature on the electoral benefits of violence, there is good reason to believe the risk of voter backlash against violence to be substantial.[10] Large majorities of citizens in Africa and elsewhere disapprove of political violence in any form (Afrobarometer, 2014). Furthermore, even in the most violent elections, the proportion of voters subject to direct coercion is usually small, so violence has the potential to trigger an electoral backlash among those voters affected only indirectly (Collier and Vicente, 2012; Burchard, 2020; Malik, 2021; Rosenzweig, 2021; Siddiqui, 2022). Even if a candidate's hardcore supporters are willing to tolerate or even embrace violence, they must contend with a potential loss of support among a broader swathe of the electorate. With credible evidence on the effects of violence on election outcomes hard to come by, the plausibility of voter backlash against violence suggests that the possibility of violence being an ineffective or counterproductive electoral tactic must be considered.

Of course, when going to the polls, voters are limited in the choices actually available to them. For one, there may not be any viable, nonviolent candidates on the ballot; given the difficulty of coordinating around a nonviolent alternative to the major candidates, such a situation could leave voters with a choice between voting for a candidate with a history of violence or presumably wasting their vote. Second, voters weigh multiple factors – not just the use of violence – when choosing among candidates who may appeal to them in some ways and not in others. They may not feel comfortable voting for a party with a reputation for mainly representing some out-group, for example (e.g., Rosenzweig, 2020; Siddiqui,

---

[10] Politicians may obscure their direct involvement in violence in an effort to reap its benefits while maintaining plausible deniability among voters. I present evidence in Chapter 5 that voters tend to be aware of credible allegations of instigating violence, and that allegations – even against in-group politicians voters are predisposed to like – tend to "stick," even if voters have a tendency to attribute greater responsibility for violence to out-group candidates than to those from their own group.

2022). Or they may prioritize concerns other than violence, where particular violent candidates may be preferred when it comes to the issues most important to them (Boas, Hidalgo, and Melo, 2018). Such considerations can explain why we often observe voting for violent parties and candidates even when voters prefer peace. Still, they don't negate the implications of the theory that (1) all else equal, the use of violence reduces support for candidates among voters, and they might therefore perform better if they refrained from it and (2) parties and candidates that are able to establish themselves as credible nonviolent alternatives will achieve electoral success. The crucial point is not that violent coercion carries *no* electoral benefits, but rather that the costs may be considerable enough to diminish the advantages that a violent strategy may provide.

The second observation underlying the theory of elite misperception is that accurately inferring voter preferences and the effects of different electoral tactics is a much more difficult task for politicians than the literature tends to assume. As I describe in more detail in Chapter 3, studies have demonstrated significant misperceptions among political elites of their constituents' views in the US, a mature democracy where public opinion data is plentiful (Miller and Stokes, 1963; Hersh, 2015; Broockman and Skovron, 2018; Hertel-Fernandez, Mildenberger, and Stokes, 2019). Furthermore, even the most sophisticated campaigns often employ ineffective tactics in their efforts to win elections (Lau, Sigelman, and Rovner, 2007; Kalla and Broockman, 2018; Krasno and Green, 2008a). As a result, I argue we should be skeptical about the assumption that politicians are able to accurately assess the relative costs and benefits of violence and act accordingly.

Why do politicians misperceive voter preferences and the efficacy of their campaign tactics? One possibility is that politicians lack sufficient information to make accurate inferences. For politicians in younger democracies, with less sophisticated campaign technology and less information at their disposal, the challenge of accurately perceiving voter preferences and the efficacy of campaign tactics may be particularly acute. But the lack of information is unlikely to fully explain this disconnect, since politicians in even the most high-information environments misperceive voter preferences as well. Instead, common cognitive biases – such as anchoring, overconfidence, and status quo bias – can explain why politicians misperceive even when they have access to relevant information by affecting their interpretation of the information available to them. Anchoring, for example, could explain why politicians continue to employ violence – even if its true efficacy is in doubt – if a conventional wisdom has emerged from prior elections that violent tactics work. Once such beliefs are established, anchoring bias could lead politicians to over rely on these initial (incorrect) beliefs, with evidence in favor of the conventional wisdom (that violence works) accepted more readily than evidence to the contrary. In fact, recent studies of politicians across multiple countries find that they are even *more* likely to exhibit several common biases – including status quo bias, sunk cost fallacy, and overconfidence – than the citizens they represent (Sheffer et al., 2018).

I argue that, in practice, (mis)perceptions about the efficacy of the various campaign tactics available to candidates emerge around the time of founding elections – the first elections held under a new multiparty regime – and persist as a result of common cognitive biases in the decision-making of politicians competing for elected office. In short, founding elections play an outsize role in shaping beliefs about what tactics are effective for winning elections in a given electoral context for years to come. Specifically, the tactics used by the winners of founding elections become the conventional wisdom about what works, whether they actually contributed to their victory or not. Parties and candidates in subsequent elections tend to copy those tactics as they seek to emulate the perceived success of the initial winners, and common cognitive biases such as anchoring, overconfidence, and confirmation bias make it difficult for the conventional wisdom to be overturned, leading to situations where politicians believe such tactics to be effective even when evidence of their efficacy is limited at best.

With respect to violence, then, the theory of elite misperception would predict that where the winner of founding elections is observed using violence as an electoral tactic, overconfidence causes politicians to interpret this fact as reliable evidence that violence is effective, regardless of whether the winner's electoral success can be expressly attributed to their use of violence, while anchoring and confirmation bias lead politicians to seek out and interpret information in such a way that confirms their prior beliefs about the efficacy of violent electoral tactics, whether or not these beliefs are accurate. In particular, they may downplay evidence of voter backlash against the use of violence in elections. Thus, politicians may continue to believe that violence is effective – and continue to employ it – even when evidence that contradicts those beliefs comes about. The theory can therefore explain the persistence of violence in electoral competition even when its efficacy is in doubt. It can also help explain why violence tends to occur in some countries much more regularly than in others; founding elections are a critical juncture whereby the electoral tactics employed by the winner – whether violent or not – tend to persist well into the future.

This theory is most likely to apply to electoral contexts with a few key features. First, the central role of elites in this account means that it is most applicable to violence that is instigated by politicians themselves. While elites tend to play a role in most significant bouts of electoral violence (Human Rights Watch, 1995b; Wilkinson, 2004), it is less likely to explain more spontaneous or grassroots violence. The theory is also primarily applicable to contexts with real electoral competition (even if the playing field is not entirely level, as in some hybrid regimes). In the absence of competitive elections (whether because an authoritarian state rules primarily via repression, or non-state armed groups have established de facto local control), voters do not have the ability to punish violent actors at the polls, so the voter backlash against violence that the theory posits cannot occur. Finally, the theory is only relevant to contexts where violence is a viable tool in politicians' toolkit, that is, contexts where – as structural theories suggest – there is weak rule of law, an adequate supply of individuals willing and able to perpetrate violence, and little chance that elites will suffer serious legal consequences for their role in organizing the violence.

While the theory of elite misperception applies most straightforwardly to so-called "pre-election" violence – that is, violence that takes place in the run-up to an election – even violence that takes place in an election's aftermath may be geared toward shaping future outcomes, and voters have the ability to take into account earlier bouts of violence (for instance in the postelection phase) when evaluating candidates in a given election cycle. As a result, the theory should provide insight into the incidence of election-related violence that takes place at multiple points in time.

1.4 EMPIRICAL STRATEGY

This book takes a multifaceted approach to testing the theory of elite misperception and several of its alternatives, focusing on the logic of election-related violence in Kenya. As Chapter 2 describes, Kenya is an important and oft-mentioned case in the literature, with several features that are characteristic of contexts where such violence regularly occurs. Specifically, Kenya is a case where politicians are pivotal actors in the outbreak of violence; where voters go the polls in flawed yet highly competitive elections; and where violence largely takes place along ethnic lines, all of which are common to cases of election-related violence around the world. It is also a context in which violence is widely viewed as an effective tactic for winning elections, so it constitutes a "hard" case for testing a theory of elite misperception based on the idea that violence is less effective than commonly believed.

The empirical approach taken here combines experimental and observational research, quantitative and qualitative data, and survey and interview evidence with both voters and politicians to evaluate how violence affects voting and election outcomes, as well as how politicians' perceptions about voters' preferences and the effects of violence on their electoral prospects match up to reality. Much of the data I analyze comes from field research conducted in various parts of Kenya between 2013 and 2018. It also includes data that I collected and coded from reports on elections and political violence in Kenya released over the last three decades. Using this data, the book presents observational analyses of the relationship between violence and election outcomes, as well as voter registration and turnout. It reports experimental results on the effects of violence and violent ethnic rhetoric on voter support for the candidates that use it. And it presents experimental and qualitative analyses of politicians' perceptions about voter preferences over – and the efficacy of – violent electoral tactics, with data that can be directly compared to the results of the voter surveys to draw inferences about how politicians' perceptions match up to reality.

I then look beyond the Kenyan case, analyzing cross-national data on violence in elections that examines the relationship between the conduct of founding elections and subsequent trajectories of election-related violence. I also present an analysis of case studies of five countries from different regions of the world with varying levels of violence in their elections in order to get a better sense for how well the findings from Kenya travel, especially whether the mechanisms posited – for how elite misperception emerges, and for how it sustains violence – appear in other contexts.

This diversified approach – summarized in Table 1.1 – allows for a more comprehensive and credible analysis of the causes and consequences of violence than any one method can provide. The observational and experimental data, for example, help to address the deficiencies of one approach or the other. In particular, the experiments help to address challenges to causal inference that plague observational research designs; specifically, violence tends to be correlated with candidate and party characteristics that are themselves related to election outcomes, making it difficult to tease out the independent effect of violence on these outcomes.

TABLE 1.1 *Summary of empirical analysis: research questions, methods, and data*

Chapter	Research question	Method	Data
Chapter 4	What is the relationship between violence and election outcomes?	Fixed effects regression	Constituency-level data on violence and election outcomes in Kenyan elections, 1992–1997
		Quantitative & qualitative analysis of electoral performance of politicians implicated in violence	Data on alleged perpetrators of 07/08 Kenyan election violence and 2013 election results
	What is the relationship between violence and turnout?	Fixed effects regression	Constituency-level data on violence and voter turnout in Kenyan elections, 1992–1997
Chapter 5	What is the effect of violence and violent rhetoric on voter support?	Survey (vignette and conjoint) experiments with voters	Survey data from purposive sample of 483 Kenyan voters from three ethnic groups
			Survey data from nationally representative sample of 2000+ Kenyan voters
	What is the effect of violence on voters' perceptions of likely candidate performance and the salience of ethnicity and security?	Survey (vignette and conjoint) experiments with voters	Survey data from purposive sample of 483 Kenyan voters from three ethnic groups

Chapter 6	How do Kenyan politicians believe violence and violent rhetoric affect voter support and election outcomes?	Survey (vignette and conjoint) experiments with politicians

Survey data from sample of 68 Kenyan politicians

Qualitative data from interviews with sample of 68 Kenyan politicians |
| | Are politicians' misperceptions due to a lack of information about the effects of violence? | Field experiment with candidates for MP |
| Chapter 7 | Is violence more likely in a country's electoral politics when violence was employed by the winner (but not the loser) of founding elections? | Cross-national regression analysis | ACLED data on election-related violence prior to the 2013 Kenyan elections

NELDA data on national election winners and AEVD data on violence in African elections, 1990–2008 |
| | Do the theory of elite misperception and the findings from Kenya apply to other contexts? | Qualitative case studies of violence and electoral politics in a diverse set of five countries | Qualitative data from accounts in academic publications, journalistic outlets, and governmental and non-governmental reports |

17

At the same time, the observational analysis helps shore up the plausibility and external validity of the experimental results, which may not fully capture the decision-making of voters in the real world. In addition, the parallel experiments conducted with both voters and politicians allow for a direct comparison, for the first time, of voters' preferences over violence and politicians' *perceptions* of those preferences.

Furthermore, the external validity of the findings from Kenya is bolstered by the cross-national quantitative analyses and the qualitative case studies of countries from multiple world regions and with varying levels of violence. More broadly, the mixed methods approach allows me to explore both the overall relationship between violence and voting outcomes, and the particular mechanisms by which the former may affect the latter. While each individual empirical approach has its strengths and weaknesses, the combined approach allows for triangulation and complementarities that strengthen the credibility of the findings overall.

1.5 PLAN OF THE BOOK

The remainder of the book is structured as follows. Chapter 2 summarizes the nature and extent of election-related violence globally and in Kenya in particular, documenting the various forms that such violence takes. It also provides important background on the Kenyan case that is the focus of this study, describing how violence in Kenya occurs and the conventional wisdom on its causes and consequences, as well as explaining why it is a particularly useful case to study. It concludes with some discussion of the special role that ethnicity often plays in the outbreak of violence in electoral competition.

Chapter 3 begins by reviewing existing theories of election-related violence and highlighting the untested assumptions of these theories that this book seeks to address. The remainder of the chapter puts forward a theory of violence as a result of elite misperception. The theory posits that violence is just as likely to hurt as to harm the electoral prospects of parties and candidates because of voter backlash against it, but that politicians may fail to perceive this. Elite misperception can explain why violence persists even when its efficacy as an electoral tactic is in doubt.

The empirical analysis begins in Chapter 4, which examines the overall relationship between violence and election outcomes. The chapter presents results from (1) a quantitative analysis of the relationship between violence and election outcomes in Kenya and (2) a close analysis

1.5 Plan of the Book

of the subsequent electoral performance of individual politicians alleged to have instigated violence. This approach – which analyzes the relationship between real-world incidents of violence and election outcomes – provides a useful complement to the survey experimental data described in Chapter 5. The analyses in this chapter demonstrate that violence does not help, but may hurt, parties and candidates in their efforts to win elected office.

Chapter 5 explores *how* violence affects voting outcomes. It first assesses the coercive effects of violence, finding mixed evidence for whether violence effectively suppresses the votes of opposition supporters. Turning to how violence affects voting behavior beyond direct coercion, the remainder of the chapter reports the results of a series of survey experiments designed to test how violence and violent rhetoric shape voter preferences over candidates for office. The results – which are robust to the use of sensitive survey techniques that mitigate the threat of demand effects or social desirability bias – show that, rather than being a useful tool for persuading voters, violence and violent rhetoric undermine candidates' support, even among their coethnic base. Furthermore, violent candidates are viewed as less likely to deliver the sorts of public and private goods that voters want them to provide. The voter backlash against violence documented in the experiments helps to explain the results from Chapter 4 showing a lack of electoral payoff for candidates that employ violence in real elections.

Chapter 6 addresses the question of why politicians continue to employ violence as an electoral tactic despite its limited or possibly counterproductive effects on their electoral performance. Analyzing original data from qualitative interviews and experiments with politicians that parallel those conducted with voters, the data demonstrate that, notwithstanding the evidence in Chapters 4 and 5 to the contrary, Kenyan politicians believe the use of violence and violent rhetoric to be at worst irrelevant – and at best helpful – in their efforts to win office. They underestimate the size and scope of voter backlash against these tactics, which explains why they continue to use them in spite of their questionable effectiveness. Furthermore, the results of a field experiment suggest that access to information alone is not enough to correct politicians' misperceptions in this domain.

Chapter 7 explores the applicability of the findings to cases beyond Kenya and assesses the potential of the theory of elite misperception to explain cross-national variation in election-related violence. It does so by (1) analyzing cross-national data on elections and violence to explore the relationship between the conduct of founding elections and violence in subsequent electoral cycles and (2) presenting case studies of election-related violence in five countries – Indonesia, Pakistan, Ghana, Nigeria, and Brazil – with historically varying levels of violence to explore whether and how the mechanisms posited by the theory of elite misperception can explain patterns of violence elsewhere in the world.

Finally, Chapter 8 summarizes the argument and findings presented in the book, explores their additional implications, and discusses their relevance to broader debates. It argues that the book's findings point to a need for research to more carefully evaluate the costs of violent electoral tactics in addition to its electoral benefits, including more microlevel research – such as that presented here – that explores voter responses to violence. In addition, scholars should ask more explicitly whether and how political elites are able to accurately assess the relative costs and benefits of violence and other electoral tactics. Future research should delve deeper into the question of how and why elites misperceive voter preferences, and when and why it is most likely to occur.

I also note that the findings suggest an alternative approach to combating election-related violence than what local and international organizations tend to pursue. Many anti-violence initiatives take a normative approach, trying to convince the relevant actors – such as political elites or violent specialists – not to incite or participate in violence because of its negative externalities, which are many. Yet this research, by highlighting the potential for voter backlash against violent electoral tactics, may be useful for efforts to reduce violence by *appealing to*, rather than *competing against*, political elites' electoral incentives. In that sense, the book paints a rather hopeful picture. If violence occurs as a result of misperception, then correcting that misperception can effectively reduce the incidence of violence in electoral competition. Peaceful elections remain achievable in divisive, hotly contested elections around the world.

2

Election-Related Violence in Kenya and around the World

Election-related violence is a common phenomenon throughout the developing world (Human Rights Watch, 1995a; Bekoe, 2012; Staniland, 2014; Birch, 2020; Birch, Daxecker, and Höglund, 2020). According to one dataset, violence by incumbents alone has plagued more than 30 percent of elections overall from 1981 to 2004 (Hafner-Burton, Hyde, and Jablonski, 2013). In Africa, 78 percent of elections from 1989 to 2001 and 58 percent from 1990 to 2008 were characterized by some level of violence (Lindberg, 2004, 72; Straus and Taylor, 2012, 23). Globally, 50 percent of elections between 1990 and 2012 saw at least three violent incidents, with deadly violence occurring in approximately 30 percent (Birch, Daxecker, and Höglund, 2020). Election-related violence occurs in countries as diverse as Kenya, Sri Lanka, Colombia, Nigeria, Bangladesh, Jamaica, Côte d'Ivoire, and India, the world's largest democracy. Even the wealthiest democracies are not immune, as is apparent from the rise of right-wing militias and political violence in the United States (Stall, Kishi, and Raleigh, 2020; Kishi, Stall, and Jones, 2020).

This chapter summarizes the nature and extent of election-related violence globally and in Kenya in particular. Touching on a number of representative cases from around the world, it documents the various forms that such violence takes and briefly references the types of explanations that have been given for why it occurs.[1] As per the definition provided in the previous chapter, I focus on *physical acts of violence* rather than the wider set of actions that might fall under the broader concepts of coercion or intimidation.

---

[1] These explanations are addressed in greater depth in Chapter 3.

This chapter also provides important background on the Kenyan case that is the focus of this book, describing the nature and extent of the violence in the country since the introduction of multiparty elections; its roots in the outsize role of ethnicity in Kenyan politics; and conventional explanations for the outbreak of violence in the Kenyan context. It also explains why Kenya is a particularly informative case to study for gaining insight into the broader logic of election-related violence. The chapter concludes by highlighting the special role that ethnicity often plays in the outbreak of violence in electoral competition.

2.1 ELECTION-RELATED VIOLENCE AROUND THE WORLD

Violence is widespread in the context of electoral competition, especially in the developing world. In India, at least a thousand Hindu–Muslim riots resulting in 30,000 casualties occurred from 1962 to 2000 (Nellis, Weaver, and Rosenzweig, 2016), with many scholars arguing that such violence is largely political in nature (e.g., Brass, 2003; Wilkinson, 2004). The most populous country in Africa, Nigeria, has seen large-scale violence around elections as well; hundreds were killed in political clashes or targeted killings in the lead up to its 2003 elections (Human Rights Watch, 2004), and at least 300 killed in violence linked to elections in 2007 (Human Rights Watch, 2007). Bangladesh saw 2,423 incidents of interparty violence from 1991 to 2001 and 2,389 deaths from such violence from 2001 to 2006 (Moniruzzaman, 2009, 85–86), while Sri Lanka saw more than 3,000 violent incidents around its 2001 elections (Höglund and Piyarathne, 2009, 294–295). Two thousand people were killed in the period around the 1984 elections in the Philippines (Linantud, 1998). In Burundi, more than 200 violent events occurred in just the four weeks preceding its 2010 elections (Travaglianti, 2014). Jamaican election campaigns have been characterized by significant violence as well, with murders, gun battles, bombings, and other attacks a common occurrence (Sives, 2010). In Indonesia, both national and local elections have been marked by various forms of violence (Wilson, 2010; Tadjoeddin, 2014).

Historically, political violence has occurred in longstanding electoral democracies such as the UK and the US, as well. Victorian England and Wales saw at least 63 riots associated with elections from 1857 to 1880 (Wasserman and Jaggard, 2007). Meanwhile, from Reconstruction to the turn of the twentieth century, lynchings and related acts of violence targeted the newly enfranchised Black population in the Southern US, a population that achieved a good deal of electoral success before again being disenfranchised as a result of Jim Crow legislation (Hagen, Makovi, and Bearman, 2013). Though the motivation behind lynching was not always explicitly tied to electoral politics, scholars have argued that "Whites turned to violence to discourage African-Americans from voting or to guarantee that their votes advanced the interests of the white supremacist Democratic party" (Tolnay and Beck, 1995, 172). The rise in recent years of right-wing militias and instances of political violence – culminating in the attack on the Capitol on January 6, 2021, by supporters of former President Trump – indicates that violence is a possibility even in long-standing democracies such as the US (Kishi, Stall, and Jones, 2020; Stall, Kishi, and Raleigh, 2020). In fact, recent research suggests there may be a link between electoral politics and the rise of such violence, where electoral competition induces right-leaning politicians to employ threat-based, anti-minority rhetoric to mobilize voters similar to that used by ethno-nationalist parties elsewhere in the world (Nemeth and Hansen, 2021).

While common, violence in electoral competition takes different forms in different contexts, and scholars have posited various motivations for its use in different settings. In the next section, I outline the different forms that violence takes in countries around the world and, foreshadowing the more extensive theoretical discussion in Chapter 3, highlight the types of explanations that have been given for the use of violence as an electoral tactic.

2.1.1 Varieties of Violence in Electoral Competition

When politicians use violence as a tactic for winning elections, it may take a number of different forms, varying in the type of violent act, the actor perpetrating the violence, and its target.[2] Election-related violence can include murder, maiming, and rape, as well as property destruction of homes and neighborhoods, businesses, and offices of political parties, candidates, or government institutions, often via arson. The 2007/08 post-election violence in Kenya, for example, included most of these, including killings, forced circumcisions, rape, and the burning of homes and businesses belonging to targeted groups (Waki Commission, 2008).

---

[2] As per the definition of election-related violence put forward in the Introduction, the focus here is on what Staniland calls "intra-systemic" rather than "anti-systemic" violence (Staniland, 2014).

Violence also varies in terms of its perpetrators, both with respect to those organizing or instigating the violence, as well as those actually carrying it out. In the most authoritarian electoral regimes, violence may be perpetrated on behalf of the ruling party by the state itself through the use of the police and other security forces. In the cases of genuine electoral competition that are the focus of this book, however, violence is often perpetrated by non-incumbent politicians as well. Furthermore, those carrying out the violence may have a more or less direct connection to the parties and candidates themselves.

Siddiqui (2022), for instance, characterizes political party violence along a spectrum related to how directly the party is involved in actually carrying out such violence. They may engage directly by deploying their own militias or cadres; they may outsource violence to violent specialists such as criminal gangs or vigilante groups; or they may form looser alliances with violent actors (e.g., warlords or gang leaders) over whom they maintain lesser control. Staniland (2014) also categorizes electoral violence by the actor carrying out the violence, including security forces acting on behalf of the incumbent; non-state armed groups allied with the ruling party, such as militias and paramilitaries; opposition parties' armed wings; and local, unaligned actors that may operate as "free agents" and take advantage of electoral conflict to achieve their own, often parochial goals.[3] In short, a range of actors may organize and carry out elite-instigated violence; it may be organized by political elites associated with the government or the opposition, and it may be carried out by groups or individuals more or less directly connected to – or more or less under the direct control of – the responsible parties and candidates.

Overall, the violence that political elites organize in competitive electoral contexts generally takes one of three forms: (1) violence perpetrated by militias directly affiliated with political parties or individual candidates for office, (2) violence perpetrated by criminal gangs allied with particular parties and candidates, and (3) civilian riots instigated by politicians, often through the use of inflammatory rhetoric. While some cases may be characterized by one such manifestation of violence or another, it is not uncommon for politicians in a given electoral environment to engage in all three.

Politicians and their parties have organized their own militias in bids to win office in countries such as Bangladesh, Sri Lanka, Pakistan, Burundi,

---

[3] I limit the discussion here to what Staniland calls "intra-systemic" violence, which maps onto the concept of election-related violence I home in on in this book (and as described in the Introduction).

and Indonesia. In Bangladesh, Husain (2002) notes that "[t]oday, all major political parties have their own armed cadres whose main responsibility is to strengthen their 'political base' and to counter the cadres of rival political parties." Similarly in Sri Lanka, where party "thugs" are hired "for the specific purpose of obstructing the work of the other party" and "the main perpetrators of electoral violence have been the established parties" (Höglund and Piyarathne, 2009, 293–294). In Pakistan, the Muttahida Qaumi Movement (MQM), a Karachi-based political party representing the ethnic Muhajir population, has employed its own party cadres – including geographically based "hit squads" – in violent attacks on opposition voters and politicians, state security forces, and members of local ethnic out-groups (Siddiqui, 2022). In Burundi, parties that had armed wings during the civil war have employed their partisan networks of loyal ex-combatants to violently coerce voters around election time (Travaglianti, 2014). In Indonesia, parties competing in the first multi-party elections after the fall of Suharto's New Order established large paramilitary units or "task forces" called *satgas*, populated with gang members known as *preman*, that clashed during the electoral period (Wilson, 2010, 203).

It's also common for political elites to ally with criminal gangs or other violent specialists that employ violence on their behalf. According to a 2007 Human Rights Watch report, Nigerian politicians "openly recruit and arm criminal gangs to unleash terror upon their opponents and ordinary members of the public" (Human Rights Watch, 2007). Reno (2011, 206–207) cites several examples of vigilante groups and gangs in various parts of the country – including the *yandaba* in the north and the Bakassi Boys in the east – being used as toughs or strongmen to threaten politicians' opponents and settle political scores. Similarly, Kenyan politicians have used their ties to gangs associated with particular ethnic groups to perpetrate violence on their behalf (Klopp and Kamungi, 2008; Waki Commission, 2008; Mueller, 2011; Dercon and Gutiérrez-Romero, 2012), while the Pakistan People's Party has employed the People's Aman Committee militia in Karachi to threaten opposition supporters and build up territorial control over particular neighborhoods (Siddiqui, 2022). In Indonesia, political parties have recruited gang members and local strongmen as local party cadres to mobilize and coerce voters (Wilson, 2010, 203), while in Jamaica, strong ties between the two main political parties (the People's National Party or PNP and the Jamaica Labour Party or JLP) and criminal gang leaders have contributed to high levels of partisan electoral violence in Jamaican politics as well, including the creation of "garrison" communities in urban slums controlled exclusively by one party or the other through their violent criminal affiliates (Sives, 2010).

In some cases, parties will even run violent criminals as candidates for office to take advantage of their coercive capacities. In India, for example, more than a quarter of its state and national legislators have faced criminal charges, with some scholars suggesting that parties nominate such candidates because of their ability to intimidate voters (Aidt, Golden, and Tiwari, 2011; Vaishnav, 2017). Politicians may also use the violent capacities of armed groups that are or have been engaged in civil conflict to further their electoral goals. In Colombia, for example, rightist politicians have established strong ties with right-wing paramilitary groups, with the latter using their coercive capacity to influence the outcomes of elections in the areas they control (Acemoglu, Robinson, and Santos, 2013). In fact, nearly a third of Colombian legislators have been under investigation, indicted, or convicted of ties with such groups (Acemoglu, Robinson, and Santos, 2013, 21).

Finally, there are several well-known cases of civilian riots being instigated or exacerbated by politicians in hopes of reshaping the electoral environment in their favor. Often, such riots take place along ethnic or communal lines. India is one such case, having suffered at least a thousand Hindu–Muslim riots resulting in 30,000 casualties from 1962 to 2000 (Nellis, Weaver, and Rosenzweig, 2016). Studies of Hindu–Muslim violence in India have pointed to the actions and rhetoric of Hindu nationalist parties such as the Bharatiya Janata Party in stoking such violence (Brass, 2003; Wilkinson, 2004; Berenschot, 2012). Paul Brass has gone so far as to posit the existence of "institutionalized riot systems" such that "riots are a part of routine politics, precipitated deliberately to gain political advantage" (Brass, 1997, 28). In Bangladesh, we observe the inverse of the situation in India, with the Bangladesh National Party (BNP) being implicated in attacks against minority Hindus that have traditionally supported its more secular rival, the Bangladesh Awami League (Datta, 2004, 83–89). Sri Lanka, too, has seen communal pogroms directed at its Tamil minority, at least partially as a result of the success of Tamil separatists at the polls. These included large-scale riots around elections in 1977 and 1981, the latter reportedly carried out by a mob including off-duty Sinhalese policemen (Kearney, 1985, 907). In Indonesia, meanwhile, the emergence of large-scale ethnic conflagrations around the transition to democratic elections and decentralized government has been attributed to local elites competing over the newly emerging opportunities for local influence and control (van Klinken, 2007).

Election-related violence may target a range of actors in politicians' efforts to improve their chance of winning office, including voters, rival politicians, and government officials. Harish and Toha (2019), for example, distinguish violence that targets (1) voters, (2) candidates, and (3) government agencies, specifically those "perceived to be responsible for creating, enforcing, and monitoring electoral rules and procedures during an election" (693). The choice of which actors to target may be based on numerous factors; for instance, violence against voters may be seen as a more appealing option when voters' preferences are easily predicted (e.g., because they tend to vote along ethnic lines), thus making it more straightforward to target groups or individuals with a higher or lower propensity to support a given candidate or party (Collier and Vicente, 2012, 121). As for which voters are most likely to be targeted with violence, most scholars suggest that voters associated with the opposition are the primary targets (Gutiérrez-Romero, 2014; Rauschenbach and Paula, 2019), though others argue that swing voters or weak supporters may be targeted most often, with candidates and parties attempting to either intimidate the most malleable voters or coerce voters into turning out for them at the polls (Robinson and Torvik, 2009; Travaglianti, 2014).

Recall that election-related violence is defined as *physical acts of violence carried out for the purpose of affecting the results of an election*, and that violence falling under that definition may occur before, during, or after the day of the election. In fact, the timing of violence relative to an election is one way in which researchers often categorize it, with cross-national data showing that most violence occurs in the period leading up to an election, followed by the post-election period, with relatively little violence falling on the day of the election itself (Straus and Taylor, 2012; Daxecker and Jung, 2018).[4] As noted earlier, this book does not define election-related violence as occurring within a specific timeframe around an election, since violence meant to affect election outcomes can take place at any point in the electoral cycle. Relatedly, it may not always be analytically useful to characterize violence as pre- or post-election, because violence in the run-up to an election may actually reflect conflict over a previous election, or violence in an election's aftermath may be geared toward shaping future election outcomes. Should the politically motivated ethnic clashes in Narok, Kenya in 1993 – which took

---

[4] It should be noted, though, that the relatively small share of violence that takes place on election day is at least partially due to the fact that it is, in fact, just a single day. Even a highly violent election day might have fewer incidents of violence than a preelection period of six months where violence occurred on a regular but relatively infrequent basis.

place *after* the 1992 elections – be classified as post-election violence, for instance, even if a primary motive was to shape the local electoral geography for future elections? The answer is not immediately clear. Still, the timing of violence may, at times, provide insight into its strategic intent and the logic of the actors engaging in it.

In addition to its timing relative to the general election day, election-related violence can take place not just around general elections (or by-elections to fill vacated seats), but during the candidate selection phase as well, whether conducted via mass primaries or processes involving a narrower selectorate (Seeberg, Wahman, and Skaaning, 2018). As will be discussed in more detail in Chapter 3, while the specific conditions that appear to increase the risk of violence at the nomination stage differ from those associated with violence in general elections (Goldring and Wahman, 2018; Mac Giollabhui, 2018; Reeder and Seeberg, 2018; Seeberg, Wahman, and Skaaning, 2018; Wanyama and Elklit, 2018; Turnbull, 2021), the overarching themes – that violence is more likely in contests viewed as higher stakes, and where the selection process is marred by weak procedures or poor implementation of those procedures – are in fact quite similar to the conditions identified by structural theories that seek to explain election-related violence more generally.

2.1.2 Motivations for Violence in Electoral Competition

Scholars have offered various motivations for the use of violence in electoral competition. Some suggest that politicians employ violence for the purely coercive electoral benefits it provides. In Nigeria, for example, politicians mobilize gangs "to attack their sponsors' rivals, intimidate members of the public, rig elections and protect their patrons from similar attacks" (Human Rights Watch, 2007, 23). In Colombia, right-wing paramilitary groups have been used to terrorize voters into voting for rightist candidates or coerce them into staying away from the polls (Acemoglu, Robinson, and Santos, 2013, 22). Armed youth wings of parties in Burundi have been used to intimidate and threaten opposition supporters and party defectors in Burundi, as well (Travaglianti, 2014, 19). In Jamaica's 2007 elections, partisan violence was used in marginal constituencies "in an attempt to 'switch' individual and community allegiance, to intimidate those who had already switched sides and to scare people away from voting" (Sives, 2010, 173).

In other cases, violence may be used not just to coerce but to persuade. It may be used, for example, to signal strength to supporters or potential supporters, a display of a party or candidate's willingness or ability to protect their own. Thus, in Burundi parties are said to use violence "in order to signal their strength and their ability to protect supporters, punish political defectors, and coerce political opponents" (Travaglianti, 2014, 3). Such a logic is perhaps most commonly cited in cases where politicians seek to appeal to a particular identity group's interest, for instance, along ethnic lines. In India, for example, scholars have posited that Hindu nationalist parties stoke Hindu–Muslim riots in order to polarize the electorate along ethno-religious lines and shore up the support of majority Hindu voters (Brass, 2003; Wilkinson, 2004; Berenschot, 2012), while in democratizing Indonesia local elites "mobilized crowds along ethnic and religious lines in order to maintain their privileged access to the state" and "change the electoral balance ... with an eye to the future" (van Klinken, 2007, 139–140). Where electoral competition is primarily between parties representing particular ethnic groups, violence may be used as a form of "ethnic outbidding" (Rabushka and Shepsle, 1972; Horowitz, 1985, 2001), where parties and candidates use violence to signal that they are best able or willing to protect their group's interests. In Sri Lanka, Kapferer (1988, 100) argues that the Sinhalese President Jayawardene was faulted by Sinhalese Buddhists for his weakness in countering Tamil interests by "not killing enough," suggesting that violent attacks on Sri Lankan Tamils would mobilize his Sinhalese electoral base. Similarly, Horowitz (2001, 241) argues that "[i]n a climate of ethnic polarization, a leader unambiguously associated with the cause of the Sinhalese would have a clear advantage, so much so that it might be reasonable to push the polarization along, even if that meant organizing violence." In India, Vaishnav (2017) argues that parties nominate violent criminals for office because voters perceive criminality as a credible signal of a coethnic candidate's ability to protect their group's interest.[5]

In sum, violence, in various forms and with various motivations, is a common feature of electoral competition through the world. I now turn to a description of election-related violence in Kenya in particular, including the history and historical roots of violence, its nature and extent over time, and conventional explanations for the outbreak of violence in multiparty electoral competition. Though every case maintains its own idiosyncrasies, Kenya, as we shall see, is representative of the cases of election-related violence this book seeks to explain: those where political elites play a primary role in instigating violence; where violence is a

---

[5] Though see Banerjee et al. (2014) for evidence against this hypothesis.

viable tool in the politician's toolkit due to weak rule of law and a lack of legal consequences; and where elections are competitive enough that voters have a genuine choice at the polls.[6]

2.2 ELECTION-RELATED VIOLENCE IN KENYA

Kenya is an important and well-studied case in the literature on election-related violence.[7] In Kenya, electoral politics – for reasons enumerated in greater detail below – has tended to revolve around ethnicity, with ethnic affiliation largely defining the major political cleavages, electoral coalitions, and patterns of voting. The country is home to more than 40 officially recognized "tribes" (ethnolinguistic groups),[8] but national-level political conflict since independence has primarily involved elites and coalitions of the largest groups, particularly the Kikuyu, Luo, and Kalenjin, from whom all the major presidential contenders have been drawn. No single group makes up anywhere near a majority; the Kikuyu are the largest at about 17 percent of the population, whereas the Luo make up just under 11 percent and the Kalenjin 13 percent (Kenya National Bureau of Statistics, 2019); however, the Kikuyu have tended to combine with closely related groups elsewhere in the Mount Kenya region (including the Embu and Meru) to make up a larger voting bloc of just over 20 percent of the population. Others, including the large Luhya and Kamba populations and many smaller groups, have often moved – or split their votes – between shifting political coalitions contesting for national power over time. The lack of a majority group means that winning national elections requires cobbling together multiethnic coalitions rather than simply mobilizing voters that share a single identity (Horowitz, 2016). Still, each of Kenya's five presidents have come from the Kikuyu or Kalenjin groups, with the leading Luo politicians and their parties historically serving in opposition.[9]

---

[6] These scope conditions are discussed in more detail at the end of Chapter 3.
[7] See, for example, Klopp (2001); Kagwanja (2003); Anderson and Lochery (2008); Cheeseman (2008); Mueller (2008); Kanyinga (2009); LeBas (2010); Boone (2011); Kanyinga (2011); Dercon and Gutiérrez-Romero (2012); Gutiérrez-Romero (2014); Harris (2013); Kasara (2016); Malik (2018); Wanyama and Elklit (2018); Mutahi and Ruteere (2019); Gutiérrez-Romero and LeBas (2020); and Klaus (2020).
[8] The true number of "official" tribes is not entirely clear and is itself a political issue (Balaton-Chrimes, 2021).
[9] The historical trajectory of Kenya's electoral politics and ethnic coalitions and their relationship to outbreaks of violence is described in more detail below. At the time this book

2.2.1 A History of Election-Related Violence

While the country has a long history of political violence, including assassinations and state-sponsored repression (Kenya Truth Justice and Reconciliation Commission, 2013), the regular occurrence of large-scale, politically motivated violence has largely been a feature of Kenyan politics only since the reintroduction of multiparty elections in the early 1990s. The first outbreaks of such violence – often referred to as "tribal clashes" – occurred in the lead up to the first multiparty elections in 1992, when President Moi and his ruling party KANU faced competition from other parties for the first time in decades. They began with an attack by Kalenjin residents (from the president's ethnic group) on non-Kalenjin residents of Miteitei farm in Nandi District of the Rift Valley province, related to a dispute over land ownership, but also following on the heels of several large rallies held by ruling party politicians in which several had called for driving out non-Kalenjin from the region for supporting the opposition (Akiwumi, Bosire, and Ondeyo, 1999d, 5–8). Homes and grain stores of non-Kalenjin residents of the farm were burned to the ground, and 279 families were forced to flee, with no efforts made to arrange their safe return (Akiwumi, Bosire, and Ondeyo, 1999d, 7). In the months that followed, additional attacks on ethnic outsiders in the run-up to the 1992 elections – including killings and the looting and burning of their homes and property – took place in various locations in the districts of Kericho, Uasin Gishu, Nakuru, Trans Mara, and parts of Nandi in the Rift Valley and Bungoma in Western region, while attacks occurred in the aftermath of the election in Enoosupukia in Narok District and Ol Moran and Njoro divisions in Nakuru. These often involved hundreds of Kalenjin "warriors" armed with bows and arrows and *pangas* (machetes) attacking non-Kalenjin farms and houses in neighboring communities. In all, about 1,500 people were killed and 300,000 displaced as a result of the "clashes" from 1991 to 1993, the bulk of them in the Rift Valley (Human Rights Watch, 1995a).

Violence flared up again around the 1997 elections, with continuing conflict in the Rift Valley and new fighting in the hitherto peaceful Coast region. The most prominent incident took place at Likoni, a town a short ferry ride across a channel from the city of Mombasa, where on August

---

went to press, the Kalenjin William Ruto had recently been elected Kenya's fifth president after an election in which ethnicity played a less prominent role in voting patterns and the construction of elite coalitions.

13 (four months before the election), an organized group of youth from the local Digo tribe attacked the local police station and armory, then proceeded to attack homes and businesses associated with outsider ethnic groups – known to be widely supportive of opposition parties – throughout the town. The final toll of the attack – carried out with bows and arrows, guns, and arson – included 5 police officers and 10 civilians dead and many more wounded; the destruction of the police station and other local government offices; and severe damage to 43 houses, 520 kiosks, 13 shops, 17 bars and restaurants, 10 butcheries, and 2 churches, and more attacks in the area (25 in total) were to follow over the next 10 months (Akiwumi, Bosire, and Ondeyo, 1999*b*, 22–30). In all, approximately 2,000 people were killed and 400,000 displaced in politically motivated ethnic violence throughout the 1990s (Human Rights Watch, 2002), with numerous reports indicating that the violence was largely instigated and organized by both senior and local KANU politicians seeking to maintain their hold on power (Human Rights Watch, 1995*a*, 2002; Akiwumi, Bosire, and Ondeyo, 1999*b*; Klopp, 2001).

The 1990s also saw the rise of urban gangs – often affiliated with particular ethnic groups – that would be hired by politicians to attack their opponents (Katumanga, 2005; LeBas, 2013). Furthermore, by the time of the relatively peaceful 2002 elections that saw the country's first transition of power from KANU to the opposition National Rainbow Coalition (NARC), election-related violence was "no longer the preserve of the ruling party. Individual politicians – belonging to both KANU and the opposition – hired or organized their own vigilante groups to attack rival candidates, intimidate prospective voters, and forcibly disenfranchise ethnic groups that were seen as likely opponents" (LeBas, 2013, 248).

While the 2002 transition elections were relatively peaceful, large-scale violence reoccurred in the aftermath of the contested 2007 election, resulting in more than 1,100 deaths and more than 650,000 people displaced (Waki Commission, 2008; Lynch, 2009). Though primarily occurring after the election, the violence in 2007/08 was similar to previous bouts of preelection violence in Kenya in terms of its organization, targeting, and motivation to reshape local electoral demography for future electoral contests (KNCHR, 2008; Harris, 2013). In fact, despite the understandable focus on the severe conflict in the post-election period, violence actually began during the campaign, concentrated in Mt. Elgon in Western Kenya and Kuresoi and Molo in the Rift Valley (Cheeseman, 2008). The violence around the 2007 election was summarized in the report of the official Waki Commission as follows:

The post-election violence was spontaneous in some geographic areas and a result of planning and organization in other areas, often with the involvement of politicians and business leaders. Some areas witnessed a combination of the two forms of violence, where what started as a spontaneous violent reaction to the perceived rigging of elections later evolved into well organized and coordinated attacks on members of ethnic groups associated with the incumbent president or the PNU party ... [T]hese were systematic attacks on Kenyans based on their ethnicity and their political leanings. Attackers organized along ethnic lines, assembled considerable logistical means and traveled long distances to burn houses, maim, kill and sexually assault their occupants because these were of particular ethnic groups and political persuasion. Guilty by association was the guiding force behind deadly "revenge" attacks, with victims being identified not for what they did but for their ethnic association to other perpetrators. (Waki Commission, 2008, viii)

Finally, though more limited in scale than earlier outbreaks, communal violence killed 500 and displaced 118,000 in the run-up to the elections in 2013 (Human Rights Watch, 2013). Dozens were killed and thousands displaced in ethnic violence in the run-up to elections in 2017 (Mutiga, 2017), and nearly 100 killed and 250 injured in the political standoff that followed, with many casualties occurring at the hands of the police in their response to opposition protests (KNCHR, 2017b).[10]

2.2.2 Colonial and Early Independence Kenya and the Roots of Ethnic Conflict

The origins of the violence in Kenya cannot be understood without reference to the role of land and ethnicity in Kenyan politics, with its roots in colonial policy and the early independence era. British rule resulted in the alienation of about half the agricultural land in Kenya to European settlers (mostly in the so-called "White Highlands") and the creation of ethnically exclusive "native" reserves as the homelands of specific indigenous tribes, where Africans not working on European farms or in urban areas were required to live (Sorrensen, 1968; Okoth-Ogendo, 1991). These policies solidified the ethnicization of Kenyan society and made access to land a primary concern (Kimenyi and Ndung'u, 2005; Kamungi, 2009; Kanyinga, 2009; Mutui, 2011).

---

[10] Mutahi and Ruteere (2019) provide a useful analysis of the reasons why election-related ethnic violence was more limited in 2017, while state/police violence against the opposition remained intense.

At independence, land and ethnicity created deep internal divisions. The smaller, pastoralist tribes native to the Rift Valley (the Kalenjin, Maasai, Turkana, and Samburu – known as the KAMATUSA) formed the Kenya African Democratic Union (KADU) and advocated for a *majimbo* or federal structure of government in which regions would be responsible for administering land in their territories, which presumably meant that the rich land being vacated by European settlers in the Rift Valley highlands would be returned to the KAMATUSA that had traditionally inhabited the area (Kanyinga, 2009). The Kenyan African National Union (KANU), on the other hand, which was supported by the large Kikuyu and Luo ethnic groups, preferred a unitary government with respect for established property rights (Kanyinga, 2009). KANU's victory in Kenya's first election and the co-optation of KADU's leadership into KANU led to the establishment of a strong central government (with a de facto and later de jure one-party state) and a rejection of the sanctity of traditional tribal lands or traditional spheres. Whether by design or by virtue of better access to resources, as a form of patronage or a means of preventing social unrest, the government settlement schemes and land-buying programs in the early independence years that redistributed land from European settlers to indigenous Africans benefited founding President Jomo Kenyatta's Kikuyu ethnic group more than any other (Kimenyi and Ndung'u, 2005; Kanyinga, 2009; Boone, 2011; Mutui, 2011). Groups such as the Kalenjin and Maasai, who had controlled much of the Rift Valley prior to the colonial takeover, felt particularly aggrieved, as did several groups native to the Coast; as a result, the central issue in Kenyan politics – land – took on a distinctly ethnic dimension. Ethnic relations suffered further damage as a result of the personal and political fallout between Kenyatta and his first Vice President, Oginga Odinga, and the assassination of the popular economy minister Tom Mboya, both ethnic Luos (Branch, 2011). That Kenyatta was perceived as favoring a small group of Kikuyu elites in land deals and government appointments – the so-called "Kiambu Mafia" – also played a role.

When Vice President Moi – an ethnic Kalenjin and former leader of KADU – took over as president upon Kenyatta's death, he gradually shifted power away from the Kiambu clique to loyalists from his own Tugen subtribe. This caused resentment among the formerly dominant Kikuyu elite, while other large groups such as the Luo continued to be cut off from power. Thus, when agitation for a return to multiparty politics arose, it was largely led by prominent Kikuyu and Luo politicians, and the nascent opposition movement generated strong popular support among these communities. The Kalenjin and their KAMATUSA allies within KANU therefore viewed the agitation as a plot to remove one of their own from power and restore the dominance of other tribes, the Kikuyu in particular. In the face of substantial domestic and international pressure, however, Moi and KANU allowed multiparty elections to take place in 1992.

2.2.3 Elections and Violence in the Multiparty Era

Multiparty elections posed a challenge to KANU, especially in ethnically mixed regions and constituencies with a sizeable proportion of ethnic groups associated with the opposition. Not only were powerful MPs – including government ministers – threatened by having to contest constituencies with sizeable populations of groups opposed to KANU rule, but President Moi himself faced the constitutional necessity of winning at least 25 percent of the vote in five out of Kenya's eight provinces, in addition to the popular vote. Thus, most analyses consider the tribal clashes of the 1990s to be part of a deliberate strategy on the part of the KANU political elite to maintain their hold on power by (1) consolidating support among the party's ethnic base and (2) weakening the opposition and its supporters (Human Rights Watch, 1995a, 2002; Klopp, 2001; Mutui, 2011). Violence had the potential to undermine the opposition by threatening and/or punishing members of those ethnic groups understood to support it; displacing voters from these groups and preventing them from registering and/or voting; and creating chaos to increase the cost of opposition demands and support KANU's assertion that democracy would cause ethnic conflict (Kamungi, 2009). Relatedly, violence could be used to mobilize KANU's core ethnic voters – the Kalenjin and Maasai in particular – by rallying them against perceived threats and injustices on the part of the large tribes opposed to continued KANU rule and giving them the opportunity to reclaim land they thought to be rightfully theirs (Kamungi, 2009; Kanyinga, 2009). While in 1992 the focus was on rallying the Kalenjin and Maasai and disenfranchising the Kikuyu, Luo, and Luhya in the ethnically diverse Rift Valley, in 1997 KANU politicians focused on shoring up their position on the Coast.[11] Much of the violence around 1992 was centered in areas on the borders between the ethnic "homelands" originally established by colonial authorities and thus locations where members of different ethnic groups lived in close proximity

---

[11] Violence *did* occur around the 1997 election in the Rift Valley as well, concentrated in the districts of Laikipia and Nakuru.

(Boone, 2011), while violence on the Coast around 1997 tapped into conflict between locally indigenous groups and those that had in previous decades migrated to the region from "upcountry" (inland) (Akiwumi, Bosire, and Ondeyo, 1999b; Laakso, 2007).

After President Moi was constitutionally barred from running for reelection, 2002 saw a relatively peaceful transfer of power to the opposition coalition's chosen candidate, Mwai Kibaki, in an election where the opposition alliance contained members of all the major ethnic groups and the two main contenders (Kibaki and KANU's Uhuru Kenyatta, the elder Kenyatta's son) were both Kikuyu. However, the grand coalition that elevated Kibaki to power collapsed shortly thereafter, and the 2007 election pitted Kibaki's largely Kikuyu Party of National Unity (PNU) against Raila Odinga's (the son of Oginga Odinga) Orange Democratic Movement (ODM), a broad coalition of ethnic groups and political leaders most closely associated with the Luo and the Kalenjin. The election campaign was characterized by ethnically charged rhetoric from politicians on both sides and the return of *majimboism*, with the ODM supporting a vague notion of devolution that some interpreted as a signal that an ODM-led government would favor the traditional land claims of the Kalenjin and Maasai over those of the mainly Kikuyu Rift Valley migrants (Klopp and Kamungi, 2008). Despite the understandable focus on the severe outbreak of violence in the post-election period, violence began during the campaign period, concentrated in Mt. Elgon in Western Kenya and in Kuresoi and Molo in the Rift Valley (Anderson and Lochery, 2008; Cheeseman, 2008). The main election-related violence, however, occurred after the results were announced. After a lull in the reporting of election results, with the last reports giving Odinga a small lead, Kibaki was abruptly announced the winner and quickly and quietly sworn in. Violence followed, consisting of: (1) spontaneous protests and rioting by ODM supporters against the perceived rigging of the election[12]; (2) violent suppression of protests by state security forces, including the use of live rounds; (3) organized attacks by mainly Kalenjin ODM supporters against mainly Kikuyu supporters of PNU in the Rift Valley; (4) counterattacks and revenge attacks – some organized, some less so – by Kikuyu youths against the Kalenjin, Luo, and Luhya; and (5) organized attacks and counterattacks by criminal gangs associated with particular ethnic groups, politicians, and business leaders against groups affiliated

---

[12] The best available evidence suggests that Odinga was, in fact, the rightful winner of the presidential election (Gibson and Long, 2009).

with the opposition (Waki Commission, 2008). Much of the violence was planned, organized, and financed by national and local politicians and business leaders (KNCHR, 2008; Waki Commission, 2008). The conflict only came to an end when Kibaki and Odinga signed a power-sharing agreement after more than two months of fighting.

In explaining the 2007/08 post-election violence, most accounts emphasize – in addition to legitimate anger over rigged election results – the recurring themes of ethnicized political conflict over land and access to power and the potential for violence to reshape electoral demographics in the most competitive constituencies (Anderson and Lochery, 2008; Waki Commission, 2008; Kanyinga, 2009; Harris, 2013; Kasara, 2016).[13] The report of the official Waki Commission investigating the 07/08 violence concluded that "the post-election violence resembled the ethnic clashes of the 1990s and was but an episode in a trend of institutionalization of violence in Kenya over the years. The fact that armed militias, most of whom developed as a result of the 1990s ethnic clashes, were never de-mobilized led to the ease with which political and business leaders reactivated them for the 2007 post-election violence" (Waki Commission, 2008, viii).

For various reasons – including increased international scrutiny, an alliance between the leading Kalenjin and Kikuyu politicians, and the existence of a more credible judicial system to handle election disputes – the 2013 election was relatively peaceful. Still, nearly 500 people were killed and 118,000 displaced in communal clashes in 2012 and early 2013 (Human Rights Watch, 2013), and the newly elected president and deputy president faced charges at the International Criminal Court for their alleged role in orchestrating the 2007/08 post-election violence, though the charges were later dropped due to the prosecution's inability to build a viable case. Despite promises to submit to the ICC process, the Kenyan government under President Uhuru Kenyatta refused to cooperate with the ICC prosecutor's requests to provide various pieces of evidence, and most key witnesses dropped out or recanted, allegedly as a result of bribery or intimidation (Mueller, 2011, 110). Though still far from the levels of 2007/08 and earlier, violence occurred before and after the contested 2017 elections as well (KNCHR, 2017a,b; Mutahi and Ruteere, 2019). While the largest outbreaks of violence have occurred in the run-up or aftermath of general elections, intraparty violence often occurs during nomination contests as well, especially in areas dominated

---

[13] See also Mueller (2008) on the institutional factors that facilitated the violence.

by one party, where winning the party nomination is the key to winning election (Wanyama and Elklit, 2018).

2.2.4 The Central Role of Political Elites

Various accounts of the violence of recent years points to the direct complicity of local and national politicians in organizing, financing, directing, or inciting the violence. Much of the violence in the Rift Valley from 1991 to 1998 was carried out by organized Kalenjin and Maasai militias that had specifically trained for their missions and were allegedly paid by KANU politicians for each person they killed or home they destroyed (Human Rights Watch, 1995a; Akiwumi, Bosire, and Ondeyo, 1999a; Laakso, 2007). The recruitment and training of Digo youths in the 1997 attacks on the Coast took a similar form (Human Rights Watch, 2003; Laakso, 2007). A Human Rights Watch report concluded – based on testimony from local politicians and individuals involved in the raids around Likoni in 1997 – that "[t]he evidence strongly suggests that government officials and KANU politicians contributed to the organization of the violence, both before and after the violence began, and – ultimately – to impunity for those behind it" (Human Rights Watch, 2003, 47).

In addition to their direct (though behind the scenes) involvement in the clashes, KANU politicians also laid the groundwork for conflict through the use of violent, ethnicized rhetoric. Nicholas Biwott, for example, an MP and government minister, said at a September 1991 rally that "the Kalenjins are not cowards and are not afraid to fight any attempts to relegate them from leadership," while MP Paul Chepkok urged attendees at the same rally to "take up arms and destroy dissidents on site" (Klopp, 2001, 485). Cabinet minister Timothey Mibei told residents of the Rift Valley to "crush any Government critic and later make reports to the police that they had finished them," while MP Willy Kamuren declared that "the Kalenjin, Maasai, Samburu and West Pokot ... were ready to protect the Government 'using any weapon at their disposal'" and "if any FORD [opposition party] member dared to visit any part of the province, they will regret it for the rest of their lives" (Akiwumi, Bosire, and Ondeyo, 1999c, 50). As a result, Bishop Ndingi Mwana a'Nzeki of the Roman Catholic Church in Nakuru described the violence in the lead-up to the 1992 elections as "politically motivated government clashes fully supported by the Kenyan Government" (Mutui, 2011, 94).

Similar involvement of politicians occurred in more recent outbreaks of violence, including in the aftermath of the 2007 elections, with leaders on both sides of the contest allegedly holding meetings, providing financing, forming alliances with criminal gangs, and inciting their supporters to commit violence against perceived supporters of the opposing party. The Kenya National Commission on Human Rights went so far as to say that the 2007/08 violence was "financed and sustained mainly by local politicians and business-people to support costs such as transport of attackers, weapons and other logistics" and that it was "largely instigated by politicians throughout the campaign period and during the violence itself via the use of incitement to hatred" (KNCHR, 2008). Rhetorical incitement occurred at rallies as well as through the media, especially through radio stations broadcast in the vernacular languages of particular ethnic groups (Waki Commission, 2008; Mutui, 2011).

One witness from the North Rift Valley who testified before the official Waki Commission into the violence "submitted videos of a campaign rally ... to illustrate what he described as a 'systematic and deliberate effort by both the politicians and the media to whip emotions both before the election and afterwards,' also citing KASS FM [a Kalenjin-language radio station] as a perpetrator," noting that Kalenjin attacks on Kikuyu residents "were coordinated using cell phones, matatu [minibus] drivers and touts" (Waki Commission, 2008, 69). Another cited "a meeting between some athletes and a prominent politician ... [that] was held 'to prepare the youth for war,'" after which "an elder informed them he was going to get guns from a friend ... and that a retired policeman would assist with using the guns and that somebody ... was sent to purchase bows and arrows," while later that week another elder "who was a point man for a prominent politician '... went around ... with some athletes and other prominent people calling on youths to be ready for war, promising them support from the MP'" (Waki Commission, 2008, 70).[14] Yet another testified that "militias were ferried in lorries owned by a local politician prominent [sic]" and that the attack on Kiambaa Church – the most deadly attack of the conflict, in which more than 30 Kikuyu residents were killed when the church they took shelter in was set ablaze – "was caused by some councillors [local elected officials] who spread propaganda that the church held Mungiki [a Kikuyu gang] ... from Central Province who were ready to attack the local Nandi [Kalenjin sub-tribe] community" (Waki Commission, 2008, 70–71). Assessments by the government's National Security Intelligence Service alleged that ODM party

---

[14] Notably, both of these witnesses were Kalenjin themselves.

leaders in the North Rift "gave money to Kalenjin youth ... to attack Kikuyu," and funded "ODM activists to organize youth for violence" (Waki Commission, 2008, 72).

Crucially, political violence in Kenya is not a purely local phenomenon outside the control of higher-level leaders. My own interviews with politicians at various levels of government revealed a widespread acknowledgment that top party officials have the ability to tamp down on local conflict should they so choose.[15] As one county assembly member stated bluntly, "[v]iolence won't happen if the ones at the top don't allow it to happen."[16] That top party leaders – including subsequently elected President and Deputy President Uhuru Kenyatta and William Ruto – were implicated by the ICC for organizing and financing the 2007/08 violence shows that, similar to the violence of the 1990s, the involvement of the political class went all the way to the top. Furthermore, the relative dearth of violence in 2013 and 2017 demonstrates the extraordinary impact of elite decisionmaking – whether by forming alliances with erstwhile political adversaries, or choosing to peacefully challenge contested election results – on whether such violence occurs (Mutahi and Ruteere, 2019).

Thus, the prevailing wisdom about election-related violence in Kenya is that it is the product of strategic maneuvering on the part of political elites, who use violence and violent rhetoric to coerce or displace opposition voters (largely non-coethnics) and to rally their coethnic base. It is therefore largely in line with existing accounts in the broader literature on the strategic use of violence in electoral competition.

2.2.5 The Case of Kenya in Comparative Context

The focus of this book is on the logic of election-related violence in contexts with a few key features. Most importantly, the study is concerned with cases where (1) political elites play a primary role in instigating violence and (2) elections are competitive enough that voters have a genuine choice at the polls. Such cases are the most puzzling because voters are presumably free to vote violent politicians out of office. As a result, politicians must consider how their use of violence affects the voting calculus of the majority of voters that are not directly affected by acts of violent coercion. Kenya is a prime example of this; politicians are pivotal actors in the

---

[15] Interviews with more than five dozen Kenyan politicians, conducted from July 2014 to June 2015.
[16] Interview with MCA, July 24, 2014.

outbreak of election-related violence, and voters go to the polls in flawed yet highly competitive elections. It is also a case of violence that takes place largely along ethnic lines, a common feature of violence in countries around the world (Human Rights Watch, 1995a). It is thus similar in many ways to numerous other cases of election-related violence from across the globe, including India, Nigeria, Indonesia, Sri Lanka, Côte d'Ivoire, and Bangladesh. As the theory put forward in Chapter 3 makes clear, the analysis of the Kenyan case should therefore be applicable to these and the many cases that share these common features.

Importantly, Kenya is in many ways a "hard" case in which to test the theory of elite misperception. This is because, in order to explain the incidence of violence, the theory of elite misperception relies on the assertion that violence costs more votes than politicians assume. Yet the conventional wisdom in the literature on Kenya is that violence is indeed a useful tactic for contesting elections, partially because candidates are unlikely to be punished by their core coethnic supporters for engaging in it. Furthermore, violence in Kenya is said to work through several of the mechanisms posited in the literature on election-related violence (Kimenyi and Ndung'u, 2005), including turnout suppression (Bratton, 2008; Collier and Vicente, 2012), displacement (Steele, 2011; Harris, 2013; Kasara, 2016), and ethnic polarization or outbidding (Rabushka and Shepsle, 1972; Fearon and Laitin, 2000; Wilkinson, 2004). Thus, finding evidence that violence is in fact ineffective or counterproductive in Kenya should be particularly noteworthy in that it represents a case in which such a finding might be least expected.

2.3 THE SPECIAL ROLE OF ETHNICITY IN POLITICAL VIOLENCE

Before theorizing about the logic of violence in electoral competition, it is important to address the oft-observed link between violence and ethnic conflict in Kenya and many other countries around the world. Often, political violence has a distinct ethnic dimension, pitting groups against one another on the basis of ascriptive identities, so explanations for the outbreak of violence must generally pay close attention to the dynamics of ethnic conflict. Relying heavily on insights from Horowitz's seminal work (Horowitz, 1985), I parse three main observations that help explain why this is the case.

First, because they are "simultaneously suffused with overtones of familial duty and laden with depths of familial emotion" (Horowitz, 1985, 60) ethnic ties tend to be strong and emotionally charged, more so than other types of identities and social ties in many societies. This is largely due to the fact that, unlike identities such as class, ethnicity is largely immutable, with movement between groups more difficult. Members of an ethnic group are therefore likely to feel a greater affinity with members of that group than with members of other social groups they may be a part of, and this can increase the probability of a conflict between individuals of different ethnicities transforming into conflict between the two groups as a whole. Fearon and Laitin (1996), for example, describe a model of interethnic relations in which intergroup cooperation rapidly devolves into indiscriminate group-based reprisals following an individual dispute between two parties. In general, the strength and emotional nature of ethnic identities makes mobilization along ethnic lines attractive for political entrepreneurs, and it can make conflict across ethnic lines particularly intense.

Second, the nature of ethnic identities implies that where political competition *does* take place along ethnic lines – as it does in many divided societies – then the contest for political power is likely to be perceived as particularly high stakes. According to Horowitz, the primary cause of ethnic conflict is group anxiety, that is, the fear of succumbing to the superior numbers or capacities of another group (Horowitz, 1985). Driven by the fear of ethnic domination and suppression, ethnic groups therefore desire power not just to compete over routine policy and the distribution of resources, but to confirm their status and avert threats in a situation where who wields power can come to define the very character of the nation. Thus, election outcomes are of critical importance to ethnic groups in divided societies, and they may therefore be more likely to employ any means necessary – including violence – to compete for political power.[17] Furthermore, when voting is driven primarily by ethnic ties, it may be less likely that voters use their vote to sanction violent, rabble-rousing candidates from their own group, thus lowering the costs of violence for those politicians who use it.

Finally, and partially as a result of the perceived high stakes, ethnic-based electoral competition tends to heighten the risk of violence breaking out. Horowitz notes that in elections *not* primarily characterized by ethnic group competition, parties divide their efforts between mobilizing known supporters and appealing for uncommitted votes, and that there is generally "a tradeoff between whipping up party loyalists to get

---

[17] Though see Ake (1993) on the democratic potential of ethnic solidarity in politics.

2.3 The Special Role of Ethnicity in Political Violence

them to the polls and soliciting the support of those whose loyalty is uncertain" (Horowitz, 1985, 332). With ethnic-based competition, however, "mobilizing known supporters and appealing to marginal voters are effectively the same thing, for there are virtually no uncommitted votes to be had on the other side of the ethnic boundary .... Accordingly, turnout becomes all-important, and there is no electoral reason to be moderate about ethnic appeals," appeals that "raise the pitch of ethnic conflict and increase the danger of violence" (Horowitz, 1985, 332). Furthermore, electoral competition in divided societies may encourage ethnic politicians to instigate violence directly in hopes of increasing the salience of ethnic divisions vis-à-vis alternative social cleavages (Fearon and Laitin, 2000; Wilkinson, 2004).

Thus, ethnic conflict – and ethnicized political competition in particular – is often an important feature of political violence in many places around the world. As is clear from the discussion above, Kenya is no exception, and the analysis in the book therefore pays close attention to the critical interplay between violence, ethnic conflict, and electoral competition.

3

Theorizing Election-Related Violence

Toward a Theory of Elite Misperception

There are a number of possible explanations for the incidence of elite-instigated violence in electoral competition. This chapter summarizes existing theories, highlights some crucial yet untested assumptions that they share, and introduces a theory of election-related violence that emphasizes the role of elite misperception about voter preferences and the efficacy of violent electoral tactics. Some theories of electoral violence are structural or macrolevel in their scope and attention to the social, political, and economic conditions under which violence is likely to occur, positing that if local conditions make violence a viable option, and the stakes of election outcomes are particularly high, then politicians will employ violence as an effective means of winning or remaining in office. Others take a more microlevel approach, identifying *how* violence may help parties and candidates win office, and therefore why they may choose to use it when available to them as an option. Both types of explanation assume that if politicians employ violence, they do so because it offers them some objective electoral benefit.

I argue that violence is a less effective tactic for winning elections than the conventional wisdom suggests. In short, voter backlash against violence is more significant than the literature tends to assume. Politicians themselves underestimate the potential for voter backlash, thus overestimating the efficacy of violence as an electoral tactic, and this misperception – which is most likely to develop in young democracies where violence was used as a tactic by the winner of founding elections – can explain why violence persists even when evidence of its effectiveness is in doubt. The theory combines microlevel insights on the effects of violence on voting and how politicians perceive those effects with macrolevel insights into how those perceptions develop and influence the incidence of violent electoral tactics over time. In doing so, it provides an overlooked yet powerful explanation for the incidence and persistence of violence in the context of multiparty electoral competition.

Recall that I define election-related violence as "physical acts of violence carried out for the purpose of affecting the results of an election." The focus in this chapter is on how violence affects voting, and on how those effects (whether real or perceived) affect politicians' decisionmaking about whether to employ violence. While this would seem to address what Harish and Toha (2019) dub "voter-targeted" violence at the expense of candidate- or government-targeted violence, the latter forms of violence can also affect voters' decisionmaking about whom to vote for. So even though the targets of coercion in candidate- or government-targeted violence may not be regular voters, such incidents still have an impact on voters that politicians must take into account; there thus remains value in analyzing them in the same general framework of electoral costs and benefits to politicians resulting from the coercive and persuasive effects of violence. Similarly, while it is most straightforward to analyze *pre*-election violence in terms of its effects on voting, post-election violence is also often meant to have an impact on future elections, and voters may take into account violence in previous elections when deciding who to support at the polls. Pre- and post-election violence can therefore be considered within this framework as well, even if the rationale for why they occur may differ to some extent.[1]

Before turning to structural and strategic explanations for election-related violence, it should be noted that violence by electoral actors can at times be unrelated to electoral competition per se (see, e.g., Siddiqui, 2022). Under such a scenario, candidates for office may engage in violence for a range of objectives not directly related to politics, for example, to sustain a criminal enterprise or to settle a nonpolitical score. It may certainly be the case that political elites employ violence in service of economic or other non-electoral motives; I argue, however, that such violence should not be considered "election-related" since it does not qualify under the definitional requirement that such violence be "carried out for the purpose of affecting the results of an election." Furthermore, politicians must still grapple with the electoral consequences of such violence, even if elections are not themselves the principal target. Where winning office

---

[1] However, as per the definition put forward in the Introduction, I do limit attention to what Staniland calls "intra-systemic" rather than "anti-systemic" violence.

remains a primary goal, politicians must take the electoral consequences of criminal or other forms of violence into account (see, e.g., Banerjee et al., 2014).

3.1 STRUCTURAL EXPLANATIONS

Many theories of election-related violence take a structural approach, explaining the political, social, and economic conditions under which such violence is likely to occur. In doing so, they often emphasize those conditions that, in particular, raise the real or perceived stakes of elections, or undermine the strength and/or legitimacy of institutions for organizing elections and managing political conflict. Such approaches posit that if local conditions make violence a viable option, and the stakes of election outcomes are particularly high, then politicians will employ violence as an effective means to win or remain in office.

Work in this vein has argued, for instance, that the likelihood of election-related violence depends on the strength of democratic institutions, rule of law, and levels of corruption (Mueller, 2008; Hafner-Burton, Hyde, and Jablonski, 2013; Burchard, 2015; Kanyinga, 2018; Birch, 2020). Birch (2020), for example, argues that elections in states with weak democratic institutions and extensive clientelism, patronage, and corruption are high-stakes affairs, since those in power maintain significant control over economic and legal resources, and incumbency is thus a highly valuable prize. In such contexts, incumbents also have the ability to sharply tilt the electoral playing field to their advantage, such that officeholders may fear that losing an election will lead to their permanent exclusion from power as their ability to contest competitive elections will be denied. Relatedly, Burchard (2015, 35) asserts that "the features of substantive democracy – protections for civil liberties, press freedoms, and effective checks and balances on political power – all promote the integrity of elections ... and reduce the likelihood that electoral violence will occur," while Hafner-Burton, Hyde, and Jablonski (2013) contend that incumbents that face strong "accountability groups," including legislatures and the courts, are less likely to employ violence because their powers to do so are more circumscribed, and because they are more likely to be held legally or politically accountable for their actions. Analyzing the Kenyan case, Mueller (2008) argues that the underlying factors that led to the 2007/08 election violence were the state's gradual ceding of its monopoly on violence; the deliberate weakening of institutions outside the presidency and the personalization of presidential power, which undermined confidence in the ability of other institutions to resolve electoral disputes; and a system of electoral competition based on ethnic patronage of state resources, which raised the perceived stakes of the election outcome. Kanyinga (2018) cites a lack of constitutionalism, weak rule of law, and poor electoral governance as conditions conducive to violence around elections in Africa at large.

Other work has focused on how electoral rules and institutional design affect the incentives for – and therefore likelihood of – violence (Hafner-Burton, Hyde, and Jablonski, 2013; Burchard, 2015; Fjelde and Höglund, 2015; Claes, 2016; Daxecker, 2020). Burchard (2015), for example, posits that elections operating under plurality or majoritarian rules are more likely to turn violent than those under proportional rules because (1) they tend to be winner-take-all affairs with clear winners and losers, rather than allocating power more proportionately; (2) they're easier to predict and therefore to affect the outcomes of with violent interventions; and (3) plurality systems specifically may have low thresholds for victory that could be more easily affected by violence.[2] Fjelde and Höglund (2015) also argue that majoritarian electoral institutions are more likely to generate violence due to the high stakes of election outcomes under such systems, especially where large ethnic groups end up excluded from power and where there is significant inequality in ownership over land. Similarly, Kanyinga (2018) argues that electoral systems geared toward greater inclusiveness in the distribution of political power are key to addressing the challenges of winner-take-all politics that make violence more likely. Daxecker (2020), meanwhile, points to the role of malapportionment (the discrepancy between the share of legislative seats and the share of population) specifically, arguing that it generates incentives for violence by increasing the heterogeneity of the voter base and reducing the electoral security of incumbents. On institutional design more generally, Burchard (2015) cites the role of independent electoral management bodies, independent and effective judiciaries, and independent and professional media in reducing violence by increasing the cost of violence through their ability to detect and punish it, while Claes (2016) argues that independent and effective election commissions are particularly important for mitigating the risk of violence.

---

[2] Note, however, that the first point suggested by Burchard is actually related to the existence of a presidential or parliamentary system. Even parliamentary systems with single-member plurality districts are not winner-take-all, since the executive is chosen by elected members of parliament. Winner-take-all elections would be those where a single candidate or party is elected nationwide, as in a presidential election.

Scholars have also focused on the nature of parties and the party system as a factor affecting the likelihood of election-related violence (Wilkinson, 2004; Fjelde, 2020; Wahman and Goldring, 2020; Siddiqui, 2022). Wilkinson (2004), for example, suggests that more fragmented party systems mitigate the incentive for ethnic parties to instigate violence against minority groups, since they may need to rely on their votes to win power. Wahman and Goldring (2020) argue that violence is most likely in constituencies where one party is dominant, as the dominant party attempts to further limit competition and maintain a high degree of territorial control, while the opposition seeks to disrupt the status quo and defend their ability to campaign in hostile territory. Fjelde (2020) posits that stronger, more organized parties are less likely to unleash violence than weaker ones because (1) they are able to implement more cost-effective tactics for mobilizing voters and (2) they have a greater ability to constrain individual political actors at both the elite and grassroots levels from deploying violence on their own accord. Finally, Siddiqui (2022) argues that parties that make exclusionary appeals to a particular ethnic group – and that don't rely on support from outside that group – are more likely to employ violence against their opponents if it is available to them as a tactic because they have less reason to fear voter backlash against it from their primary base of support.

Related to explanations of violence focused on the nature of the party system are those that seek to explain variation in the incidence of violence at the nomination stage (Goldring and Wahman, 2018; Seeberg, Wahman, and Skaaning, 2018; Mac Giollabhui, 2018; Reeder and Seeberg, 2018; Wanyama and Elklit, 2018; Turnbull, 2021). In general, such explanations call attention to the same overarching conditions highlighted by structural theories of election-related violence more broadly – that is, weak electoral processes and management and high-stakes elections – but the specific conditions that make for deficient processes and increased stakes differ. For example, in a dominant party context where the main nexus of electoral competition is intraparty rather than interparty, there may be more violence at the nomination stage since the stakes of winning the dominant party's nomination are so high (Goldring and Wahman, 2018; Mac Giollabhui, 2018; Seeberg, Wahman, and Skaaning, 2018; Wanyama and Elklit, 2018; Turnbull, 2021).[3] Furthermore, when weakly organized parties conduct their own nomination processes, the credibility

---

[3] Others have argued that the converse of this is true for violence during general elections, where closer elections may generate more violence (Wilkinson, 2004).

of such processes is often low and the likelihood of violence in response to contested results therefore high (Mac Giollabhui, 2018; Wanyama and Elklit, 2018).

Other scholars have pointed to how particular economic arrangements affect electoral politics in ways that make violence more or less likely, including systems and patterns of land tenure and ownership (Kanyinga, 2009; Boone, 2011; Klaus and Mitchell, 2015; Klaus, 2020). Kanyinga (2009) and Boone (2011) argue, for example, that the dynamics of the post-independence reallocation of land that had been seized from the native population by the colonial government in Kenya led to deep-seated, long-simmering tensions between ethnic groups (some of whom benefited more than others, and some of whom considered themselves more indigenous to that land than others) that led to land-related political violence during multiparty elections. Land conflict may be particularly conducive to violence around elections when the tenure system gives government officials (and therefore election winners) substantial control over the security of tenants' land claims (Boone, 2011; Klaus, 2020). In fact, a system in which land security is dependent upon who controls the government may be essential to mobilizing violence along such lines, even when grievances over land exist, since only in such cases may politicians credibly claim to have the ability to award or revoke land rights should they be elected to office (Boone, 2011; Klaus and Mitchell, 2015; Klaus, 2020).[4]

Finally, international factors may play a role; in particular, the presence or absence of international election observation may affect the likelihood of violence (Daxecker, 2012; Smidt, 2016; von Borzyskowski, 2019).[5] Smidt (2016) describes a complex relationship between international observation and violence, where the presence of observers generally reduces violence on the part of the incumbent – but not the opposition – because violent actions by state forces are more easily observable than those by agents of the opposition, and incumbents expect greater criticism from observers than does the opposition. On the other hand, in the presence of fraud, international observation makes incumbent violence more likely than opposition violence, since the government will already expect criticism regarding rigging and has little to lose by also employing violence, whereas the opposition has less reason to resort to violence

---

[4] Or, as the case may be, protect land claims against an opposition who may seek (or be portrayed as seeking) to take them away.

[5] Smidt (2020) also explores how exposure to UN peacekeepers may reduce violent election-related protest and rioting though their election education campaigns.

because they expect observers to respond to electoral malpractice. Daxecker (2012) and von Borzyskowski (2019) suggest that international election observation can increase the risk of post-election violence by casting doubt on an election's credibility, though von Borzyskowski also notes that international technical assistance in the run-up to elections can help reduce the risk of violence by strengthening electoral institutions and the credibility of the outcome.

As I discuss in more depth below, the theory I put forward to explain election-related violence – which explains violence in terms of elite misperception about its efficacy as an electoral tactic – assumes that the structural conditions are in place such that violence is a viable option for contesting elections. In other words, institutions are weak enough – and the stakes high enough – that employing violence is possible and, perhaps, desirable if it in fact assists in politicians' efforts to win or maintain power. Thus, in the following section, I summarize existing theories of elite-instigated electoral violence that similarly take its possibility for granted and seek to explain why it does or does not occur as a result of the strategic incentives politicians face when competing in elections.

3.2 STRATEGIC, MICROLEVEL EXPLANATIONS

In general, there are two overarching ways in which politicians might use violence as a tool to help win elections: they can *coerce* voters, preventing them from voting or forcing them to vote against their preferences, or they can *persuade* voters, employing violence to shape voter preferences or demonstrate their willingness and ability to provide what voters want. Alternatively, violence could be an indirect byproduct of other tactics that politicians find useful, such as the use of hostile ethnic rhetoric. Yet as we shall see, violence can also occur even if its value as an electoral tactic is limited, as long as politicians *believe* it to be a useful tool.

3.2.1 Violence as Coercion

A first set of explanations for the strategic use of violence in electoral competition points to the purely coercive power of violence to affect whether and how people vote. Such theories explain violence in terms of its ability to force voters to vote a certain way (or not vote at all), regardless of their true preferences; they pay less attention to how violence may affect voter preferences themselves.

One such explanation argues that politicians may use violence to force voters to change their vote for fear of reprisals (Acemoglu, Robinson, and Santos, 2013; Ellman and Wantchekon, 2000; Wantchekon, 1999). In Colombia, for example, Acemoglu, Robinson, and Santos (2013) describe a situation in which right-wing paramilitaries increased vote share for right-wing political candidates by credibly threatening reprisals if their preferred candidates did not win. Analyzing election results from the mid-1990s to the mid-2000s, they document a positive association between local paramilitary activity and vote share for third-party candidates and for incumbent President Álvaro Uribe, both favorites of the paramilitary groups. In El Salvador, Wantchekon (1999) argues that the right-wing Alianza Republicana Nacionalista (ARENA) won the first multiparty elections after the country's civil war despite the left-wing Frente Farabundo Martí para la Liberación Nacional (FMLN) more popular position on land reform, the leading policy issue of the day, because of voters' legitimate fear that an electoral loss would lead ARENA – and not the FMLN – to resort to violence. Similarly, Ellman and Wantchekon (2000) ascribe the warlord Charles Taylor's victory over former World Bank economist Ellen Johnson Sirleaf in the 1997 presidential elections to the threat of violence should he lose (Sirleaf would go on to win the presidency in 2005). In Jamaica, politician have used criminal gangs to construct single-party dominant "garrisons," zones in poor urban neighborhoods of Kingston where residents demonstrate support and vote for only one party by overwhelming margins, since doing otherwise will trigger severe violent reprisals from the gangs that control the neighborhood and are aligned with one party or the other (Sives, 2010).

Though such accounts are plausible, at least two points are worth noting. First, the effect of actual violence on election outcomes in situations where coercion is said to operate is hard to pin down, since much of the impact ascribed to violent actors in such situations is related to their coercive *capacity* rather than the use of violent coercion itself. In other words, it is the *threat* of violence rather than its actual use that does most of the work. In El Salvador and Liberia, for instance, voters are said to have voted for ARENA and Charles Taylor, respectively, because of fears that these actors might reignite those countries' civil wars following an electoral defeat, not necessarily because they violently coerced during the election campaign. In Colombia, meanwhile, paramilitaries used their control over localities to influence election results not only with violence, but with fraud as well (Acemoglu, Robinson, and Santos, 2013, 22).

Second, and relatedly, the situations in which violent coercion succeeds in forcing voters to vote against their true preferences appear to be largely limited to those in which an armed group – be it an insurgent group, paramilitary, or criminal gang – has established such extensive *de facto* control over a particular area that, violence aside, the conditions for holding a nominally free and fair election have completely broken down. Yet such conditions are not present in many important cases where violence occurs yet votes are cast and counted more or less as they are supposed to. Furthermore, such a situation allows violent actors to control the electoral process with more than violence alone. In Colombia, for example, Acemoglu, Robinson, and Santos (2013, 22) note that – in addition to threatening violent reprisals – paramilitaries likely influenced vote outcomes by denying access to polling stations so they could manipulate the vote counting, or by forcibly collecting individuals' voter cards and using them to fill in their ballots for them, tactics that would be much more difficult to pull off had they lacked such extensive control. Again, in such situations, it is unclear whether it is violence itself – or, rather, the mere potential for coercion – that may lead citizens to vote against their true preferences. In some ways, the logic is similar to that laid out in Kalyvas' (2006) important study of civilian behavior in civil war settings, where civilians generally act in support of an armed actor where that actor establishes the greatest level of control, not where it engages in the highest levels of violence. In short, coercion may induce voters to vote against their true preferences, but it is likely most effective in situations where the establishment of local dominance makes the actual use of violence largely unnecessary.

Another possibility is that politicians use violent coercion not to change how people vote, but to reduce voter turnout, especially among supporters of other political parties, either before or on election day (Chaturvedi, 2005; Bratton, 2008; Collier and Vicente, 2014, 2012; Condra et al., 2018). Politicians know that some voters are more likely to vote for them than others as a result of their ideology, ethnicity, location, or other characteristics. Based on these characteristics, individuals or groups of voters can be grouped into categories such as core, swing, or opposition voters, and violence may be used to reduce turnout among the latter relative to the former, thus shaping the electorate in one's favor.[6]

---

[6] Robinson and Torvik (2009) are of the view that violence may in fact be most effective when used to reduce turnout among *swing* voters, as opposed to strong supporters of the opposition, whereas Travaglianti (2014) argues that violence in Burundi aims to coerce *greater* turnout among *core* supporters. Violence may also be used by incumbents to provoke opposition boycotts, undermining opposition turnout via elite-led collective action (Hafner-Burton, Hyde, and Jablonski, 2018).

The evidence for this mechanism is mixed. Studying the relationship between violence and turnout with a cross-national regression across 47 countries in Africa, Bekoe and Burchard (2017) find no significant relationship between pre-election violence and turnout.[7] They suggest that the generally nonexistent average effects are due to the differing goals that such violence may have across contexts, where it may sometimes be used to depress turnout or displace voters, but other times used to pressure voters to go to the polls. Also analyzing cross-national Afrobarometer data from Africa, Burchard (2020) likewise finds that voters who fear violence report being no more or less likely to vote than those who do not.

Analyzing a randomized experiment around the 2007 Nigerian general election in which a local NGO conducted an anti-violence campaign that encouraged voters to act collectively against violence and vote against violent candidates, Collier and Vicente (2014) find that the intervention reduced perceptions of violence in those areas where it was implemented compared to those where it was not, as well as some evidence that it increased voter turnout.[8] The authors interpret these findings as evidence that violence reduces turnout in the setting they study. But while the evidence is suggestive of a relationship between violence and turnout, the randomized treatment is an anti-violence campaign, not violence itself. As a result, levels of violence in the study area are "post-treatment," making it possible that some other aspect of the anti-violence campaign – rather than the reduction in perceived violence itself – is responsible for the increase in turnout in treated areas.

Bratton (2008) also analyzes the relationship between violence and turnout in the Nigerian election of 2007 – in his case using survey data on voters' experience with violent intimidation and their intent to vote – finding that respondents who reported being subjected to "threats of negative consequences in order to get you to vote a certain way" were significantly less likely to report that they planned to vote in the upcoming election.[9] This was the case even when respondents had been subjected to threats in the run-up to previous elections held in 2003. Of course, the difficulties with attributing the lower levels of turnout intentions to violent intimidation in this setup are manifold, among them the possibility of selective

---

[7] They also find no relationship between the incidence of pre-election violence and turnout across constituencies and districts in the 2007 Kenyan election.
[8] The experiment was randomized within pairs of enumeration areas, with treatment randomly assigned to one area within each of 12 pairs.
[9] The survey Bratton analyzes was conducted two months before the 2007 elections.

reporting of voting intentions and/or experience with intimidation, selective targeting of voters with intimidation, and measurement error due to voting intentions being measured two months prior to the election.

Also relevant are Condra et al. (2018) and Robbins, Hunter, and Murray (2013), who study the turnout effects of insurgent and terrorist violence, respectively. Employing an instrumental variables approach related to weather patterns that make insurgent attacks in Afghanistan more or less viable, Condra et al. (2018) find that insurgent violence on the morning of – and in the month leading up to – elections is associated with a lower turnout in the districts where it occurs. In contrast, in a cross-national regression analysis of 51 countries, Robbins, Hunter, and Murray (2013) find that terrorist violence is associated with an *increase* in voter turnout, suggesting this is due to attacks increasing the salience of politics and thus leading to greater participation in elections.

Finally, politicians may use violent coercion to forcibly displace voters – primarily opposition supporters or members of groups that are likely to be – from their homes, thereby producing a more favorable electorate in a given locality not just in a forthcoming election, but perhaps in elections further into the future, as well.

The best evidence for the successful implementation of such a strategy comes from Kenya. Studies by Kimuli Kasara and J. Andrew Harris on the dynamics of the 2007/08 violence in the Rift Valley Province, in particular, have demonstrated (1) that election-related violence in Kenya has clearly targeted specific groups with particular political preferences and (2) that such violence has changed the demographic makeup of the areas in which it occurs in a way that may improve the electoral prospects of those who have perpetrated the violence (Harris, 2013; Kasara, 2016).

Both Kasara and Harris investigate the local targeting of violence in 07/08 using highly disaggregated data on fires as a proxy. Kasara (2016) finds that the violence – as proxied by fire intensity – was targeted in locations that were electorally pivotal and contained a greater number of internal migrants from other regions of the country. Such locations also saw higher levels of displacement, as measured by the number of internally displaced persons (IDPs) that ended up in IDP camps. Harris (2013) analyzes the dynamics of violence at the polling station level in the northern Rift Valley using data from official voter registers and a novel technique to extract ethnicity from voter surnames, finding that violence (again proxied by fire incidence) was more common around polling stations with larger number of ethnic "outsiders," and that such violence resulted in a significant drop in the local Kikuyu population relative to other ethnic groups. The results support the conventional wisdom suggesting that most of the violence in this region involved ODM supporters acting against perceived supporters of the Kikuyu-dominated PNU, and that such violence may have succeeded in reshaping local electoral demography in favor of non-Kikuyu groups and political elites.[10]

Steele (2011), meanwhile, studies violence as a tool for displacing opposition voters in Colombia, a conflict setting. Analyzing the consequences of counterinsurgency forces targeting supporters of an insurgent-backed party in the country's northwest, she finds that the strategy found some success displacing such voters in the region's main city, but not in rural areas, where the residents who were targeted either remained or returned after a short time away despite the constant threat of attack. And in another example of violence meant to displace opposition voters, Bratton and Masunungure (2007) analyze the effects of Operation Murambatsvina in Zimbabwe, an effort by Robert Mugabe's ruling ZANU-PF to, among other goals, forcibly displace young urban dwellers in the informal economy (likely supporters of the opposition) to rural areas where they could be more easily monitored. However, using survey data measuring whether respondents had recently relocated, the authors find that, despite the destruction of homes and businesses that the operation entailed, no more Zimbabweans appear to have migrated from urban to rural areas following the operation than did in the period before (Bratton and Masunungure, 2007, 36–37). The study suggests that local demographics can prove quite durable in the face of violence meant to reshape the makeup of the local population.

Overall, while logic suggests that the coercive effects of violence are surely important, the empirical record is limited and somewhat mixed. Furthermore, it is important to note that direct coercion usually only affects a small proportion of the voting population. Bratton (2008), for example, finds that just 4 percent of voters overall, and 13 percent in the most affected region, experienced instances of intimidation in the quite violent 2007 elections in Nigeria. It is therefore crucial to understand how violence shapes voter preferences more broadly for a more complete accounting of the effects of violence on election outcomes, and a number of theories attempt to do just that.

---

[10] Since the group that formed ODM's primary base of support in the Rift Valley – the Kalenjin – ended up aligning with the Kikuyu in the subsequent 2013 elections, however, it is difficult to determine definitely whether these demographic changes actually improved the electoral prospects of Kalenjin politicians and associated parties at the expense of their Kikuyu counterparts.

3.2.2 Violence as Persuasion

Out-Group Violence as a Good

One possibility – and perhaps the most unsavory – for how violence might be used to bolster voter support is that some element of a politician's constituency actually receives some expressive benefit from particular acts of violence, so producing such violence increases the politician's support among that group of voters. Horowitz (1985) and Petersen (2002), for example, have emphasized the role of interethnic resentment and hatred in generating intergroup political violence. This possibility is perhaps most likely to occur in the context of extreme levels of animosity between different groups in society, such as ethnic groups with a history of intergroup conflict (Kaufmann, 1996). The idea is that, in contexts where group identities are highly salient and intergroup animosity exceptionally high, members of a particular group might obtain some expressive benefit from violence committed against a hated out-group. Thus, a politician responsible for such violence might benefit from increased support among members of the in-group to which he provided the "good" of out-group violence. Kapferer (1988, 100), for example, suggests that Sinhalese Buddhists in Sri Lanka faulted Sinhalese President Jayawardene for capitulating to Tamil interests by "not killing enough"; more generally, Horowitz (2001, 243) asserts that "the most likely factional motive for organizing ethnic riots is the one that depends most heavily on preexisting proviolence affect." However, this type of explanation must contend with the fact that violence is, in general, highly counter-normative; recall the 77 percent of African citizens across 33 countries cited above who asserted that the use of violence is never justified in their countries' politics. Thus, the idea of out-group violence as a good appears fairly implausible under all but the most extreme circumstances. Still, the evidence for such an explanation should be considered.

Violence as a Signal of Candidate Type

A second explanation that considers violence as a persuasive tool asserts that violence may be used to signal certain candidate traits that voters desire (Vaishnav, 2017).[11] Especially in low-information, low-credibility environments where voters have limited information about candidates and campaign promises lack credibility, violence may be one of very few tools that candidates have to visibly and credibly signal what they can

---

[11] See also (Hoffman and McCormick, 2004) on suicide terrorism as a form of strategic signaling.

and will do once in office.[12] Politicians might use violence to signal, for example, that they are willing and able to defend their coethnics against security threats from other groups. Or they might use it to signal their toughness or ability to get things done. Analyzing the prevalence of violent criminals in Indian politics, Vaishnav (2017) suggests that candidates use violence to signal all of these things – their toughness, their ability and willingness to defend the common man, and their ability to get things done – since poor voters have limited information with which to evaluate candidates with respect to what they see as these all-important traits. As a result, it is important to analyze how violence shapes voters' perceptions of candidates and their likely behavior once in office.

Violence as a Means of Ethnic Polarization

A third possibility is that politicians use sectarian violence to polarize the electorate along ethnic lines and increase the importance voters place on security concerns (Fearon and Laitin, 2000; Oberschall, 2000; Horowitz, 2001; Klopp, 2001; Brass, 2003; Wilkinson, 2004). They do so in order to shore up support among members of their group, particularly those that might lean toward other parties on the basis of other issues or identities. The polarization hypothesis is based on two main observations. First, social psychology has found that exposure to violence increases individuals' identification with their cultural in-group and against out-groups (Greenberg et al., 1990). Second, sectarian violence is likely to increase the weight voters put on issues of security, increasing support for politicians – usually coethnics – deemed most likely to provide that security in the face of the perceived threat (Wilkinson, 2012, 367).[13] As such, it is important to analyze the effect of violence on the strength of ethnic identity and the salience of security vis-à-vis other political issues.

Violence as a Side Effect of Divisive Rhetoric

Even if violence per se is not an explicit strategy of candidates for office, it is possible that, in hopes of consolidating the coethnic vote, politicians

---

[12] See Kramon (2016) for a similar logic with respect to the use of electoral handouts.
[13] Increasing the weight they attach to security issues might be just one way in which being exposed to violence might make voters more receptive to certain types of appeals and certain types of information more so than others. For example, voters might pay more attention to information about threats (e.g., from other groups) because of an increased sense of loss aversion, or be more receptive to clientelist or particularistic appeals. Young (2019) finds that feeling fear – a presumably common psychological response to violence – reduces opposition supporters' willingness to participate in dissent against an autocratic regime.

use heated ethnic rhetoric that increases intergroup animosity to the point that violence breaks out (Rabushka and Shepsle, 1972; Horowitz, 1985; Benesch, 2011). For example, Horowitz (1985, 332) argues that in the context of ethnic-based electoral competition, "turnout becomes all-important, and there is no electoral reason to be moderate about ethnic appeals" that "raise the pitch of ethnic conflict and increase the danger of violence." In this view, violence is not a direct effect of politicians' actions but rather an indirect outcome of another tactic – ethnic rhetoric – that candidates may find useful in their campaigns. It is therefore important to explore (1) whether ethnic rhetoric is in fact effective in consolidating the coethnic vote and (2) whether such rhetoric increases the likelihood of violence breaking out.

3.3 VIOLENCE AS A RESULT OF ELITE MISPERCEPTION

All of the strategic explanations outlined above turn on two key assumptions: (1) that election-related violence is an effective tactic for politicians contesting for office and (2) that political elites accurately assess the relative costs and benefits of a violent electoral strategy and act accordingly.

Violence is, unfortunately, a common occurrence in elections around the world. Since politicians frequently employ it as a tactic, it seems reasonable to assume that they benefit from doing so. Perhaps as a result, strategic explanations for the incidence of election-related violence have focused almost exclusively on its electoral benefits, with much less attention to its costs.[14]

Yet convincing evidence on the efficacy of violence as an electoral tactic is limited, and microlevel studies of how violence affects individuals' voting decisions are few. This is in no small part due to the difficulty of devising credible research designs to answer this question; the incidence of election-related violence is far from random, being correlated with characteristics of candidates, parties, and the electoral units in which

---

[14] Collier and Vicente (2012), Malik (2021), and Siddiqui (2022) are notable exceptions. Collier and Vicente (2012) consider the possibility that violence reduces support for candidates among "soft" supporters, whereas Siddiqui (2022) argues that parties that form "exclusionary" linkages with voters (i.e., those that mobilize only part of the electorate and appeal to voters primarily on the basis of group identity) are unlikely to suffer backlash from their voters, but those that rely on cross-group appeal very well might. Malik (2021) suggests that backlash will mainly occur in areas subject to previous bouts of violence where voters are able to attribute violent outbreaks to politicians.

they run. For instance, if politicians employ violence only in the most competitive elections, then violence may be associated with smaller vote margins even if, in reality, it increases or reduces a party or candidate's vote share. While some of these characteristics may be observable, others are not, making studying the effects of violence on voting difficult using observational techniques. Employing randomized experiments to answer the question is not much easier, given the obvious ethical problems with implementing a study where the variable of interest – violence – is randomized.

A second inferential challenge has to do with measurement. In particular, it is difficult, in many cases, to generate a valid measure of the incidence or intensity of violence, particularly at the local level. Different types of datasets on violence – including media-based, crowd-sourced, and machine-coded variants – may systematically underreport violence in different ways that threaten to bias estimates that employ such data (Eck, 2012; Weidmann, 2015, 2016; Muchlinski et al., 2020). Thus, studies of violence and voting face the duel challenges of measurement and endogeneity that make generating valid inferences about the causal effect of violence on vote outcomes difficult. Perhaps as a result, rigorous, systematic studies of the effect of violence on election outcomes are largely lacking, with one review of the literature on election-related violence concluding that "[t]he most basic [outstanding] question is whether the use of violence actually advances the goals of those who deploy it" (Staniland, 2014, 113).

Despite these challenges, a handful of studies have attempted to analyze the effect of violence on election outcomes. Many focus on the well-studied case of India and seek to understand the effect of Hindu–Muslim riots on vote share for secular parties such as the Indian National Congress versus Hindu nationalist parties such as the Bharatiya Janata Party (BJP), with the expectation that violence might benefit majority Hindu parties by polarizing the electorate along ethno-religious lines. Of these, all find that Hindu–Muslim riots increase vote share for the BJP at the expense of the Congress (Dhattiwala and Biggs, 2012; Blakeslee, 2013; Nellis, Weaver, and Rosenzweig, 2016; Iyer and Shrivastava, 2018), suggesting that instigating riots may be a useful strategy for Hindu nationalist parties such as the BJP.[15] However, Dhattiwala and Biggs (2012) and

---

[15] Several studies have posited that electoral incentives determine whether Indian politicians instigate or suppress Hindu–Muslim violence; see Brass (2003), Wilkinson (2004), and Nellis, Weaver, and Rosenzweig (2016).

Blakeslee (2013) only analyze the effects of violence in one election in one state, and Iyer and Shrivastava (2018) is the only study to employ plausibly exogenous variation in violence to identify its electoral effects.[16]

Other studies include Acemoglu, Robinson, and Santos (2013), which finds that the presence of right-wing paramilitary groups, which used violent coercion in their attempts to influence voting in Colombia, has been associated with greater local vote share for third-party candidates (which tend to be right leaning) and for the rightist presidential candidate Álvaro Uribe. While suggestive, the interpretation of this result is somewhat ambiguous, since the independent variable measures paramilitary presence rather than violence itself, and the presence of paramilitary forces could work through several different channels in addition to outright violence. In Nigeria, meanwhile, Bratton (2008) and Collier and Vicente (2014) find that the threat of violence reduces voter turnout and generally benefits opposition parties at the polls, but the results from both studies are difficult to interpret. Bratton (2008) simply asks Nigerian voters prior to an election whether they had been threatened to vote in a certain way and looks at whether the answer is correlated with voters' intention to vote and who they plan to vote for. We do not know *who* made the threat, nor do we know whether it took the form of actual violence or some other form of intimidation. It's also possible that voters who received threats were already less likely to vote or more likely to vote for the opposition; the study's research design cannot rule out the possibility. As for Collier and Vicente (2014), the authors implement a field experiment which, at first glance, would appear to generate exogenous variation in violence that can be used to estimate its effects on voting, but the research design is not very well suited to answering this particular question. To begin with, the randomized intervention the authors study is a campaign encouraging voters to oppose violent politicians, rather than one that intervenes to directly reduce violence by targeting violence-instigating politicians, for example. Second, the main independent variable in the study is not violence itself, but the *perceived* threat of violence. Thus, the effects that are measured are of perceptions about violence, rather than actual violence. Third, since the anti-violence campaign includes multiple messages, including a plea to not vote for violent

---

[16] Dhattiwala and Biggs (2012) and Nellis, Weaver, and Rosenzweig (2016) essentially analyze district fixed-effects models, while Blakeslee (2013) employs an instrumental variables approach, but the latter is far from credible. In particular, the exclusion restriction is almost certainly violated in his setup, which employs proximity to a BJP campaign route as an instrument for riots (as well as the campaign itself).

politicians, the exclusion restriction for an estimation strategy that uses treatment assignment as an instrument for violence is violated since voting outcomes could have been affected directly by this messaging rather than levels of violence alone.

Overall, then, existing evidence on the relationship between violence and electoral outcomes is quite limited. The relative dearth of studies with credible causal identification strategies, combined with a likely bias against the publication of null results, suggests that whether violence is an effective tactic for winning competitive elections remains an open question.

In fact, despite the literature's focus on the benefits of violence for the parties and candidates that use it, there is good reason to believe that its electoral costs can be substantial. Violence is highly counternormative, with large majorities of citizens in Africa and elsewhere expressing disapproval of political violence in any form. Seventy-seven percent of citizens surveyed across 33 African countries for the Afrobarometer survey, for example, declared that the use of violence is never justified in their country's politics (Afrobarometer, 2014), while candidate vignette experiments have demonstrated that – even in contexts where politician-instigated violence is common – voters are less likely to support candidates that use it (Banerjee et al., 2014; Gutiérrez-Romero and LeBas, 2020). Combined with the fact that, even in some of the most violent elections, the proportion of voters subject to direct coercion is usually quite small,[17] the possibility that violence may trigger a sizable electoral backlash among those voters affected only indirectly (e.g., by hearing about attacks) deserves serious consideration (Rosenzweig, 2021; Siddiqui, 2022). Even if a party or candidate's hardcore supporters are willing to tolerate or perhaps even embrace violence, they must still contend with a potential loss of support among a broader group of voters for whom violence is unacceptable.

Of course, when going to the polls, voters are limited in the choices actually available to them. There may not be any viable, nonviolent candidates on the ballot, for instance; given the difficulty of coordinating around a nonviolent alternative to the main candidates, such a situation could leave voters with a perceived choice between voting for a candidate with a history of violence or likely wasting their vote. Voters also

---

[17] Bratton (2008), for example, finds that just 4 percent of voters overall, and 13 percent in the most affected region, experienced instances of intimidation in the quite violent 2007 elections in Nigeria.

weigh multiple factors in addition to the use of violence when choosing among candidates, who may appeal to them in some ways and not in others. They may not feel comfortable voting for a party with a reputation for mainly representing some out-group, for example (Siddiqui, 2022). Or they may prioritize concerns other than violence and prefer particular violent candidates when it comes to the issues that are most salient to them (Boas, Hidalgo, and Melo, 2018; Gutiérrez-Romero and LeBas, 2020). These factors could explain why we often observe significant electoral support for violent parties and candidates for office; even so, violence may still generate electoral costs for politicians, on average, that they could avoid were they to eschew it, and nonviolent alternatives could find success competing against those that continue to employ it.[18]

It may also be the case that politicians seek to obscure their direct involvement in violence in an effort to reap its benefits while maintaining plausible deniability among voters. While plausible, I present evidence in Chapter 5 that voters tend to be aware of credible allegations of instigating violence, and that allegations – even against in-group politicians voters are predisposed to like – tend to "stick," even if voters have a tendency to attribute greater responsibility for violence to out-group candidates than to those from their own group.

Finally, sometimes the goal of politician-instigated violence may be less about influencing voters and more about intimidating rivals or signaling to other elites their resolve or a capacity for imposing costs should they stand in the way of their political objectives.[19] Even in such cases, the ultimate goal generally remains winning elected office, so (1) voter backlash to such violence must still be considered when assessing its efficacy and (2) we should expect empirical evidence that it helps rather than hurts parties and candidates win elections. In other words, even if influencing voters isn't the primary intent when politicians instigate violence, how voters respond – and how that affects election outcomes – remains crucial for understanding its efficacy as an electoral tactic.

In short, my argument is not that violent coercion carries *no* electoral benefits, or that the costs are certain to outweigh the benefits, but simply that the electoral costs may be substantial and possibly large enough to offset whatever benefits a violent strategy may provide. Even where politicians maintain some core of support no matter how violent their tactics

---

[18] Siddiqui (2022), for example, documents the unraveling of support for the violent MQM in recent years as a viable nonviolent alternative for Muhajir voters in Karachi, Pakistan has emerged.

[19] I thank an anonymous reader of the manuscript for emphasizing this possibility.

become, a large enough loss of support among the broader electorate can threaten their ability to win office. In sum, the assumption that election-related violence is an effective tactic for politicians contesting for office may not hold.

There is also reason to doubt a second assumption underlying existing theories of election-related violence, that is, that politicians are able to accurately assess the relative costs and benefits of violence and act accordingly; or, put differently, that they have adequate information about its efficacy as an electoral tactic and objectively assess that information when deciding what strategy to pursue. In reality, inferring voter preferences and the effects of electoral tactics is more difficult for politicians than is often assumed. As Boas (2016, 25) notes, "[e]lections are complicated strategic terrain, and there is rarely a single, unambiguous course of action that will maximize one's chances of victory." In fact, a growing body of research suggests that (1) politicians in even the most mature democracies frequently misperceive public opinion and (2) campaigns often pursue tactics that research shows to be ineffective or even counterproductive.

On the first point, a number of recent studies on political elites' perceptions about public opinion in the US – a mature democracy in which public opinion data is widely available – have found that elites severely misperceive the electorate's views on a range of salient issues. Hertel-Fernandez, Mildenberger, and Stokes (2019), for example, find that Congressional staffers – key conduits between legislators and their constituents – significantly misperceive constituents views about a diverse set of issues, including healthcare, climate policy, gun control, and the minimum wage. Meanwhile, Broockman and Skovron (2018) find that candidates for state legislatures from across the US – including both incumbents and challengers – sharply misperceive public opinion among the electorate in their districts on a broad array of issues including same-sex marriage, gun control, abortion, and immigration policy. Their findings are consistent with those of Miller and Stokes' seminal study from more than 50 years ago (Miller and Stokes, 1963). Importantly, Hertel-Fernandez, Mildenberger, and Stokes (2019) and Broockman and Skovron (2018) find not just inaccuracy but *bias* in political elites' perceptions; they don't just misperceive the electorate's views, but misjudge them *in one particular direction* (in the case of the US, believing that the electorate holds more conservative views than they actually do). This finding is important because it implies that elites may not only have difficulty perceiving public opinion in general, but that a consensus may develop about public opinion on a particular issue that may in fact be incorrect. That such misperception occurs in a democracy as mature as the US – and in a context with access to large quantities of relevant information, such as public opinion polling – suggests that such misperception may be particularly likely to occur in newer democracies and those where public opinion data is less widely available (Geer, 1996).

Another line of research has documented in recent years the ineffectiveness of a number of tactics commonly used by politicians' campaigns. The work of Lau et al., for instance, has found negative campaigning to be an ineffective tactic for winning votes, despite its ubiquity in most campaigns (Lau and Pomper, 2002; Lau, Sigelman, and Rovner, 2007). In their seminal field experiment on campaign tactics for turning out voters, Gerber and Green (2000) find phone calls and – to a lesser extent – direct mail to be ineffective in achieving their aims, whereas Krasno and Green (2008*b*), analyzing a natural experiment that harnesses the geographic idiosyncrasies of US state boundaries and media markets, find the volume of television ads to have little to no effect on turnout, despite the hundreds of millions of dollars spent on them in each election cycle. Most notably, recent research analyzing data from nearly 50 field experiments on a range of voter contact and advertising campaigns in the US finds the average effect of such efforts to be zero (Kalla and Broockman, 2018). Isolating the effects of particular campaign tactics in the absence of rigorous research is hard (Gerber and Green, 2000; Gerber, Green, and Kaplan, 2004), and if some of the most sophisticated, well-funded, information-rich campaigns in the world's oldest democracy frequently pursue ineffective tactics in their efforts to win office, it would not be surprising if politicians in newer democracies – with fewer resources and less information at their disposal – would end up doing the same. In short, there is good reason to believe that politicians in many contexts – and perhaps newer democracies and lower information environments in particular – may misperceive voter preferences and the effects of the campaign tactics they employ.

To be sure, a lack of access to reliable information might explain why political elites misjudge public opinion and the efficacy of various campaign tactics. In a field experiment in New Mexico, for instance, Butler and Nickerson (2011) find state legislators to be uninformed about constituent opinion on a spending bill they study, resulting in no connection between constituent opinion and the way a representative votes. Providing legislators with new polling data about their constituents' opinions changes this, resulting in a better match between constituent preferences and legislators' voting behavior. Geer (1996) also highlights the role of information, arguing that public opinion polling has an important effect on American politicians' political behavior.

Yet information alone – or the lack of it – may not fully explain why politicians misperceive voters' preferences or the efficacy of various campaign tactics. The fact that much of the literature documenting elites' misperceptions comes from the US – a high-information environment with a long history of elections – suggests that "even the most sophisticated campaigns often misperceive voter preferences" (Hersh, 2015, 11). Furthermore, contrary to what Butler and Nickerson (2011) found with state legislators in New Mexico, Kalla and Porter (2020) – in an experiment targeting state legislators from across the US – find no effect of providing detailed information about constituents' policy preferences on legislators' systematic misperceptions about those preferences. Why else might politicians systematically misperceive voter preferences and the efficacy of campaign tactics?

Even if politicians have access to reliable information, well-known cognitive biases may affect how they interpret that information and muddy their ability to draw accurate conclusions from it. Models such as those by Ortoleva and Snowberg (2015) and Eyster and Rabin (2010) demonstrate how individuals can come to false conclusions about the true state of the world simply by putting too much weight on certain types of information, such as personal experiences or the actions of others. Overconfidence, confirmation bias, and anchoring could all contribute to misinterpretation of what information is available to politicians about voter preferences and the efficacy of their campaign tactics.

Anchoring, for example, could explain why politicians continue to employ violence even if its true efficacy is in doubt if a conventional wisdom has been established from earlier election cycles that violence does, in fact, work. Once such beliefs are established, anchoring bias would cause politicians to rely heavily on this initial set of beliefs, and evidence in favor of the conventional wisdom (that violence works) would be accepted more readily than evidence to the contrary. Confirmation bias operates similarly, such that if the majority of politicians holds beliefs in line with the conventional wisdom (which they should, if it is indeed the conventional wisdom), then they may seek out or interpret information in line with those existing beliefs, even if incorrect, to a greater extent than information that contradicts them.

Overconfidence could contribute to the same outcome if politicians take the signals they observe – of instances of violence and whether or not the candidate or party associated with it wins – as unbiased samples of the full distribution of instances of violence/nonviolence and election outcomes, even when certain elections and instances of violence are more likely to be observed and the characteristics of these instances are correlated with the outcome of the election itself. For example, election winners generally get significantly more attention in the media and elsewhere than those who lose, so violent candidates who win are more likely to be observed than the (possibly much larger) number of violent candidates who lose. If this bias is systematic, but observers (i.e., politicians) do not take this into account, then they put too much weight on those observations; they will infer that violent candidates winning is the norm when the reality may be that they win at a lower rate than nonviolent ones, but nonviolent losers are less likely to be observed or widely discussed.

Interestingly, while cognitive biases affect decision-making among all humans to an extent, recent research suggests that at least some such biases – including status quo bias, sunk cost fallacy, and overconfidence – are even more prevalent among political elites than among the citizens that they represent (Sheffer et al., 2018). Furthermore, these biases have been shown to play out in domains where politicians must make strategic decisions; Treisman (2020), for example, finds that cognitive biases can help explain why autocrats fumble in their efforts to prevent democratic breakthroughs.

With these insights in mind, I propose a theory of election-related violence as a function of elite misperception. Once we acknowledge that the efficacy of violence may be undermined by voter backlash against it – and that the ability of political elites to accurately gauge voter preferences and the effects of violence on their electoral prospects is limited – it becomes clear that violence can occur even when it is ineffective or possibly counterproductive. I posit that, in many cases, this is in fact the case; election-related violence is ineffective or counterproductive for parties and candidates in competitive elections, but it occurs nonetheless because politicians underestimate the potential for voter backlash against it. Election-related violence could therefore be explained by politicians' misperceptions about the effect of violence on their ability to win elections.

I argue that elite misperception about the efficacy of violence – beliefs that violence is an effective electoral tactic when in reality it is not – develop from the circumstances of a country's initial experience with multiparty elections, and that politicians' misperceptions persist as a result of common cognitive biases such as anchoring, confirmation bias, and overconfidence. Founding elections – that is, the first competitive multiparty elections that take place after a bout of single-party or authoritarian rule – often play an outsize role in shaping electoral politics in the years and decades that follow.[20] The cleavages along which political competition occurs, the quality of elections, and the electoral tactics – both licit and illicit – in subsequent elections are more likely to approximate those of first elections than to deviate sharply from them, barring some shock to the system (Boas, 2010; Riedl, 2014; Boas, 2016; Bleck and van de Walle, 2018). In particular, the campaign tactics used by winning parties and candidates in founding elections are likely to be copied by incumbent and opposition parties and candidates alike in subsequent electoral cycles as they seek to emulate their perceived success, a process that Boas calls "success contagion" (Boas, 2010, 2016). Thus, if the winners of founding elections employ violence as a tactic, then violence is likely to become a standard tool in the toolkit of those competing for elected office; if the winners of founding elections do not (even if the losers do), then parties and candidates are less likely to employ violence in elections going forward.[21]

Even if the determinants of violence in founding elections are entirely contingent, whether or not it occurs has direct implications for the likelihood of violence in subsequent elections, even holding the underlying propensity for conflict constant. Importantly, this logic does not require that the tactics employed by election winners are effective in actual fact; all that is necessary is that they be *perceived* as such because they are associated with successful parties and candidates. As Boas (2016, 25) explains, success contagion "predicts that when making tactical decisions among two or more plausible alternatives, candidates will choose the option that is consistent with the established model of national campaigning. Whether such decisions ultimately help or harm the candidate's electoral chances does not change the decision-making logic that went into them."

---

[20] Founding elections are the first competitive multiparty elections held after *any* bout of single-party or authoritarian rule. For example, if multiparty politics are interrupted by a coup that puts in place a military regime for some period of time, if a country reverts to multiparty elections, then the first elections held after the return from military rule would be the founding elections. As should clear, a given country could have *multiple* founding elections in its history if regimes shift between single-party/authoritarian and multiparty competition more than once.

[21] There are various, sometimes idiosyncratic reasons why some founding elections turn violent whereas other do not. One determinant may be the relative inclusiveness or exclusiveness of the ruling coalition under the previous authoritarian regime (Brosché, Fjelde, and Höglund, 2020).

Electoral politics in Kenya exemplify this scenario. President Moi and his ruling KANU party won the country's first multiparty elections after a decades-long hiatus in 1992 (as well the following election in 1997) while instigating violence to achieve its electoral goals. Regardless of whether the violence actually helped Moi and KANU in its efforts to retain power in the face of competitive elections (and evidence presented in Chapter 4 suggests that it did not), the use of violence by the founding election's winner established a conventional wisdom among Kenya's political elites that violence is an effective electoral tactic. Take the violence in the Coast region in the run-up to Kenya's second multiparty elections in 1997, for example. A Human Rights Watch report found that local KANU politicians – in an echo of the rhetoric used in the Rift Valley from 1991 to 1993 – called for *majimbo* and "exhorted Mombasans to [violently] force outside groups back up country" (Human Rights Watch, 2003, 27–28), while those recruited to participate in the raids testified that "[i]t was already known from the Rift Valley how to chase people out – by clashes – *so it was copied* [emphasis added]" (Human Rights Watch, 2003, 30). Evidence from interviews with Kenyan politicians presented in Chapter 6 further shows the extent to which Kenyan politicians have internalized the belief that – its destructive impact notwithstanding – the country's electoral history demonstrates that violence works for winning elections. Contenders for office after 1992 have thus operated under the conventional wisdom that violence is an effective electoral tactic, even if the evidence for its efficacy is limited.

Why, though, do parties and candidates continue to employ violence – or other electoral tactics for that matter – when the evidence for their effectiveness is contestable at best? Why do they not adjust as circumstances change or new information comes to light? There are two main possibilities.

The first is that politicians lack sufficient information about voter preferences and the relative efficacy of different campaign tactics. Learning what works and what doesn't based on observation of tactics and election outcomes alone is difficult in any context, given the problems of inferring cause and effect when multiple factors are at play. Thus, even after multiple electoral cycles, politicians may not have credible, convincing evidence about the efficacy of various electoral tactics that they can act on with confidence. But the information problem may be particularly acute in young, low-income democracies. In such contexts, there is often less polling, less sophisticated campaign technology, and limited scholarship on voting behavior and the efficacy of different campaign tactics.

Having experienced few iterations of the electoral process also means that politicians have less information with which to make inferences about the tactics that are most effective in garnering votes. Even in mature democracies such as the US – with a long history of electoral competition, extensive polling and data-rich campaigns, and ample research on voting behavior and electoral tactics – a lack of information may lead politicians to misperceive voter preferences (Butler and Nickerson, 2011). It would therefore not be surprising for that to be the case in new or young democracies especially; under conditions of great uncertainty, it may be logical for politicians to emulate the tactics of previously successful candidates, even if the evidence in favor of their efficacy is limited.[22]

But a lack of information is certainly not the whole story, nor even the primary explanation for why political elites misperceive public opinion and the efficacy of their campaign tactics. In fact, "even the most sophisticated campaigns often misperceive voter preferences" (Hersh, 2015, 11), and research has shown that access to greater information alone does not lead to greater accuracy in politicians' beliefs (Kalla and Porter, 2020). Instead, the cognitive biases highlighted earlier likely play a role in enshrining the tactics of potentially dubious value employed by the winners of founding elections as standard practice for election cycles to come.

Anchoring, for example, can explain why politicians continue to employ violence even when its effectiveness is in doubt if the conventional wisdom established in the founding election cycle is that instigating violence works. When such beliefs are established in the first elections under a new multiparty regime because of the winning candidate or party employing violence, anchoring bias can lead politicians to rely heavily on this set of initial beliefs, as evidence in favor of the conventional wisdom (that violence works) is accepted more readily than evidence to the contrary.

Confirmation bias could contribute to this dynamic as well. If the results of founding elections generate a conventional wisdom that violence works, then in subsequent elections a majority of politicians will hold beliefs in line with that conventional wisdom (if indeed it is the conventional wisdom). In that circumstance, confirmation bias will lead them to seek out or interpret information in line with their existing beliefs, even if incorrect, to a greater extent than information to the contrary,

---

[22] Uncertainty may also affect the electoral strategies politicians choose by encouraging them to hedge against the risks of any one strategy (Lupu and Riedl, 2013).

producing a situation in which beliefs about the efficacy of violence are robust in the face of evidence that may arise against them.[23]

In short, the tactics founding election winners employ generate a conventional wisdom about what works in a country's electoral politics; anchoring ensures that, once such beliefs are established, evidence in favor of the conventional wisdom is accepted more readily than evidence to the contrary. Thus, if the election winner employs violence – regardless of whether it contributed to its victory or not – then anchoring would make politicians more likely to accept evidence in line with the initial conclusion that violence works and less likely to accept information that suggests otherwise. Similarly with confirmation bias, such that if the majority of politicians hold beliefs in line with the conventional wisdom established as a result of founding election results, then they may seek out or interpret information in line with their existing beliefs – even if incorrect – to a greater extent than information that contradicts them.

Cognitive biases that affect how politicians interpret new and existing information can therefore help explain the persistence of incorrect beliefs about voter preferences and the efficacy of campaign tactics, even when the evidence is limited – or contrary to – those beliefs. With respect to violence, this means that – where the winner of founding elections is observed using violence as an electoral tactic – politicians interpret this fact as reliable evidence that violence is an effective electoral tactic, regardless of whether the winner's electoral success can actually be attributed to their use of violence. Furthermore, anchoring and confirmation bias leads politicians to seek out and interpret information in ways that confirm their beliefs about the efficacy of violent electoral tactics, whether or not these beliefs are accurate. As a result, learning leading to a change in tactics generally does not occur in the absence of some significant shock to a country's political system that alters the conventional wisdom about the drivers of success in election campaigns. The conventional wisdom – one that may be incorrect or incomplete, at best – can persist over many electoral cycles absent such a shock.

---

[23] The cognitive bias of overconfidence (or correlational neglect) may also serve to reinforce incorrect beliefs about the efficacy of violence, as highlighted above, though this mechanism is less related to the impact of founding elections, so I don't discuss it in detail here. But the greater observability of violent candidates who win than violent candidates who lose – and individuals' tendency to not consider selection effects in what they observe – are likely to bolster beliefs that violence is effective, even if the full range of evidence suggests that it is not.

3.3 Violence as a Result of Elite Misperception

The Kenyan example helps demonstrate how this process occurs in practice. Following President Moi and KANU's victory in the country's first multiparty elections after the transition – elections in which they employed violence for purposes of electoral gain – the conventional wisdom became that violence, as unsavory as it may be, was effective for winning elections. Once established via the process of success contagion outlined above, common cognitive biases make the conventional wisdom difficult to override, even if evidence arises that might contradict it. Violence in election campaigns became the status quo (at least in some areas), and any new information about the effects of violence on parties' and candidates' ability to win office is evaluated in light of the conventional wisdom forged in those early elections. A combination of confirmation bias and overconfidence in the informativeness of their observations helps explain why most politicians interpret instances of violent, rabble-rousing candidates winning elections as evidence of the efficacy of such tactics while downplaying instances of their losing as exceptions to the rule. Even systematic evidence of voter backlash against violence may not effectively sway elites' opinions about its effects.

Violence may therefore emerge around founding elections as politicians seek to compete for office under conditions of high uncertainty about what makes for a successful campaign. Whether violence occurs in such elections is a function of many, often contingent factors, yet once violence becomes part of an "established model" of campaigning due to its association with the winning party or candidate (Boas, 2016), it can persist even where its true efficacy is in doubt as politicians' miscalculate due to biases in the way they interpret the information available to them.[24] Compounding the problem is the fact that the direct results of violent coercion (such as voters being displaced or prevented from turning out at the polls) are much easier to observe than the more indirect effects (such as voters voting against candidates for instigating violence), and it is the latter that creates the greatest potential for unintended consequences in the form of voter backlash. By this logic, escaping a cycle of repeated violence may require unusually strong evidence – for

---

[24] One implication of the theory for subnational variation in the incidence of election-related violence is that violence may be most likely to occur in those subnational units where violence was employed by the winners of founding elections in those particular units. For instance, constituencies where the winning MP candidates in founding elections employed violence would be more likely to see violence in subsequent elections than those where this was not the case, independent of the underlying factors contributing to likelihood of violence breaking out.

example, a landslide defeat of a prominent party or candidate associated with violence – to break the conventional wisdom and make nonviolence the strategy of choice in the most competitive elections. It's therefore possible for an equilibrium in which violence is ineffective or counterproductive yet remains endemic to elections to persist for a substantial period of time in the absence of such a shock to a country's electoral politics.

One somewhat counterintuitive implication of the idea that founding elections establish the standard model of campaigning in subsequent electoral cycles is that more experienced, mainstream, insider candidates are generally more likely – and political newcomers or outsiders less likely – to follow conventional wisdom. As a result, new parties or outsider candidates (who are more willing to think outside the box) may be less likely to employ violence than insider candidates or established parties in contexts where election-related violence has become the norm. I analyze this empirically in Chapter 6 and find suggestive evidence that this is the case. Chapter 7 also examines the violent MQM party's rapid decline in Karachi, Pakistan, after years of dominance, catalyzed by the emergence of a new, explicitly nonviolent party in a traditionally violent electoral context. The case highlights both the theory's implication about which parties and candidates are most likely to employ violence in contexts where it's prevalent, as well as potential mechanisms by which violent equilibria may eventually be overcome.

In sum, there is good reason to believe that employing violence is just as likely to hurt as to harm the electoral prospects of parties and candidates because of voter backlash against it, but politicians may fail to perceive this because of a combination of a country's electoral history and common cognitive biases that complicate the process of updating beliefs rooted in the conventional wisdom. The theory of elite misperception described here has the potential to explain the persistence of violence in contexts where its efficacy as an electoral tactic is in doubt. It can also explain variation in the use of violent electoral tactics across countries; in short, the theory predicts that countries where the winner of founding elections employed violence are likely to see violence reoccur in subsequent elections. Importantly, whether or not the *loser* employs violence should have no effect, a prediction that can be used to distinguish between the explanatory power of this theory versus others that are consistent with the persistence of election-related violence over time.

To conclude, it should be noted that the theory of elite misperception is most likely to apply to electoral contexts with a few key features. First, due to the central role of elites in this account, an obvious requirement is that elites are important actors in initiating what violence occurs in the course of electoral competition. This describes most contexts in which election-related violence occurs (see, e.g., Brass, 2003; Human Rights Watch, 1993, 1995b), but would exclude cases of truly spontaneous or grassroots violence.

Second, the theory is most applicable to instances with genuine electoral competition (i.e., those where there is a real chance for more than one party to compete), as well as where no political actor has established a local monopoly on violence (i.e., where neither the ruling party, nor an opposition group, has the unfettered ability to control the local population through the use of force). This excludes authoritarian regimes that do not hold competitive elections or that rule primarily through force.[25] It also excludes contexts where a single political actor – whether through an affiliated insurgent group, paramilitary, or criminal gang – has established *de facto* local control so that the conditions for holding a nominally free and fair election have broken down completely. In either case, voters do not have the ability to punish violent actors at the polls, so the effects of violent coercion are more straightforward. As a result, India, Nigeria, or Indonesia – where elections are flawed but competitive – are places where the theory of elite misperception may apply. It is less likely to explain violence in places like Zimbabwe, Colombia, or Jamaica – where elections are not free or fair, or where violent actors such as paramilitaries or gangs maintain total control over the areas in which they operate.

Third, as noted above, elite misperception – and any other theory about the strategic use of election-related violence, for that matter – applies only where violence is a viable tool in the politicians' toolkit. As structural theories of election-related violence suggest, this is generally the case in places with (1) weak rule of law, especially those lacking strong or impartial security services; (2) an adequate supply of people willing and able to commit violent acts; and (3) a low likelihood that politicians will face serious legal consequences for their role in promoting violence. Where these conditions do not hold, politicians face much higher barriers to violence, barriers that make election-related violence unlikely for reasons beyond politicians' electoral calculus alone.

---

[25] It does include, however, hybrid regimes that *do* hold competitive elections, even if the playing field is uneven.

In short, where violence is a realistic option, yet elections are competitive enough that voters have a real choice at the polls, elite misperception can explain the use of violence as an electoral tactic. The foregoing analysis demonstrates the power of this theory in explaining this phenomenon.

4

Violence and Election Outcomes

A focus of this book is on *how* – via coercion and persuasion – violence affects election outcomes. Yet it is important to begin by examining the evidence for the overall relationship between violence and election outcomes in Kenya.[1] Doing so can give us a prima facie sense of whether, in general, violence appears to improve or diminish candidates' electoral prospects, or whether it has limited effect one way or the other. It also complements the survey experimental evidence analyzed later by studying the relationship between real-world violence and voting outcomes. While the strength of the experiments is in controlling for any observable or unobservable confounders that could bias estimates of the effect of violence on elections, they study voter reactions to hypothetical candidates with or without allegations of instigating violence, not real candidates competing in real elections, and not situations in which voters are exposed to actual violence. Thus, while the analysis here is less able to account for potential confounders, it can complement the experimental results by probing hypotheses about the effects of violence using data from real elections and instances of violence.

This chapter analyzes the relationship between violence and vote outcomes in two ways. First, it analyzes the relationship between violence and election outcomes in the first two multiparty elections in Kenya – held in 1992 and 1997 – where what violence occurred was committed almost exclusively on behalf of the ruling Kenyan African National Union (KANU). Second, it describes a close analysis of the subsequent

---

[1] Chapter 3 presented the limited existing evidence in the literature on this question more broadly.

electoral performance – in the 2013 general elections – of Kenyan politicians that were alleged to have participated in some way in the large-scale outbreak of violence in the aftermath of the 2007 elections. This analysis shows that (1) there is no significant relationship between violence committed on behalf of KANU and the party's electoral performance and (2) Kenyan politicians implicated in the outbreak of violence in 2007/08 performed poorly in subsequent elections held in 2013, in both an absolute sense and in comparison with their peers. There is therefore little prima facie evidence that violence is an effective electoral tactic in Kenya or elsewhere.

Kenya is a useful case for studying whether the conventional wisdom on the utility of violence as an electoral tactic is sound. As mentioned in Chapter 2, Kenya is a "hard" case in the sense that the conventional wisdom would lead us to believe that violence is an especially effective tactic there. Evidence that violence is in fact relatively ineffective or even counterproductive for Kenyan politicians – as the theory of elite misperception suggests – should therefore be particularly persuasive evidence that violence is not as effective a tactic as generally believed.

The Kenyan case also benefits from the availability of certain types of data and uniquely informative research designs. In particular, the clear links between KANU politicians and the violence of the 1990s allows for clarity on the identity of the perpetrating party in those years, as well as the one that should benefit if violence is an effective electoral tactic. In addition, the wide-ranging investigation of the Waki Commission of the violence in 2007/08 – and the leaking of its individual-level allegations by Wikileaks – allows for a unique analysis of the effects of orchestrating violence on the electoral prospects of *individual candidates*, something that is usually impossible due to problems of attribution. There is therefore much to learn from analyzing the relationship between violence and voting in Kenyan elections.

4.1 VIOLENCE AND ELECTION OUTCOMES IN KENYA IN THE 1990S

To examine the overall relationship between violence and election outcomes in Kenya, I begin by analyzing the first multiparty elections held in 1992 and 1997. This includes incidents of violence described in Chapter 2, such as killings and the looting and burning of non-Kalenjin's homes and properties in the Rift Valley in the run-up to the 1992 elections, and the killing and property destruction by Digo youths at Likoni around elections in 1997. I focus on these first two election cycles because

4.1 Violence and Election Outcomes in Kenya in the 1990s

it drastically simplifies our ability to estimate how violence perpetrated on behalf of a political actor affects the electoral prospects of that actor. This is because in these elections – as described in Chapter 2, and unlike those held in later years – what violence occurred was committed almost exclusively on behalf of a single party: the KANU in power at the time. Thus, if violence is a useful campaign strategy, we would expect the incidence of violence in these elections to increase local KANU vote share and the likelihood of a KANU win at the expense of other parties. I therefore analyze the relationship between pre-election outbreaks of violence and KANU election outcomes at the constituency level in the 1992 and 1997 elections. I estimate a model that includes constituency fixed effects that focuses on how variation *within* constituencies affects subsequent election results.

In the dataset, a constituency-election observation is coded as being affected by violence if violent clashes occurred in that constituency from 1990 until the 1992 election (for the 1992 election cycle) and from the 1992 election until the 1997 election (for the 1997 election cycle) according to the Akiwumi Report, the most comprehensive account of the 1990s political violence in Kenya (Akiwumi, Bosire, and Ondeyo, 1999b). The coding was done by hand, based on a thorough, cover-to-cover reading of the report. Where a constituency was specifically named, violence was coded as having occurred in that constituency. When the name of the constituency was missing, what information was given (such as the town, ward, or location) was used to match the incident to the proper constituency. I noted the page number of the report where the information for each event was recorded to allow me and other researchers to recheck the accuracy of the coding.

Using the violence data, as well as data on election results from the 1992 and 1997 elections, I estimate the following model:

$$Y_{it} = \alpha_{it} + \beta_1 \text{Violence}_{it} + \varepsilon_{it} \quad (4.1)$$

where Y_{it} is one of three measures of KANU electoral success (vote share for the KANU parliamentary candidate, the likelihood that the KANU parliamentary candidate wins their election, and vote share for the KANU presidential candidate, Daniel arap Moi) in constituency i in year t,[2] Violence$_{it}$ equals one if violence occurred in constituency i in the years

---

[2] I do not estimate the effect of violence on the likelihood of winning the presidential vote in a parliamentary constituency, since winning the presidential vote in a constituency has no relevance to winning the presidential election overall.

prior to year t and zero otherwise, α_{it} represents constituency and year fixed effects, and ε_{it} is an error term. The estimated effect of violence on KANU electoral outcomes is therefore based solely on those constituencies that were affected by violence prior to the 1997 election but not 1992, or vice versa.

The universe of cases this analysis includes are shown in Figure 4.1. The constituencies affected by violence prior to the 1992 and 1997 elections are shaded in the first and second panels, respectively, while in the

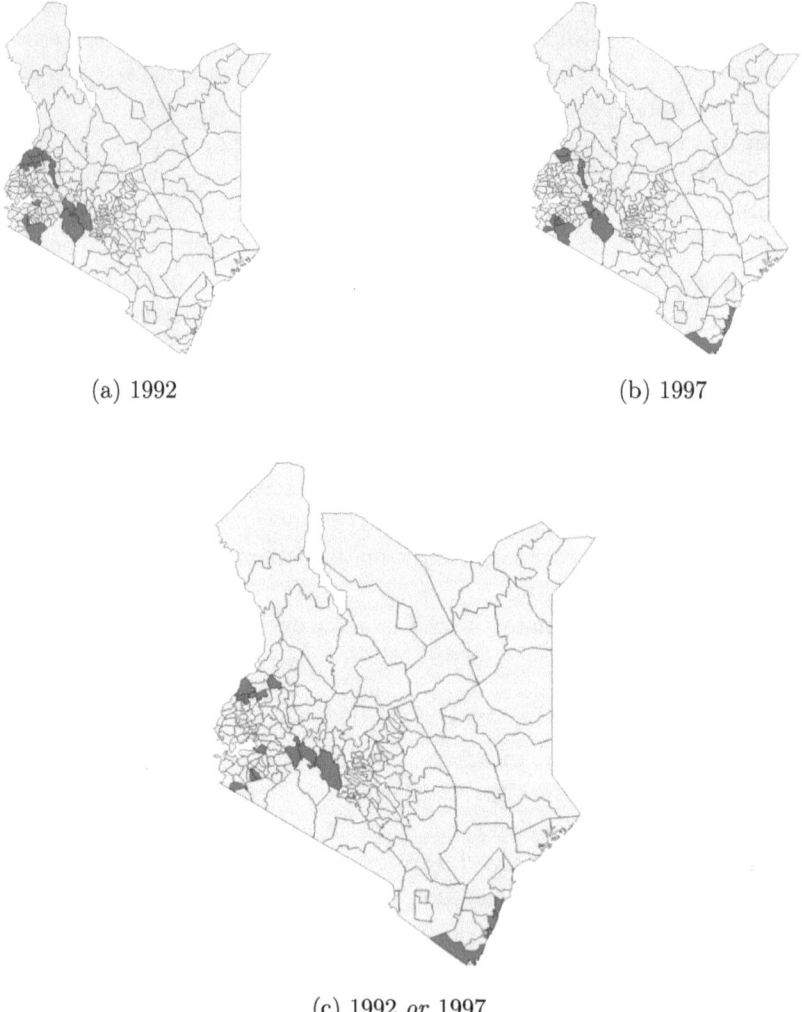

(a) 1992   (b) 1997

(c) 1992 *or* 1997

FIGURE 4.1 Map of violence in Kenyan parliamentary constituencies, 1992–1997

4.1 Violence and Election Outcomes in Kenya in the 1990s

third, constituencies are shaded if they were affected by violence in *either* 1992 *or* 1997 (but not both), that is, those constituencies within which the effects of violence are identified in fixed effects analysis. Only seven of the 22 constituencies that saw violence in the run-up to the 1992 and 1997 elections experienced such violence in both election cycles, meaning that the fixed effects regression identifies effects off more than two-thirds of violence-affected constituencies. Seven constituencies saw violence prior to 1992 but not 1997, and nine in the run-up to 1997 but not 1992. As described in Chapter 2, the violence around 1992 was centered in areas on the borders between the ethnic "homelands" originally established by colonial authorities, locations in the diverse Rift Valley where members of different ethnic groups lived in close proximity (Boone, 2011); violence on the Coast around 1997 occurred in areas with tension between locally indigenous groups and those that had in previous decades migrated to the region from "upcountry" (inland) (Akiwumi, Bosire, and Ondeyo, 1999*b*; Laakso, 2007).

The fixed effects model is meant to control for time-invariant constituency-level characteristics that may confound estimates of the effect of violence on election outcomes. This is most useful if the primary confounders are stable across units over time; there is some evidence that this may be the case, given the concentration of much of the violence in particular parts of the Rift Valley and Western Kenya, and the fact that the constituency presidential voteshare for KANU is correlated at 0.96 between the election years analyzed. It cannot control for time-varying confounders that may be correlated with both the incidence of violence and election results; still, this analysis is, as far as I know, the first systematic quantitative analysis of the relationship between violence and election outcomes in Kenya. What does it show?

Table 4.1 summarizes the results. Despite the conventional wisdom that KANU benefited electorally from instigating tribal clashes around the 1992 and 1997 elections, the results do not support this narrative. I find no statistically significant effect of violence on KANU vote share in parliamentary or presidential elections, nor on the likelihood of a KANU parliamentary candidate win in a constituency. The conclusions from a model with constituency fixed effects but no election-year fixed effects are the same (Appendix Table B.2), as are those from a model that estimates the relationship between violence that occurs at *any* point prior to the election (i.e., including during the previous electoral cycle) and election outcomes (Appendix Table B.3). A simple analysis of the relationship between violence and election outcomes in Kenya thus reveals little prima

TABLE 4.1 *Violence and KANU election outcomes, 1992–1997*

	(1) MP vote share	(2) Likelihood of MP win	(3) Presidential vote share
Violence	0.00125	0.0776	0.00655
	(0.0454)	(0.106)	(0.0376)
Constant	0.428***	0.502***	0.432***
	(0.00972)	(0.0227)	(0.00806)
Constituency fixed effects?	Yes	Yes	Yes
Election-year fixed effects?	Yes	Yes	Yes
Observations	334	334	334

Standard errors in parentheses
* $p < 0.10$, ** $p < 0.05$, *** $p < 0.01$

facie support for the idea that violence is an effective campaign strategy. Still, this bird's eye view may obscure the ways in which violence might be effective in particular ways in particular circumstances. It may also be the case that the benefits of violence accrue to the particular candidates that employ it rather than their party as a whole. What can we say about the electoral prospects of individual politicians who engage in violence? I explore this question below.

4.2 THE 2007/08 POST-ELECTION VIOLENCE AND 2013 ELECTION OUTCOMES

One way to explore the impact of violence on election outcomes is to see how politicians who employ violence fare in their campaigns for office. Not only does this type of analysis allow us to get a sense of how violence affects the prospects of individual candidates (rather than parties in general), it also allows us to disentangle the effects of violence that occurs on both sides of the electoral divide, as has often been the case in Kenyan elections in the last decade and a half, including the large-scale outbreak of violence in the aftermath of the 2007 election campaign. Still, doing so requires information on the specific politicians that are actually involved in organizing political violence, information that, due to its sensitive nature, is usually quite difficult to get. This would have been the case in Kenya, as well, except that an embargoed document with a full list of alleged perpetrators of the 2007/08 post-election violence was obtained and posted by WikiLeaks. In short, this list, which was submitted to the

Waki Commission – the main body set up to investigate criminal culpability for the violence – as an annex to an investigative report by the Kenya National Human Rights Commission (later released publicly with the list of alleged perpetrators redacted), was compiled in secret, submitted to Kofi Annan (the mediator of the post-election political accord), and finally submitted to the ICC prosecutor's office after the Kenyan government failed to take action on the allegations in the report as required by the post-election accord. I therefore use this list to explore how politicians who employ violence fare electorally by analyzing the performance of those alleged perpetrators who subsequently competed for office in the next Kenyan elections in 2013.[3]

This method, of course, is not perfect. As a list of alleged perpetrators, the document may be incomplete or implicate individuals who were not in fact responsible for the alleged crimes. However, it was compiled by an independent organization as a result of an extensive investigation, so the quality of the information is likely to be relatively good. Second, definitive proof of a politician's involvement in violence is usually very difficult to come by, yet allegations of involvement against likely perpetrators are more widespread, and it is generally these allegations that voters based their judgments on. While the list of alleged perpetrators was officially secret, those named are the individuals that most voters would have been aware of the allegations against. Thus, we can be fairly certain that the voters these politicians were appealing to in their 2013 campaigns were aware of the allegations against them and were able to take this information into account when deciding at the polling booth. All this suggests that analyzing the 2013 electoral performance of the alleged perpetrators of the 2007/08 post-election violence should be informative about how violence affects the electoral prospects of the politicians that use it.

A review of the KNHCR list reveals 26 politicians alleged to have participated in some way in organizing the 2007/08 violence. Of these, 20 ran for elected office in the subsequent 2013 elections. Of the six that did not, three died in the intervening period.[4] We therefore have a list of 20 politicians implicated in the 2007/08 violence that competed in the subsequent elections. These include 12 sitting MPs, three former MPs, two former MP candidates, two district councillors, and one prominent party activist. Of these, 13 ran in 2013 for the same office they previously held

---

[3] Since most of the violence occurred in the aftermath of the 2007 election, it is the effects of the violence on the subsequent 2013 election results that are of most interest.
[4] Two, MPs and government ministers Kipkalya Jones and Lorna Laboso, were killed in the same helicopter crash.

or contested, six ran for the newly created position of Senator, and one former MP candidate ran for member of county assembly.[5] How did these allegedly violent candidates do? Did their alleged involvement in violence help them win election, for example by mobilizing their coethnic base or instilling fear in opposition voters? Or did their history of violence make their efforts to win office less successful by provoking a voter backlash?

The 2013 electoral results for politicians implicated in the 2007/08 violence are striking and largely unequivocal: out of the 20 that ran for office in 2013, just six (30 percent) won election (Table 4.2 summarizes the

TABLE 4.2 *Alleged perpetrators of 07/08 election violence and 2013 electoral performance*

Politician	Position in 2007	Office contested in 2013	2013 election outcome
Sally Kosgei	MP	MP	Lost
Fred Kapondi	MP	MP	Lost
Henry Kosgey	MP	Senator	Lost
William ole Ntimama	MP	MP	Lost
John Pesa	MP	MP	Lost
Ramadhan Kajembe	MP	Senator	Lost
Peter Mwathi	MP	MP	Lost
Stanley Githunguri	MP	Senator	Lost
Najib Balala	MP	Senator	Lost
Chris Okemo	MP	Senator	Lost
James Cheruiyot Koske	former MP	MP	Lost
Wesley Kipkemoi Ruttoh	MP candidate	MCA	Lost
Mike Brawan	MP candidate	MP	Lost
Jayne Kihara	MP candidate & former MP	Senator	Lost
Franklin Bett	MP	Did not run	Did not run
Boaz Kaino	MP	Did not run	Did not run
Elizabeth Ongoro	MP	Did not run	Did not run
Omondi Anyanga	MP	MP	Won
Kabando wa Kabando	MP	MP	Won
Stephen Leting	Ward councillor	MCA	Won
Moses Cheboi	Former MP	MP	Won
Jonathan Kuria Warothe	Ward councillor	MCA	Won
Mary Wambui	Party activist	MP	Won

[5] Note that the equivalent of the district councillor under the new constitution, which governed the 2013 elections, was the member of county assembly, or MCA.

results for the 23 surviving candidates).⁶ These outcomes are particularly striking given the likelihood that those politicians who chose to run again in 2013 are likely to have been more viable than those who chose to sit the elections out. For comparison, 60 percent of incumbent MPs won their reelection campaigns in 2013; even when we include non-incumbent former winners, the election rate was 52.5 percent. The election rate for allegedly violent politicians was therefore substantially lower than the election rate for previous officeholders overall.⁷

Even in those instances where allegedly violent politicians *did* win election, there is evidence in several cases that their alleged involvement in the 07/08 violence hurt more than it helped. Kabando wa Kabando, MP for Mukurweini constituency, for example, won his election in a squeaker, besting his closest competitor by less than 1 percent of the vote. This was a smaller margin than he won by in 2007, despite having the nomination of the "Kikuyu party" of presidential candidate Uhuru Kenyatta – the TNA – in his Kikuyu-dominated constituency. Similarly, Omondi Anyanga, MP from Nyatike constituency, won his election with less than 50 percent of the vote despite having the nomination from the "Luo party" – the ODM – of presidential candidate Raila Odinga in his heavily Luo constituency. He had won the previous election in 2007 with 60 percent of the vote.

The election outcomes for several other allegedly violent politicians are revealing. Peter Mwathi, the incumbent MP from the heavily Kikuyu

---

⁶ Observers of Kenyan politics might point out that Uhuru Kenyatta and William Ruto were indicted by the ICC for their alleged orchestration of the 2007/08 post-election violence and yet won election as president and deputy president. This is true, though presidential politics take on a different dimension from political competition at other levels. There were only two viable presidential candidates – Uhuru Kenyatta and Raila Odinga – so the choice was clear. Furthermore, despite not being implicated by the ICC, there were widespread allegations in Kenya that Odinga was at the very least culpable in the violence as well. My own survey data shows that many Kenyans – including more neutral groups such as the Maasai – saw Odinga as nearly as responsible for the violence as Kenyatta and Ruto. 32.6 percent of Maasai respondents believed Kenyatta was responsible for the violence, while 21 percent said the same for Odinga. Among Kikuyu respondents, a full 52 percent believed Odinga to be responsible.

⁷ It may be noted that many of these violent politicians won their elections in 2007, when the large-scale violence occurred. However, since the violence in most constituencies occurred in the aftermath of the election, it should not have affected these candidates' electoral prospects in that election. Even where violence *did* occur in the run-up to the 2007 election, such as in Kuresoi constituency, there is little evidence that violence helped those candidates allegedly involved in it. Wesley Kipkemoi Ruttoh, an alleged perpetrator of the violence in Kuresoi, lost the 2007 election for MP in that constituency.

Limuru constituency, failed to even win the primary for the TNA nomination, losing by a large margin. Running in the general election on another party's ticket, he lost by nearly 50 percentage points. Wesley Kipkemoi Ruttoh, who ran for MP in Kuresoi constituency in 2007, chose to run for the lower-level office of MCA (member of county assembly) from the Kalenjin-dominated Kiptororo Ward. He lost despite having garnered the nomination of the URP – the "Kalenjin party" led by deputy presidential candidate William Ruto. Finally, John Pesa, incumbent MP from the heavily Luo Migori constituency holding office as an ODM party member, lost the primary election for the ODM nomination to a Somali candidate who went on to win the seat in the general election, a rather surprising outcome given the prominence of ethnic voting in Kenyan politics.

Lynch (2014) cites two additional examples of instances in which voters in 2013 chose to vote against incumbent MPs (and nominees of the most popular local party) because of allegations of violence against them – Fred Kapondi in Mt. Elgon constituency and Luka Kigen in Rongai. In the former, voters chose independent candidate John Serut because he was "more development-conscious and peaceful" than Kapondi, who was said to have organized a powerful local militia known as the Sabaot Land Defense Force. In the latter, Kigen had allegedly incited local Kalenjin against their Kikuyu neighbors, so voters elected a candidate that asked voters to "shun leaders interested in manipulating the ethnic composition of the constituency in favor of one tribe" (Lynch, 2014, 102).

These examples and the general pattern therefore highlight two important facts. First, contrary to what one would expect if the use of violence provided politicians an electoral advantage, allegedly violent candidates appear to perform worse than nonviolent ones when competing for office. Second, voters appear willing to vote against coethnic candidates or the parties most associated with their group when that candidate has a history of violence. Thus, the evidence from recent Kenyan elections suggests that the use of violence may hurt politicians more than it helps them in their efforts to win elected office. The following two chapters drill down deeper to explore *how* – through coercion and persuasion – violence affects the electoral prospects of the politicians that use it.

4.3 SUMMARY OF FINDINGS

Analyzing data on violence and election outcomes from several Kenyan elections, this chapter investigated the proposition that the use of violence improves electoral performance. The analysis suggests that violence does not provide any significant benefit to those parties or candidates that use it. Violence does not appear to improve election outcomes for the parties that engage in it, and candidates with a history of violence appear to perform worse at the polls than candidates without it. Thus, there is little prima facie evidence that violence is an effective tactic for winning competitive elections. The following chapter, which analyzes the specific channels – coercion and persuasion – by which violence may affect election outcomes, explores why this may be the case.

5

How Violence Affects Voting

Coercion, Persuasion, and Backlash

Chapter 4 provided some tentative evidence from real elections about the overall relationship between violence and election outcomes. But in order to more fully understand the relationship between violence and voting, it is necessary to investigate the specific mechanisms by which violence affects voting; specifically, coercion and persuasion. This chapter analyzes the direct effects of violent coercion – that is, whether and how violence coerces voters away from the polls or into voting for particular candidates – as well as how violence affects voter support for the candidates that use it. Understanding *both* the coercive as well as the persuasive effects is crucial, because when election-related violence occurs, the number of people subject to direct coercion is nearly always small relative to the size of the broader electorate. Bratton (2008), for example, finds that just 4 percent of voters overall, and 13 percent in the most affected region, experienced instances of intimidation in the quite violent 2007 elections in Nigeria. As a result, whatever effects direct coercion has must be put into context alongside how violence affects the voting calculus of a much larger – and therefore more electorally relevant – group of voters: those that are aware of, but not directly affected by, the violence (Siddiqui, 2022).

The analyses in this chapter find the effects of violent coercion on key outcomes such as voter turnout to be relatively muted, whereas violence provokes broad and consistent voter backlash against the candidates that use it. These findings help explain why violence does not appear to help parties and candidates win elections, on average, and how it may in fact undermine their chances of winning office.

5.1 VIOLENCE AS COERCION

I begin by analyzing the direct effects of violent coercion. Violence may shape election outcomes by altering voter preferences or sending a message about a candidate's abilities or intentions once in office (i.e., by *persuading* voters), but here we are concerned with the more straightforward ability of violence to affect voting through the direct application of force alone (i.e., by *coercing* voters). There are three primary ways in which violence might have such an effect. First, violence may be used to force voters to vote against their preferences for fear of violent reprisals (Wantchekon, 1999; Acemoglu, Robinson, and Santos, 2013; Ellman and Wantchekon, 2000). Second, it may be used to reduce voter turnout, especially among supporters of opposing candidates, either before or on election day (Bratton, 2008; Collier and Vicente, 2014, 2012).[1] Finally, violence may be used to shape the electorate – not just in one election but in future elections as well – by forcefully displacing voters from the places where they live (Steele, 2011; Harris, 2013; Kasara, 2016). Chapter 3 found that the existing evidence for these mechanisms is mixed. To what extent do they help us understand the logic of election-related violence in Kenya?

Of the three ways in which violent coercion may operate to affect voting – changing vote choice, affecting turnout, and displacing voters – the latter two are most likely to operate in a context such as Kenya that holds competitive elections under a secret ballot. In particular, with the secret ballot and the absence of a dominant local violent actor (such as a rebel group, paramilitary, or authoritarian security force that operates unchecked at the local level), it is hard to imagine how violence could be used to force voters to vote against their true preferences. This is because, in such contexts, violent actors do not have total control over the electoral process, nor the ability to monitor and then respond to how people vote. Of course, even when violent actors lack this capability, if voters do not *believe* their vote is secret, they may still vote against their true preferences for fear of violent reprisals. So, what do Kenyan voters believe about the secrecy of their vote?

In fact, despite various flaws in the electoral process, only 11 percent of Kenyan voters believe that it is "somewhat" or "very" likely that powerful people can find out how they voted.[2] While this is lower

---

[1] Also see Travaglianti (2014) on the use of violence to *increase* turnout among core voters.
[2] Results come from the Afrobarometer Round 5 Survey conducted in Kenya in 2011. Data available at www.afrobarometer.org.

than the average of 18 percent across the diverse set of 34 African countries surveyed for the Afrobarometer, voter confidence in the secrecy of the ballot is high in otherwise problematic electoral contexts across the continent.

What about the effect of violent coercion on turnout and displacement? The analyses by Harris and Kasara cited earlier suggest that violence in Kenya around the 2007 elections *did* displace large numbers of voters, from targeted groups such as the Kikuyu in particular, at least in the short term. Yet the long-term impact on local electoral demography and the makeup of the electorate in subsequent elections is less clear. As informative as Kasara and Harris' analyses are, they study the ethnic makeup of Internally Displaced Persons (IDP) camp residents in 2008 and registered voters in 2010, respectively, so we don't know for sure how violence may have affected the demographic makeup and relative turnout levels in the general elections of 2013.[3] In particular, we do not know to what extent IDPs or other displaced persons ended up returning to the areas from which they were displaced prior to the subsequent elections in 2013. As noted above, there is some evidence that local electoral demography may be fairly resilient to violent intervention (Bratton and Masunungure, 2007). Furthermore, the electoral effect of what displacement occurred in 07/08 is difficult to tease out since the main antagonists in the violence (the Kalenjin and Kikuyu communities) formed an electoral alliance in advance of the 2013 elections, so they contested elections across the country as allies rather than competitors. If violence committed by Kalenjin militia against Kikuyus in the North Rift was meant to help Kalenjin-dominated parties at the expense of Kikuyu-dominated ones, for example, the fact that such parties sought not to compete against one another in 2013 obscures whatever electoral impact the violence may have had.

While the relationship between violence, displacement, and voter turnout in recent years is difficult to pin down, the violence and elections of the 1990s give us – as we saw in Chapter 4 – greater empirical leverage. The analysis in Chapter 4 showed that violence perpetrated on behalf of the ruling KANU party in the run-up to elections did *not* improve the party's electoral prospects in the places where it occurred. Yet, the question remains whether the violence failed to help KANU *in spite of* its success in displacing and suppressing turnout among supporters of

---

[3] The register that Harris analyzes was used for the 2010 referendum on a new constitution, but not competition for elected office.

the opposition, or whether the violence failed in suppressing opposition voting in the first place.

To answer this question, I turn again to the dataset I constructed on the incidence of politically motivated ethnic violence and election outcomes across Kenyan constituencies in the first two multiparty elections in the 1990s.[4] This time, instead of estimating the relationship between violence and KANU vote share or likelihood of victory at the constituency level, I look at three measures of turnout, one of which is a proxy for displacement. Specifically, I look at the relationship between violence prior to an election and (1) the total number of votes cast for president and MP, (2) voter turnout, as measured by the number of votes divided by the number of registered voters, and (3) the number of registered voters in a constituency. Again, I analyze the relationship in a model with constituency and year fixed effects, which should control for any time-invariant characteristics of constituencies that would otherwise confound the estimates. I also control for whether the race for MP was uncontested, which has a direct effect on turnout and the number of votes cast. What does the analysis show?

Table 5.1 presents the results, which show no significant relationship between the incidence of violence prior to an election and the total

TABLE 5.1 *Effect of violence on voter turnout in Kenyan elections, 1992–1997*

	(1) Votes cast	(2) Voter turnout	(3) Registered voters
Violence	4058.9	0.0163	3998.0
	(3887.6)	(0.0249)	(4705.5)
MP election uncontested	−25661.8***	−0.378***	
	(3894.8)	(0.0249)	
Constant	56003.5***	0.668***	82211.8***
	(865.1)	(0.00554)	(1008.5)
Constituency fixed effects?	Yes	Yes	Yes
Election-year fixed effects?	Yes	Yes	Yes
Observations	334	334	334

Standard errors in parentheses
* $p < 0.10$, ** $p < 0.05$, *** $p < 0.01$

---

[4] Surprisingly, despite assertions in the literature that ethnic clashes in the 1990s depressed turnout where they occurred, there has not yet been any systematic analysis of the relationship between violence and turnout in the 1992 and 1997 elections.

number of votes cast, voter turnout, or the number of registered voters in a constituency. The same is true if we look at constituencies that experienced violence at any point prior to the election (i.e., for the 1997 elections, this would include constituencies that experienced prior to the 1992 election cycle but not between 1992 and 1997; see Table B.2). That there is no significant relationship between violence and turnout suggests that violence was not successful in intimidating voters away from the polls. In addition, the lack of a relationship between violence and the number of registered voters suggests that violence did not displace large numbers of voters for long enough that they were unable to register to vote in the subsequent elections. Alternatively, while violence may have stopped some from voting, it may have mobilized others so that the net effect was neutral. Koch and Nicholson (2016), for example, describe a psychological mechanism by which exposure to violence might mobilize voters and increase their likelihood of turning out to vote.[5]

Of course, it's possible that different groups of voters were differentially affected, so that while members of some ethnic groups were displaced, those belonging to other groups came in to take their place, creating a net neutral effect on the number of registered voters. This could have been the case with respect to voter turnout as well, with increased turnout among unaffected groups making up for any decrease in turnout among those most affected. Without data on the ethnic makeup of registered voters or those that actually turned out to vote, it is impossible to know for sure, though the earlier analysis of the relationship between violence and election outcomes in these same elections demonstrates that, either way, the violence did not ultimately have the intended effect of bolstering KANU's electoral prospects.[6] Indeed, the failure to effectively suppress turnout may be one reason why.

In short, the results show that violence does not, in the aggregate, suppress turnout or reduce the number of registered voters in Kenyan elections. Combined with the results on election outcomes described in Chapter 4, the evidence overall is therefore consistent with three (not mutually exclusive) scenarios: (1) violence does not effectively suppress

---

[5] Though Koch and Nicholson (2016) analyze a different treatment in a different context – foreign war deaths in the US and Britain – the psychological mechanism linking exposure to war deaths to increased turnout may plausibly apply to violence and voter turnout in Kenya.

[6] Extending Harris' (2013) analysis – which predicts the ethnicity of registered voters based on surnames – from the 2010 to the 2013 voter register would help to shed some light on the question of displacement, at least.

turnout and voter registration among those affected by it; (2) violence *does* prevent those directly affected from voting, but it also mobilizes voters with similar political preferences to register and turnout out at a higher rate, resulting in a net neutral effect on turnout; and (3) violence reduces turnout and voter registration among the targeted group, which is offset by increases among non-targeted groups, but some nontrivial proportion of the non-targeted groups shift support away from the party associated with the violence. The experimental evidence presented below suggests that this third scenario – voter backlash against violence – is at least partially responsible for the limited efficacy of violent electoral tactics as documented in the observational analysis presented thus far.

5.2 VIOLENCE, PERSUASION, AND VOTER BACKLASH

In this section, I study how violence affects vote choice by analyzing the effects of violence on voters' preferences over, and perception of, candidates for office. In particular, I investigate the effect of violence on the likelihood of voting for the candidates that use it, either among the general voting population or specific segments of it.[7] I also analyze potential mechanisms that might link a candidate's history of violence to voter support for that candidate by examining the effect of violence on voters' perceptions of candidates across a range of characteristics and on the salience of voters' ethnic identity and security concerns.

Furthermore, I explore the possibility that violence arises as an indirect consequence of heated ethnic rhetoric that politicians may find useful for rallying their coethnic base, rather than something that politicians produce directly. Even if politicians gain nothing from violence *per se*, they may still benefit from the use of such rhetoric if it rallies their coethnic base, but it may also increase the likelihood of violence breaking out. If so, violence could arise as a byproduct of politicians' ethnicized campaign rhetoric rather than an integral part of their strategy.[8]

As described in Chapter 3, there are several ways in which violence may persuade voters – rather than simply coerce them – into voting for

---

[7] Siddiqui (2022) points out that violence is likely to turn off some types of voters more than others, which affects political parties' calculus regarding whether to employ violence via the types of voters they rely on and the types of linkages they form with those voters. Gutiérrez-Romero and LeBas (2020) find evidence (as I do here) that coethnic voters are less likely to punish violent politicians than non-coethnic ones. They also find that poorer voters and copartisans are less likely to sanction violence.
[8] Such a strategy could be, but need not necessarily be, a complement to the use of violence to polarize the electorate along ethnic lines.

a candidate for office. Various theories predict that violence might persuade voters to support a candidate if certain voters view violence against a hated out-group as an intrinsic good; if violence signals certain traits about the candidate that voters (or some segment of them) find desirable; or if violence helps candidates consolidate the coethnic vote by polarizing voters along ethnic lines and increasing concerns about physical security. All these theories share the prediction that the use of violence increases voter support for a candidate, at least among certain types of voters such as coethnics. If a candidate's use of violence signals certain desirable traits to voters, however, we should also expect voters to perceive violent candidates to perform better than nonviolent candidates if elected to office. And if violence successfully polarizes voters along ethnic lines and increases the salience of security vis-à-vis other issues, then voters exposed to violence should attach relatively greater importance to their ethnic identity and the issue of security. If violence is a byproduct of politicians' efforts to consolidate the coethnic vote through the use of antagonistic ethnic campaign rhetoric rather than the result of direct instigation, we would expect the use of such rhetoric to (1) increase candidates' support among coethnic voters and (2) increase the likelihood of violent conflict.

I have argued, however, that violence is likely to result in significant voter backlash against the candidates that use it, and that this backlash may be large enough to diminish the benefits that coercion may provide. Violence may occur in spite of this because politicians fail to perceive voters' true preferences over violence and the effects of violent tactics on their level of support. I therefore predict that violence reduces support for candidates that use it, including – crucially – among voters that they rely on to win office.[9]

Inferring the effects of violence on voting is challenging, with numerous factors that threaten the validity of attempts to estimate this relationship with observational data. The incidence of violence and the choice to use it are not random, but rather associated with candidate characteristics and local political conditions that may themselves be correlated with election outcomes, thus confounding estimates of its electoral effects. For instance, violence may be more commonly used by incumbents or challengers, or by candidates with greater or fewer resources, both of which also affect the likelihood of electoral success. Similarly, violence may be more likely in more or less competitive areas or those with more or less ethnic diversity, each of which is likely to affect election outcomes.

---

[9] Note that this does not preclude some segment of a party or candidate's base that will support them regardless of their use of violence; the key point is that violence may cost them enough marginal voters so as to threaten their ability to win office.

To tease out the effects of violence on vote choice, I therefore take an experimental approach, analyzing the effects of violence and heated ethnic rhetoric on voters' preferences over candidates in a series of survey experiments conducted with a sample of Kenyan voters (see Gutiérrez-Romero and LeBas (2020) for a similar approach). In particular, I investigate how violence and violent ethnic rhetoric affect the likelihood of voting for candidates for office, either among the general voting population or specific segments of it.

Such experiments cannot tell us – without additional assumptions – precisely how voters would choose to vote in real elections in which violence is instigated by some candidates and not others, since the experimental "treatment" is an allegation of violence, rather than actual violence, and respondents are evaluating whether to vote for a candidate in the context of an interview rather than in the voting booth. Controlled experiments are also unable to fully evaluate the range of mediating factors that might lead voters to vote for violent candidates in some circumstances but not in others, especially the effects of direct coercion. For instance, it cannot capture the ability of violence to forcibly prevent people from voting, for example, by displacing residents from their homes. Still, they have the advantage of being able to home in on how allegations of violence affect voter support for candidates by controlling (via the randomized design) for a host of potential confounders that are usually bundled together with violence, making inferring the effects of violence on vote choice very difficult with observational data. They are thus well-suited to understanding how violence affects voter support among those not subject to direct coercion, a group that is nearly always more numerous and electorally pivotal. Furthermore, pairing the experimental results with observational (both quantitative and qualitative) data, as I do in this study, can help with triangulation; they can reveal whether findings are consistent and robust across different empirical approaches, with their varying strengths and weaknesses, as well as provide some insight into the balance between coercive and persuasive effects. The following sections summarize the experimental results.

5.2.1 The Effect of Violence on Vote Choice

For evidence on the effects of violence on vote choice, I begin by analyzing a survey experiment conducted with 483 eligible voters in Kenya.[10]

---

[10] All of the voter experiments were preregistered on the EGAP study registry. The protocol for the experiments was approved by the Yale University Human Subjects Committee (Protocol No. 1308012598), and the broader research project was

The sample was drawn from the towns and surrounding areas of Nakuru, Kisumu, and Narok and included equal numbers of men and women as well as older and younger and more- and less-educated voters.[11] These locations were chosen mainly to sample from the dominant ethnic groups in the area: the Kikuyu in Nakuru, the Luo in Kisumu, and the Maasai in Narok.[12] These groups were selected so as to ensure sample representation of some of Kenya's most politically salient ethnicities (the Luo and the Kikuyu, historically bitter rivals in the national political arena) as well as a less salient one (the Maasai, who often split their vote between rival camps). The locations were also chosen because of their position as focal points of violence in recent years in the hope that the findings from these locales might be of special significance for understanding the dynamics of political violence in Kenya. The survey was written in English or Kiswahili, but all enumerators came from the same tribe as their respondents and were fluent in their tribal language.[13] Summary statistics for the sample – and data on national averages for comparison – can be found in Table 5.2, which shows that the sample's characteristics are similar to national averages, except for access to electricity, which is significantly higher due to respondents' location in urban and peri-urban areas.[14]

The experiment was designed to test for the effect of violence and its interaction with ethnicity – the dominant predictor of vote choice in Kenya – on voter support for, and perceptions of, candidates for office. It does so by presenting respondents with a vignette about a candidate for county governor that randomly varies the candidate's ethnicity and

---

approved by the Kenya National Commission for Science, Technology, and Innovation (NACOSTI/P/13/8198/105) to ensure that it met local standards. Among other precautions, the voter survey was anonymous (it did not collect any identifiable information), and the informed consent script made explicit that there was no penalty for refusing to participate and that respondents could end participation at any time or refuse to answer any individual question.

[11] "Older" voters were those 35 and above, while "more educated" voters were those that had completed secondary school. These cutoffs are roughly equal to the median age and educational attainment of the Kenyan population.

[12] Sampled respondents were 37 percent Nakuru-area Kikuyu, 26 percent Kisumu-area Luo, and 37 percent Narok-area Maasai.

[13] Some evidence from surveys across Africa shows that respondents give more honest and less socially desirable answers to coethnic interviewers (Adida et al., 2016), though see Rosenzweig (2020) for evidence to the contrary. The results do not rely on enumerator effects one way or the other; below I present evidence from endorsement experiments that mitigate the problem of social desirability more directly.

[14] For additional information on the sampling strategy, see Appendix A.

5.2 Violence, Persuasion, and Voter Backlash

TABLE 5.2 *Descriptive statistics for Kenyan voter survey, N = 483*

Variable	Mean/proportion	Median	National average
Age	34	34	31
Education	Some secondary	Secondary	Some secondary
Radio	0.92	Yes	0.81
Income	$164/month	$115/month	$113/month
TV*	0.72	Yes	0.60
Vehicle*	0.24	No	0.15
Mobile phone*	0.97	Yes	0.85
Electricity*	0.72	Yes	0.40
Running water*	0.32	No	0.30
Owns home*	0.50	No	–

Notes: * denotes a binary variable. National average is calculated from various sources as follows: Age is median age as at the 2009 National Population and Housing Census. Education is median education level from the nationally representative Afrobarometer Round 6 survey conducted in 2014. Income is per capita GDP from the World Bank Development Indicators for 2014. Note that per capita GDP is mechanically lower than average income in the sample since the sample includes working-age adults only, while per capita income includes children in its calculation. If only Kenyan adults are considered, average individual income in 2014 was $195/month. Radio, TV, Vehicle, and Mobile phone ownership are from the 2014 Afrobarometer Round 6 survey, as is access to Electricity, which is the percentage of respondents with a connection to the grid and that actually receive power from the grid at least occasionally. Running Water is the percentage of households stating that they had access to piped water in the 2009 National Population and Housing Census. Nationally representative data on home ownership was unavailable.

history of violence (see Appendix C for wording).[15] With respect to ethnicity, voters were assigned with equal probability to either a coethnic or non-coethnic candidate.[16] With respect to violence, respondents were assigned – again with equal probability – to a candidate with one of the following four attributes: (1) allegations of arming youths to *attack* people from other tribes during the last campaign; (2) allegations of arming youth to *defend* against attacks from other tribes during the last campaign; (3) allegations of youths committing violence against other tribes in the candidate's electoral ward during the last campaign; and (4) no mention of violence. Candidates' associations with violence were presented as

---

[15] LeBas (2010) and Gutiérrez-Romero and LeBas (2020) use a similar approach.
[16] Respondents had a 50 percent probability of being assigned a candidate from their own tribe and a 12.5 percent chance of being assigned a candidate from each of four other tribes. Multiple tribes were included in the non-coethnic condition so that comparisons with the coethnic condition purporting to estimate the effect of coethnicity would not be biased by sentiments particular to one tribal out-group or another.

allegations rather than as facts because this is the way in which voters actually receive information about candidates; rarely, if ever, do voters have solid proof of politicians' involvement, so the information available to them in both the vignettes and the real world is open to personal interpretation.

The design produced three nested dimensions of theoretically relevant variation in the candidate's history of violence: (1) whether or not violence occurred during the candidate's campaign; (2) whether or not what violence did occur was directly attributed to the candidate; and (3) whether violence directly attributed to the candidate was framed as offensive or defensive. The candidate's ethnicity was also randomized independent of their history of violence in order to capture potential trade-offs between voters' preferences over violence and their strong tendency to support coethnic politicians. Thus, the experiment overall is a 2 × 4 factorial design, but most of the main treatment effects are estimated between collapsed categories (e.g., between "attributed violence" – offensive plus defensive violence – and "no violence"; see Table 5.3). Balance tests on more than 30 pretreatment covariates for each of the main treatment conditions are summarized in Figures B.1, B.2, and B.3.

The main outcomes of interest in the experiment are answers to a series of questions measuring respondents' support for the candidate for governor described in the vignette. These outcomes include three measures of support: (1) the likelihood that the respondent would vote for the candidate described; (2) the likelihood that their neighbors would

TABLE 5.3 *Experimental design*

		Violence treatments			
		Violence			No violence
		Attributed violence		Unattributed violence	No violence
Ethnicity treatments	Coethnic	Coethnic candidate + offensive violence	Coethnic candidate + defensive violence	Coethnic candidate + unattributed violence	Coethnic candidate + no mention of violence
	Non-coethnic	Non-coethnic candidate + offensive violence	Non-coethnic candidate + defensive violence	Non-coethnic candidate + unattributed violence	Non-coethnic candidate + no mention of violence

5.2 Violence, Persuasion, and Voter Backlash

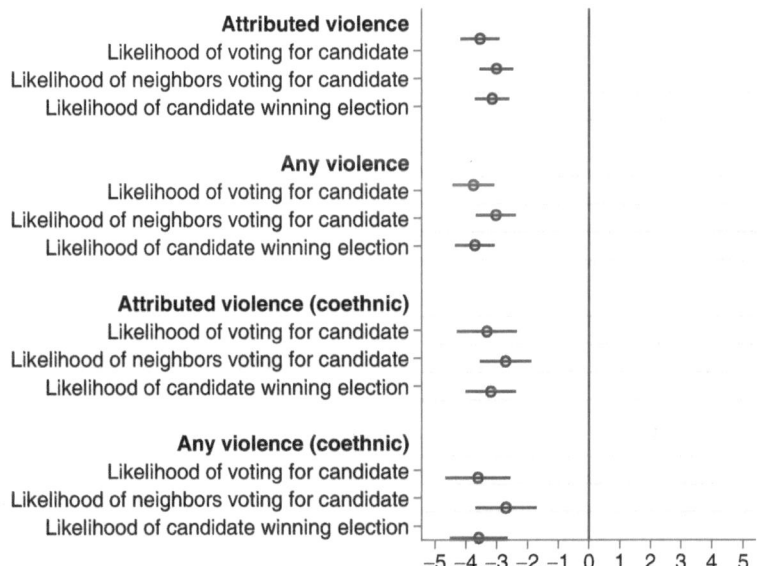

FIGURE 5.1 Effect of violence on vote choice
Note: Estimates are based on difference in means between treatment (either attributed or any violence) and control and are displayed with 95 percent confidence intervals. The attributed violence treatment pools data from the offensive violence and defensive violence conditions (results separated by offensive versus defensive violence are reported in Figure B.5). The *x*-axis measures change on a scale from 1 to 10.

vote for the candidate[17]; and (3) the likelihood that the candidate would win the election, each measured on a scale from 1 to 10 (see Appendix C).

What do the results tell us about how employing violence affects candidates' support among voters? In short, violence has a strong negative effect on candidate support, including among coethnic voters (Figure 5.1). This is true regardless of whether or not the violence is directly attributed to the candidate, as well as whether it is framed as defensive or offensive (Figure B.5). There is therefore strong evidence that violence, rather than helping candidates to persuade voters to vote for them, actually causes candidates to lose support from all types of voters, even those in their coethnic base.[18] This is important because it demonstrates that Kenyan politicians can't simply assume that they can employ violence against

---

[17] This question is included because it may be less subject to social desirability bias than a question about the respondent's own preference over candidates.
[18] This suggests, among other things, that ethnicity may not be the sole determinant of Kenyans' vote choice (Bratton and Kimenyi, 2008).

out-groups that would vote against them while maintaining the support of the core supporters in their in-group.[19]

With any such design, however, come concerns about social desirability bias driving the results.[20] We might also worry about the representativeness of the sample. To address these issues, I replicated and extended the above experiment with a nationally representative sample of over 2000 Kenyans in which support for candidates is measured with endorsement experiments – a method designed to elicit true preferences with respect to sensitive topics (Rosenfeld, Imai, and Shapiro, 2016).[21] This approach elicits respondents' true attitudes toward a politician by asking them about their support for public policies that the politician has endorsed. By asking respondents about their support for a policy rather than the politician, their attitude toward the politician is obscured, yet we can still measure preferences for one type of politician versus another across individuals since – as social psychology has shown – individuals are more likely to support policies when they maintain positive affect toward the endorser (Rosenfeld, Imai, and Shapiro, 2016). To increase the power of the tests I run, I measure support for candidates with questions about respondents' attitudes toward three distinct policy proposals that are combined into an index (Appendix C). Because I use this method to measure support for violent versus nonviolent candidates, the estimand of interest is the difference in average support for the three policies respondents are asked about when the policies are endorsed by a candidate with or without a history of violence, with the latter being randomly assigned. This approach allows us to infer voter support for violent versus nonviolent candidates while avoiding concerns that the attitudes measured are due to some form of desirability bias.

---

[19] Siddiqui (2022) points to the importance of this dynamic in affecting whether parties have an incentive to employ violence in contesting elections.

[20] Though it should be noted that recent evidence suggests that the threat of social desirability bias and demand effects may be more modest than it is often made out to be (De Quidt, Haushofer, and Roth, 2018; Mummolo and Peterson, 2019; Blair, Coppock, and Moor, 2020), and that conjoint experiments like the ones analyzed here are effective at mitigating such bias, even in the absence of additional indirect measurement techniques (such as endorsement experiments) that may be used to deal with the sensitivity of certain topics (Horiuchi, Markovich, and Yamamoto, 2021).

[21] I ran a slightly modified version of the experiment that would make better sense when fielded countrywide as opposed to specific locations. This included increasing the number of possible candidate ethnicities to each of the 11 tribes that make up at least one percent of the Kenyan population. The effective sample includes only respondents from such tribes (nearly 93 percent of those surveyed). See Appendix C for wording.

5.2 Violence, Persuasion, and Voter Backlash

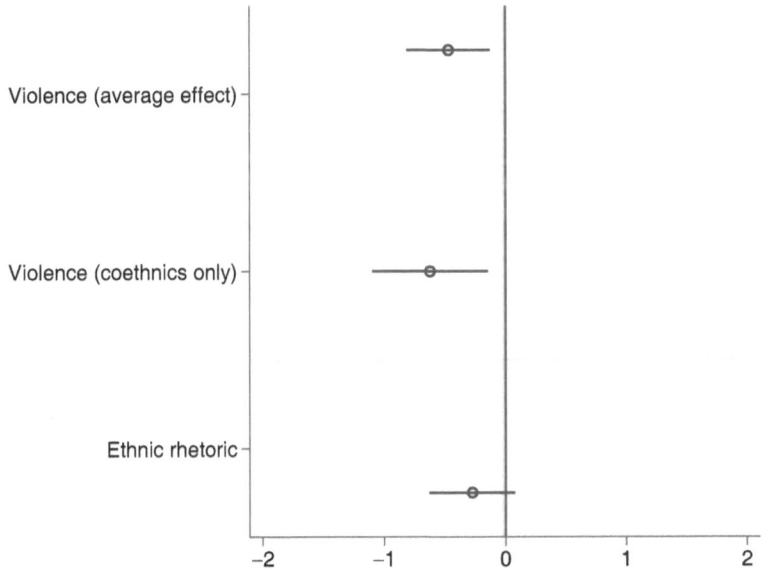

FIGURE 5.2 Effect of violence and ethnic rhetoric on support for candidate-endorsed policies
Note: Estimates are based on difference in means between the pooled violence treatments and control and are displayed with 95 percent confidence intervals.

The analysis is summarized in Figure 5.2, which shows that the negative effect of violence on candidate support is robust to measuring attitudes with endorsement experiments, mitigating concerns about social desirability bias (and a nonrepresentative sample) driving the results. The average effect of a candidate's use of violence across respondents is negative and statistically significant, as is the effect for coethnics only.[22] The estimated effect for non-coethnics is negative as well, though not statistically significant, likely reflecting lower levels of baseline support for non-coethnic candidates; however, the difference between the effect for coethnics and non-coethnics is indistinguishable from zero.

That the negative effect of violence on candidate support holds for coethnic voters suggests that candidates stand to lose supporters they need to win elections should they pursue a violent strategy. In fact, the results for young, less educated, coethnic men – the group one might expect to be least turned off by violence – are consistent with those of the overall

---

[22] The effect is estimated as the difference in means between the pooled violence treatments and the control group.

sample (Figure B.6), suggesting that violent politicians' erosion of support may be quite broad based.

How well do the experimental results capture real-world voting behavior? The best evidence to date suggests that results from the types of experiments employed here correspond well to the decision-making of voters in the real world (Hainmueller, Hangartner, and Yamamoto, 2015). But there may still be reasons to be skeptical. For one, it may be that voters are less inclined to support particular politicians that employ violence, but what if they are attractive candidates in other respects? And what if they must choose between, say, a violent coethnic and a nonviolent noncoethnic, given the propensity for Kenyans to vote along ethnic lines? In real elections, a complex set of factors may come into play (Boas, Hidalgo, and Melo, 2018). A conjoint experiment conducted with the same nationally representative sample helps address this question,[23] since it asks respondents to make a choice between two candidates for office, rather than simply rating the likelihood of voting for a given candidate without information about the alternatives, while also allowing us to see whether characteristics of the candidate and their opponent condition the effect of violence on voter support.

In the experiment, respondents are presented with two potential candidates for president, with information about each candidates sex, age, religion, tribe, education level, and record in office, including whether or not they have a successful history of providing public goods to their parliamentary constituency and whether or not they have a history of organizing political violence. The candidates' current office (MP), sex (male), age (50s), and educational level (bachelor's degree) are held constant, while their ethnicity, record of public goods provision, and allegations of violence are allowed to randomly vary. Specifically, candidates are either from the respondent's tribe or one of four other tribes[24]; are assigned either a positive record of public goods provision, a negative one, or no information about their record one way or the other; and are said to have either organized youths to commit violence or to have run a peaceful campaign when running in the last election (see Table 5.4 for a

---

[23] See Hainmueller, Hopkins, and Yamamoto (2014) for details about the design and analysis of conjoint experiments.
[24] Each candidate has a 50 percent probability of being from the respondent's tribe and a 12.5 percent probability of being from one of four other tribes, so chances are 50/50 that the candidate is the respondent's coethnic.

5.2 Violence, Persuasion, and Voter Backlash

TABLE 5.4 *Conjoint experiment design*

	Candidate 1	Candidate 2
Sex	Male	Male
Age	50s	50s
Religion	Christian	Christian
Tribe	[Kikuyu/Luo/Maasai/Kalenjin/Luhya]	[Kikuyu/Luo/Maasai/Kalenjin/Luhya]
Education level	University (Bachelors)	University (Bachelors)
Record in office	[The candidate has a record of delivering public goods to his constituency such as health clinics and improved roads./The candidate has not yet delivered improvements in public goods such as health clinics and roads to his constituency./] [In the last election, he was said to have organized youths to commit violence./In the last election, he was said to have run a peaceful campaign.]	[The candidate has a record of delivering public goods to his constituency such as health clinics and improved roads./The candidate has not yet delivered improvements in public goods such as health clinics and roads to his constituency./] [In the last election, he was said to have organized youths to commit violence./In the last election, he was said to have run a peaceful campaign.]

summary of the design). Respondents are then asked to choose which of the two candidates they prefer to see as president of Kenya.

Focusing on the *least likely* situation in which we would expect voters to punish violent politicians – the case where a candidate is a coethnic with a positive record of public goods provision – I find that having instigated violence reduces the likelihood of choosing the candidate by 23 percentage points (p-value of 0.00).[25] Thus, even when candidates are attractive on other dimensions – and even when voters must actually choose between candidates – violence sharply reduces voter support for the candidates that use it.

Additional evidence that the experiments accurately capture the reality of how violence shapes voting preferences in Kenya comes from a question that asked respondents who they thought was responsible for the

---

[25] Following Hainmueller, Hopkins, and Yamamoto (2014), I estimate the conditional average marginal component effect (AMCE) of the violence treatment, conditional on a candidate being a coethnic and having a positive public goods record.

violence described in the vignette. The allegations against the candidates in the vignettes were described as exactly that – allegations – rather than as facts precisely because it is almost always allegations, rather than indisputable facts, that Kenyan voters are forced to grapple with when evaluating candidates for office, and these allegations are interpreted through the lens of voters' political (often ethnic) allegiances. Voters are generally aware of when politically motivated violence occurs and the politicians who are said to be involved but must come to their own decision about who was truly responsible. To see whether the vignette experiments capture this aspect of voting in Kenya, I therefore asked respondents to say who they thought was responsible for the violence described in the candidate vignette.[26]

The results, which show responses for respondents assigned to the "unattributed violence" and "defensive violence" treatment conditions and are summarized in Figure 5.3, are encouraging.[27] They show that,

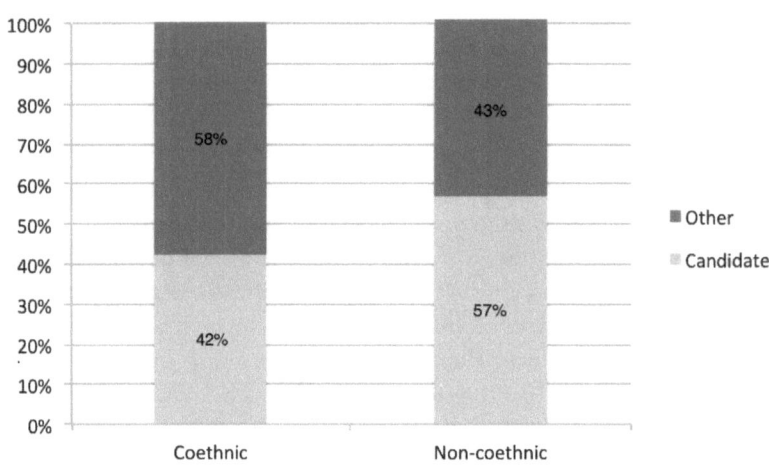

FIGURE 5.3 Attributed responsibility for violence described in the vignettes
Note: The figures presented here come from respondents assigned to the "unattributed violence" and "defensive violence" treatment conditions. N=246.

---

[26] This question was of course only asked of those respondents assigned to one of the violence treatments. It was also asked only in the experiments conducted with the sample of Kikuyu, Luo, and Maasai voters.
[27] I show results for these two treatment conditions because unlike in the "offensive violence" condition, responsibility for the violence described is most open to interpretation.

as would be expected as voters evaluate allegations, only a proportion (about half) of respondents believe the candidate described to be responsible for the violence mentioned in the vignette. Furthermore, there is a clear difference in the percentage of respondents who attribute responsibility to the candidate based on whether or not the candidate is a coethnic, which reflects the lens through which Kenyan voters evaluate allegations against candidates in the real world. This suggests that the voter decision-making demonstrated in the vignette experiments employed here are reflective of how such decisions are made in the real world.

Scholars of Kenyan politics pondering these results might reasonably wonder whether the sharp negative reactions to violent candidates among Kenyan voters is a consequence of the highly traumatic 2007/08 post-election violence and subsequent anti-violence campaigns and that, in the past, the use of violence would have provoked a lesser backlash from voters. Furthermore, voter responses to violence may vary by geography; perhaps violence occurs more in some places than others because it results in less voter backlash there than elsewhere. As the evidence on the relationship between violence and KANU vote share in the 1990s showed, however, there is little reason to believe that, even then, violence was an effective tactic. Furthermore, survey data suggest that public opinion on political violence changed little as a result of the 2007/08 conflict and subsequent sensitization campaigns. Responses to an Afrobarometer question asking whether political violence is ever justified shifted only slightly over time: those expressing the view that violence is never justified went from 76.5 percent in 2005 to 82.5 percent in 2011, the last time the question was asked. And in a panel survey of Kenyan voters that interviewed respondents both before and after the 2007 elections, those respondents who were directly affected by the violence were actually *more* likely to say that political violence may be justified (Gutiérrez-Romero, 2014), the opposite of what we would expect if exposure made voters more averse to violence.

Perhaps most relevant, however, is that the negative effects of violence on voter support found in the experiments analyzed here do not vary according to whether respondents had been previously affected by violence or not. Results from the endorsement experiments show that respondents that had been personally affected by violence are equally as likely to reduce their support for violent candidates as those unaffected

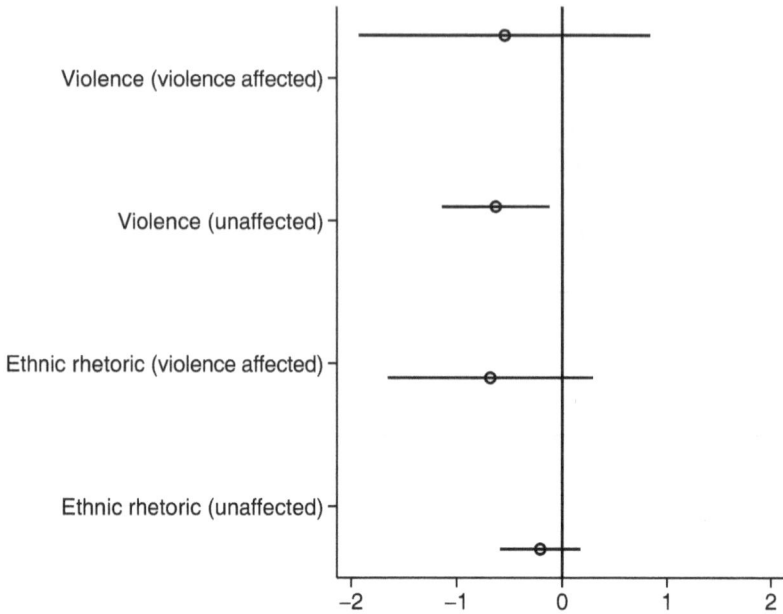

FIGURE 5.4 Effect of violence and ethnic rhetoric on support for candidate-endorsed policies, violence affected vs. unaffected respondents, coethnics only
Note: The figure shows results of the policy endorsement experiment separately for respondents who have been affected or not by election-related violence in the past and is limited to coethnic respondents only. Estimates are based on difference in means between the pooled violence treatments and control and are displayed with 95 percent confidence intervals.

by violence in the past (Figure 5.4).[28] All told, there is therefore little reason to believe that the effects of violence on voter support reported here are (1) unique to the post-07/08 election violence political environment or (2) less applicable to some areas than others, most notably those where violence has been more or less common in the past.

In their totality, these results demonstrate a large, consistent, and broad-based voter backlash against violence. Crucially, they demonstrate that the coercive effects of violence must be large enough to offset the loss of support that this backlash entails. The evidence presented in Chapter 4, for instance, suggests that voter backlash can undermine the

---

[28] The survey asked respondents – prior to treatment – whether they had ever been personally affected by violence in any of the following ways: (a) personal injury, (b) displaced from your home, (c) personal property destruction, or (d) some other way that they were asked to specify.

efficacy of violence as an electoral tactic, even when its coercive effects are quite clear.

They are also in contrast to most existing models, which largely fail to consider the possibility of such backlash. Most compatible with the findings may be the work of Collier and Vicente and Siddiqui. Collier and Vicente (2012) posit that violence will not cost candidates the votes of their core supporters but will cost them the votes of weak supporters. To an extent, this is what our data suggest, though it should be noted that in the Kenyan context, coethnics would likely be considered core supporters and therefore unlikely to sanction violence on the part of their preferred candidates. Closer perhaps is Siddiqui (2022), which recognizes the possibility of parties losing voter support from employing violence, particularly those that rely on mobilizing voters across group lines. While Kenyan parties tend to rely on coethnic voters for their base of support, they don't generally form the sort of exclusionary linkages with these voters that Siddiqui suggests limit the threat of voter backlash against violence, since Kenyan parties need to appeal to more than just their core ethnic base to win elections (at least for the presidency, the top electoral prize) (Horowitz, 2016).

The results presented here are important because they demonstrate that the coercive effects of violence must be large enough to offset the loss of support that this backlash entails. The evidence presented in Chapter 4, for instance, suggests that voter backlash can undermine the efficacy of violence as an electoral tactic, even when its coercive effects are quite clear.

5.2.2 Testing Potential Mechanisms of Persuasion

The results described above suggest that violence is *not* an effective tactic for persuading voters; in fact, it appears to turn off voters of all kinds. Still, it may be possible that, under some circumstances, violence can signal traits that are desirable to certain key voters. In those areas most afflicted by ethnic tensions, for example, it might be essential to coethnic voters that candidates signal their willingness and ability to engage in violent action to protect them against attacks from other groups. Furthermore, previous studies have suggested that violence may help consolidate coethnic voters by increasing the salience of ethnic identities and voters' concerns about their physical security. Though the results above show that violence reduces support for candidates among non-coethnic and coethnic voters alike, it may be worth testing these posited mechanisms directly.

To this end, I analyze the effects of violence in the candidate vignette experiment on respondents' perceptions about the likely performance and behavior of the described candidate once in office. This includes four measures of the candidate's likely provision of private goods and 13 measures of the candidate's likely overall effectiveness (see Appendix C). As we are also interested in analyzing the effect of violence on the salience of ethnic identity and security concerns, I also analyze the effect of violence on seven measures of the strength of respondents' ethnic attachment and the importance they place on security relative to other issues.

Violence as a Signal of Candidate Type

I first analyze the effect of a candidate's use of violence on voters' perceptions about the likelihood that the candidate will provide common private goods during the campaign and once in office. For both coethnics and voters overall, the general perception is that violent candidates are more likely to buy votes by providing gifts during the campaign period, but less likely to provide personal assistance once in office (Figure 5.5). Having a history of violence reduces the perception among voters of the likelihood

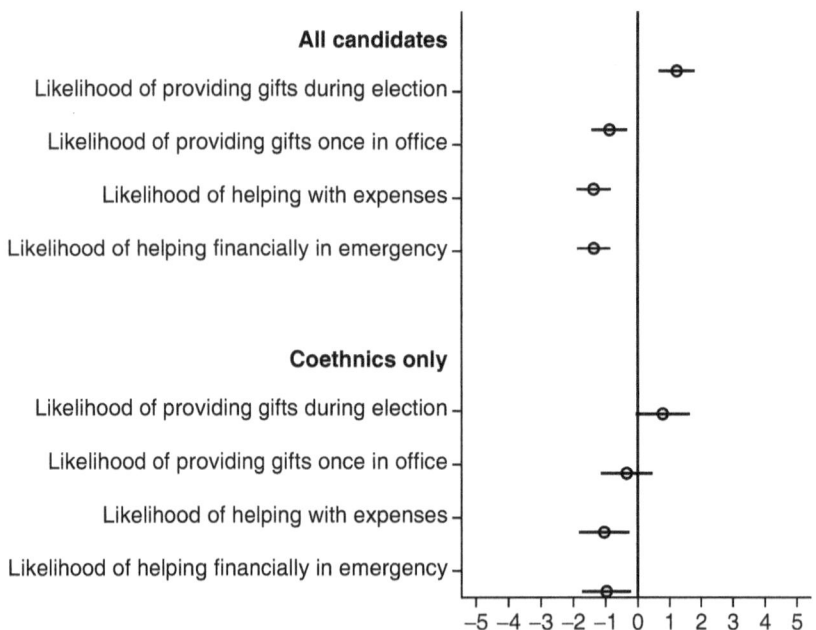

FIGURE 5.5 Effect of violence on voter perceptions of candidates' private goods provision

Note: Estimates are based on difference in means between the attributed violence treatment and control and are displayed with 95 percent confidence intervals.

that candidates will provide gifts once in office, as well the likelihood that they will help pay school fees or health expenses or provide financial assistance in an emergency. Of course, such beliefs would not provide an electoral advantage to candidates, even if voters desire gifts during the campaign. This is because voters know whether or not a candidate *has* in fact provided them with a gift before they go to the polls; using violence to signal that this will occur makes little sense. Instead, it's likely that voters simply associate illicit behaviors such as vote-buying and violence with particular candidates, so that if a candidate is engaged in one activity, he is more likely to be engaged in the other.[29] At the same time, the fact that voters believe violent candidates to be *less* likely to provide personal assistance once in office puts them at a distinct disadvantage, since such assistance is in some ways the Kenyan version of constituency service.[30]

Violence also disadvantages candidates with respect to voters' perceptions about their ability to provide public goods and be effective leaders overall. Figure 5.6 shows that violence makes voters less confident that candidates will perform well across a range of indicators, including providing local public goods, ensuring the security of their community, being a strong leader, and taking into consideration the views of people like them. These negative results hold both for the sample as a whole and for coethnics specifically (Figure 5.7). Particularly notable is that even coethnic voters believe violent candidates to be less likely to provide security to their community, undermining the notion that politicians employ violence to demonstrate to coethnics that they're willing and able to defend them from insecurity.[31]

Violence as a Means of Increasing the Salience of Ethnicity and Security

Does violence increase the salience of ethnic identities and voters' concerns about their physical security? I estimate the effects of exposure

---

[29] Vote buying is common in Kenya, but it is usually conducted in relative secrecy under the cover of darkness as a result of its illegality.

[30] The mobile phones of the elected officials that I interviewed would frequently buzz with messages from constituents asking for financial assistance to pay for family members' health bills, funeral services, school fees, etc. These officials considered it to be a standard part of their job. During one interview, a Kenyan MP showed me three SMSs he had received from his constituents in just the last hour asking for personal assistance for purposes such as a relative's hospital bill.

[31] "Community" (*jamii* in Swahili) has a particular connotation in the Kenyan context, generally referring to one's tribe.

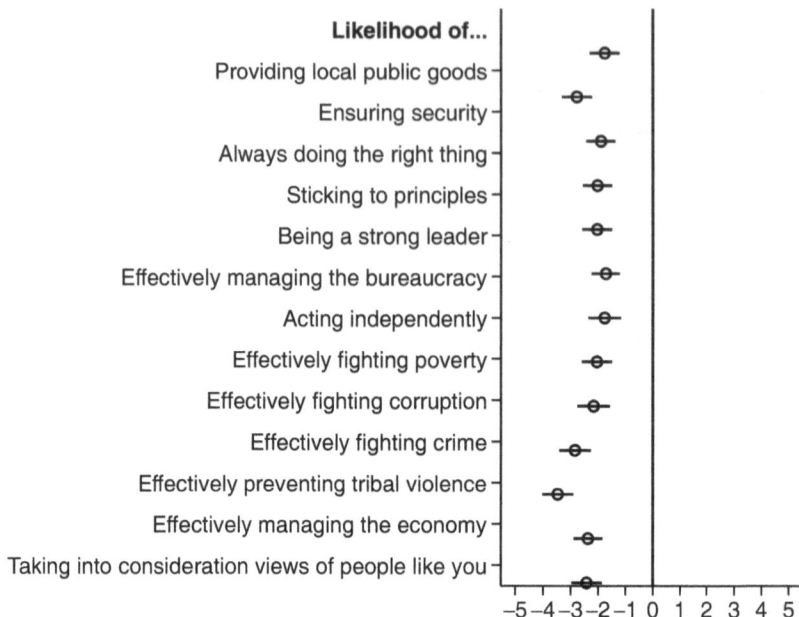

FIGURE 5.6 Effect of violence on voter perceptions of candidates' ability and effectiveness
Note: Estimates are based on difference in means between the attributed violence treatment and control and are displayed with 95 percent confidence intervals.

to violence (or, rather, a description of violence in the vignette) on the strength of respondents' ethnic identity and the relative importance they place on the issue of security. Specifically, I estimate the effect of violence on respondents' trust in their own tribe versus others; on their propensity to identify as a member of their tribe rather than as Kenyan; and on their preference for particularistic versus universalistic policies. I also estimate the importance respondents attach to security relative to other major concerns (poverty and corruption).

I find no evidence that violence polarizes voters along ethnic lines. In fact, the one statistically significant result on the outcomes of interest suggests that exposure to violence *reduces* voters' support for policies favoring their own community over the country as a whole (Figure 5.8). I also find no evidence that exposure to violence increases the importance voters attach to security relative to other issues of concern. The results suggest that violence is not an effective tool for Kenyan politicians seeking to polarize the electorate and consolidate their ethnic base.

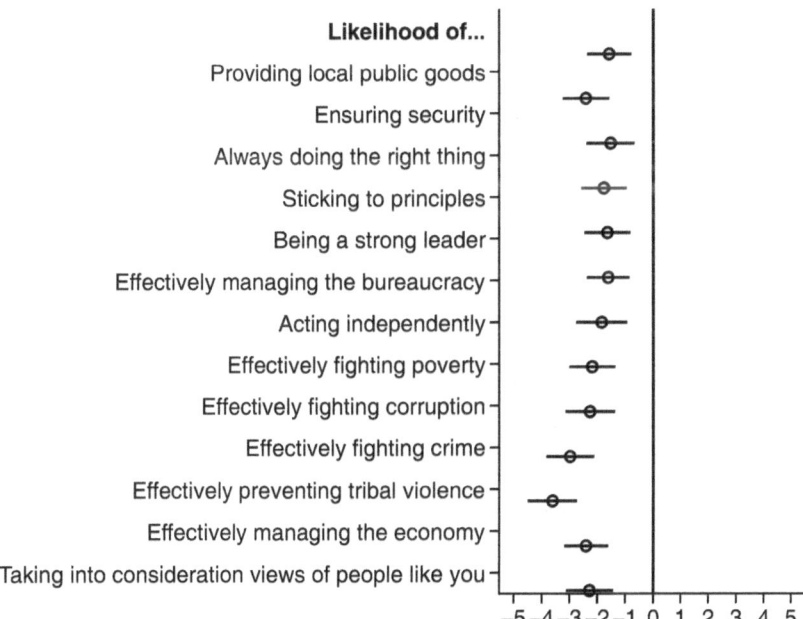

FIGURE 5.7 Effect of violence on voter perceptions of candidates' ability and effectiveness (coethnics only)
Note: Estimates are based on difference in means between the attributed violence treatment and control and are displayed with 95 percent confidence intervals.

5.2.3 The Effects of Ethnic Rhetoric on Voting and Violence

The evidence thus far is quite clear in showing that violence reduces support for the candidates that use it, diminishing the benefits of coercion. But even if violence itself is not a useful tactic for winning elections, politicians may still receive some benefit from heated ethnic campaign rhetoric that is both useful for rallying the coethnic base *and* a catalyst for violent conflict. In other words, violence could occur as a byproduct of politicians' campaign tactics rather than an integral part of their strategy. Does heated ethnic rhetoric actually help politicians win coethnic votes? And does such rhetoric increase the likelihood of violent ethnic conflict? Results from two additional experiments provide some answers to these questions.

In the first experiment, conducted with the same sample of 483 Kenyan voters described above, respondents were presented with a vignette about a coethnic candidate for MP from their constituency that randomly varied the candidate's campaign rhetoric and association with violence. In

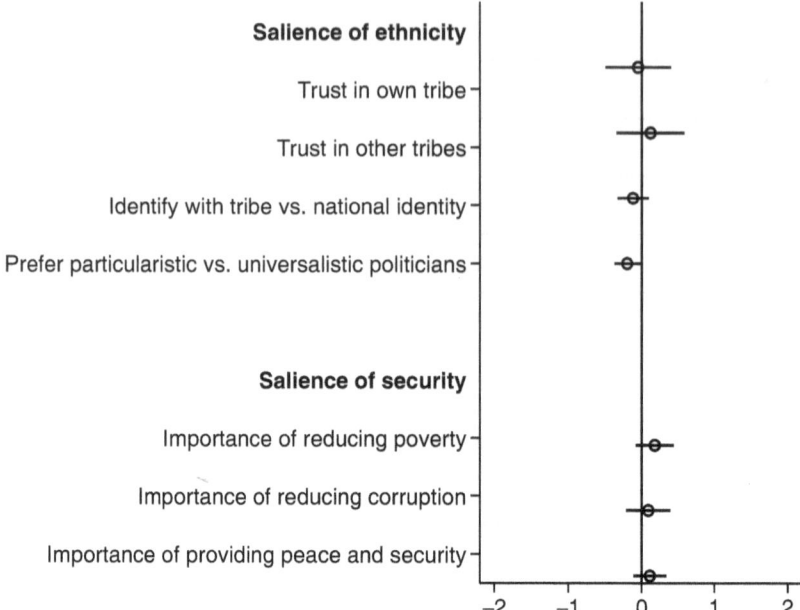

FIGURE 5.8 Effect of violence on the salience of ethnicity and security
Note: Estimates are based on difference in means between the violence treatment and control and are displayed with 95 percent confidence intervals.

the control condition, there is no mention of the candidate using ethnic rhetoric or being associated with violence. In a second condition (the "rhetoric" treatment), the candidate cites the candidate's promise to ensure that his coethnics get their fair share of land and government jobs, which he asserts have been stolen by people from other tribes, and there is again no mention of violence. This particular message was chosen because perceived injustices in the distribution of land among tribes is by far the greatest source of conflict between ethnic groups in Kenya (Kanyinga, 2009; Boone, 2011; Klaus, 2020), and unequal representation in government employment is a second major source of interethnic tension. A third condition (the "rhetoric plus violence" treatment) has the candidate making this same ethnic appeal and suggests that similar speeches by the candidate led to ethnic violence in the past. A final treatment condition (the "violence" treatment) leaves out the candidate's use of heated ethnic rhetoric but maintains the suggestion that past speeches he made led to violence. The result is a 2 × 2 experimental design.

The main purpose of the experiment is to test (1) whether the use of heated ethnic rhetoric increases support among coethnic voters and (2)

5.2 Violence, Persuasion, and Voter Backlash

whether such rhetoric increases the likelihood of violence.[32] The main outcomes of interest are therefore three measures of candidate support (the same as in the first vignette experiment about violence presented above) and two measures of the likelihood of violence. The first measure simply asks respondents to rate the likelihood of violence occurring in the next election the candidate runs in. The second asks respondents whether they agree or disagree with the following statement: "In this country, it is sometimes necessary to use violence in support of a just cause." The question is based on the observation that, if heated ethnic rhetoric is to increase the likelihood of violent conflict by stirring ethnic animosity and making violence a realistic option, it should make regular citizens more accepting of violence as a tool to achieve certain aims.

If heated ethnic rhetoric increases candidates' support among coethnic voters, then we would expect candidates in the rhetoric treatment condition to enjoy greater support than those in the control condition. If ethnic rhetoric increases the likelihood of violence, then we would expect respondents to anticipate a greater likelihood of violence in the next election and be more amenable to using violence for a just cause in the rhetoric condition as compared to the control.

Figure 5.9 shows that heated ethnic rhetoric – as captured by a promise to provide coethnics with land and government jobs purportedly "stolen" by members of other tribes – does *not* increase candidate support among coethnic voters. Instead, the use of such rhetoric *reduces* coethnic support. Survey respondents reported that they and their neighbors would be less likely to vote for the candidate in the rhetoric condition than the one in control. They also expressed the belief that such a candidate would be less likely to win the election for MP. There is therefore no evidence that heated ethnic rhetoric helps candidates consolidate support among their coethnics; in fact, it erodes their support.

To address the same concerns raised earlier with respect to representativeness and social desirability bias, the ethnic rhetoric experiment was also replicated using the same nationally representative sample and the same sensitive item techniques (endorsement experiments) described above.[33] The results from this analysis are consistent with the idea that

---

[32] A secondary purpose, if ethnic rhetoric were found to be useful, would be to evaluate whether the benefits of such rhetoric outweigh the costs of being associated with the violence that might arise from it. The results indicating that ethnic rhetoric is not useful in the first place make this analysis moot.

[33] See Appendix C for the specific outcome questions used.

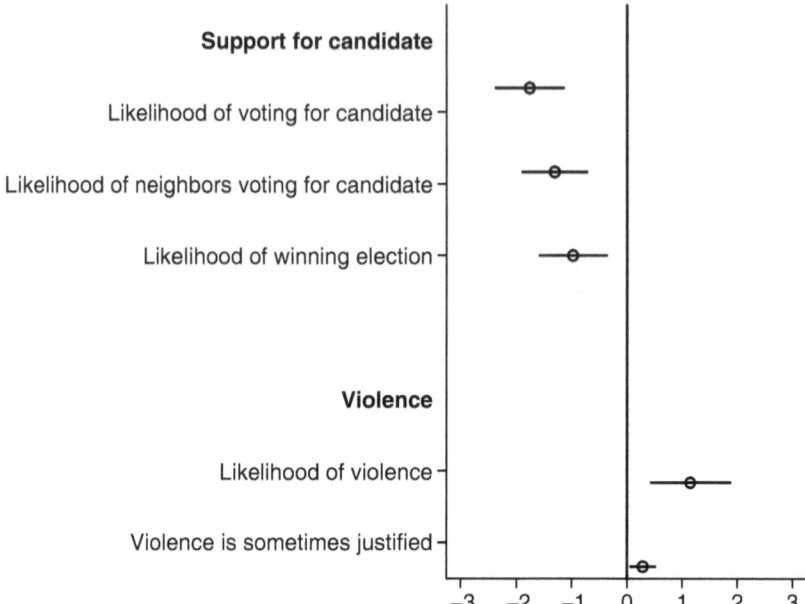

FIGURE 5.9 Effect of ethnic rhetoric on vote choice and violence
Note: Estimates are based on difference in means between the violence treatment and control and are displayed with 95 percent confidence intervals.

ethnic rhetoric is at best irrelevant, and at worst counterproductive, for the candidates that employ it. Figure 5.2 shows that the estimated effect of ethnic rhetoric on voter support, while not statistically significant, is negative (one-sided p-value of 0.116). As with the violence treatment, the effects of ethnic rhetoric on candidate support among young, less educated men and among respondents affected by violence in the past are similar to those for the sample at large (Figures B.5 and 5.4). There is therefore no evidence that heated ethnic rhetoric helps candidates consolidate support among coethnics; if anything, it erodes their support.[34]

While heated ethnic rhetoric provides no apparent benefit to candidates for office, it *does* appear to increase the likelihood of violent conflict. Figure 5.9 shows that voters in the rhetoric condition were significantly more likely than those in the control to anticipate that the next election the candidate runs in would be characterized by violence.

---

[34] These results are largely consistent with Horowitz and Klaus (2020) on the efficacy of ethnic appeals in Kenya.

They were also more likely to agree with the statement that violence is sometimes necessary in support of a just cause, suggesting that antagonistic ethnic rhetoric increases the propensity for violence among those exposed to it. We can therefore conclude that, though ethnic rhetoric is not an effective tactic for Kenyan politicians seeking to win over coethnic votes, it does increase the likelihood of violence breaking out. If politicians choose to engage in it, such rhetoric may make violence more likely to occur.

5.2.4 Implications for Voting and Elections in the Real World

It is worth returning at this point to the results of the observational analysis on the relationship between violence and voting presented in Chapter 4 and the first part of this chapter in light of the experimental results presented here. In particular, comparing the observational results to the experimental finding that violence generates strong and broad-based voter backlash can help us evaluate how this backlash compares against the potential electoral benefits of violent coercion. If violence is not associated with better electoral outcomes in the observational data, then there is a good chance that the backlash documented in the experiments occurs in real elections and is large enough to diminish the benefits violent coercion may provide.

Recall that the results presented in Chapter 4 showed no relationship between violence and election outcomes for the responsible parties, and some evidence of an electoral disadvantage for individual politicians with a history of violence. At the same time, results presented in the first part of this chapter showed no relationship between violence and aggregate turnout or voter registration. Our conclusion was that this evidence is consistent with three, potentially overlapping possibilities: (1) violence does not effectively suppress turnout and voter registration among those affected by it; (2) violence *does* prevent those directly affected from voting, but also mobilizes voters with similar political preferences to register and turnout out at a higher rate, resulting in a net neutral effect on turnout; and (3) violence reduces turnout and voter registration among the targeted group, which is offset by increases among non-targeted groups, but some nontrivial proportion of the non-targeted groups shift support away from the party associated with the violence. The experimental findings in this chapter demonstrate that the third scenario can at least partly explain the observational results: politicians that employ violence suffer a sizable and broad-based backlash from voters. As a result, whatever benefit they may get from, for example, suppressing turnout among opposition voters must be weighed against the loss of voter support that such a strategy entails. The experimental results are therefore consistent with the observational findings, giving us confidence that they are not just the result of the experimental setup but actually reflective of voters' decision-making in real elections. They also shed further light on these findings, helping us to better understand *why* violence may not help politicians win elections, even if it successfully prevents opposition voters from turning out at the polls. At the same time, evidence from the observational analysis demonstrates that the willingness of voters to sanction violent politicians does not simply evaporate in real elections, where voters may be forced to trade off candidates' history of violence with other candidate or party characteristics. In short, the combination of experimental and observational results suggest that, in general, violence does not help – but may hurt – candidates for office, and that this is at least partially due to voter backlash against it.

5.3 SUMMARY OF FINDINGS

This chapter analyzed the effects of violence – via coercion and persuasion – on voting. In Kenya, existing research finds that violence may displace targeted groups in a way that benefits some parties and candidates at the expense of others. Yet, the durability of these demographic changes, and therefore their effect on subsequent election outcomes, is less certain. Systematic analysis of the effects of violence on voter turnout and registration in the Kenyan elections of the 1990s found no effect on these outcomes in the aggregate.

On persuasion, the analysis found consistent evidence of a large and broad-based voter backlash against violence, including among the coethnic voters that politicians rely on to win elections. Furthermore, while antagonistic ethnic rhetoric *does* appear to increase the likelihood of violence breaking out, it is *not* a useful strategy for mobilizing coethnic support. These results suggest that voter backlash against violence and violent rhetoric may undermine the efficacy of violence as an electoral tactic, and they help explain why violence is not associated with better outcomes for candidates in real elections.

6

Elite Misperception and Election-Related Violence

The results described in the previous chapters only deepen the puzzle of why election-related violence occurs. The experimental evidence suggest that violence and violent rhetoric result in significant voter backlash, and the observational analysis suggests that violence is at best ineffective – or at worst counterproductive – for winning votes. Why, then, do we observe many politicians directly instigating violence or employing rhetoric that creates the conditions for it to break out?

The answer lies in Kenyan politicians' perceptions – or, rather, misperceptions – about voter preferences over violence and ethnic conflict. This chapter analyzes original data from experiments and qualitative interviews conducted with Kenyan political elites. The results show that, despite clear voter preferences against candidates that employ violence and hostile ethnic rhetoric, Kenyan politicians believe the use of these tactics to be at worst irrelevant – and at best helpful – in their efforts to consolidate coethnic support and win elections. These beliefs help explain why election-related violence is common in Kenya despite its apparently limited utility as an electoral tactic. Furthermore, access to more information alone does not appear to affect politicians' propensity to employ violence in their campaigns, suggesting that cognitive bias – rather than lack of information – best explains why politicians' misperceptions persist.

6.1 POLITICIANS' (MIS)PERCEPTIONS ABOUT THE EFFECTS OF VIOLENCE AND ETHNIC RHETORIC ON VOTE CHOICE

To assess politicians' perceptions about voter preferences over violence and the effects of violent tactics on their ability to win office, I ran a modified version of the survey experiments conducted with voters with a sample of 68 Kenyan political elites, including 42 MCAs (Members of County Assembly), 21 MPs, one Senator, one former MP, two former MP candidates, and a former gubernatorial candidate, constructed as follows. Efforts were made to contact MPs and Senators if their contact information was available on the parliamentary website or provided by their colleagues. They were interviewed primarily in the capital city of Nairobi. County-level politicians were mainly recruited by in-person visits to county assemblies and governors' offices, mostly in the counties where the voter survey was conducted (Nakuru, Kisumu, and Narok), as well as Nairobi. Interviews were conducted by me, a small number of highly trained research assistants, or both, in various locations, most commonly the politicians' offices in the national parliament or county assemblies. Several of the interviewed politicians were alleged to be involved in previous bouts of violence themselves, though this was never asked about in the survey or more open-ended discussions that followed.[1]

In the elite version of the first experiment, the violence treatment is simplified to be binary (violence/no violence).[2] In the elite version of the second experiment, the violence-only treatment is dropped while the control, rhetoric, and rhetoric plus violence conditions remain. Following both experiments, politicians were asked about the likelihood that coethnics and non-coethnics would vote for the candidate described and that the candidate would win the election for MP.

The interview protocol also asked respondents to comment on the rationale underlying their answers, offering a rich source of data on how Kenyan elites perceive the rewards and drawbacks of violent and ethnically charged campaign strategies. More than two dozen in-depth interviews conducted with politicians prior to the survey contributed further knowledge about the role of violence in Kenyan electoral competition.

---

[1] This was both for the safety of myself and the research team, as well as to encourage the interviewed politicians to speak as candidly as possible about the topics at hand, without worrying about incriminating themselves.

[2] This eliminates the offensive/defensive violence distinction as well as the attributed/unattributed violence dimension. Also, since politicians are asked to comment on how they believe *voters* will act, the ethnic match between candidate and respondent is irrelevant. Instead, I randomly vary whether the constituency the candidate runs in is dominated by his tribe or ethnically mixed in order to determine whether ethnic demographics matter for politicians' beliefs about the efficacy of a violent strategy (heterogeneous treatment effects are not reported due to the small sample size).

6.1.1 Politicians' Perceptions about the Effect of Violence on Vote Choice

The preponderance of experimental and qualitative evidence suggests that Kenyan politicians see little potential for violence and ethnically charged rhetoric to hurt them at the polls, at worst having no effect on their ability to win elections. Some believe these tactics – heated ethnic rhetoric in particular – to in fact be quite effective in mobilizing coethnic support and increasing the likelihood that they prevail. For instance, though based on a small sample, the experimental results presented in Figure 6.1 indicate that politicians believe violence has no significant effect, on average, on the likelihood of a candidate winning the coethnic vote or on the

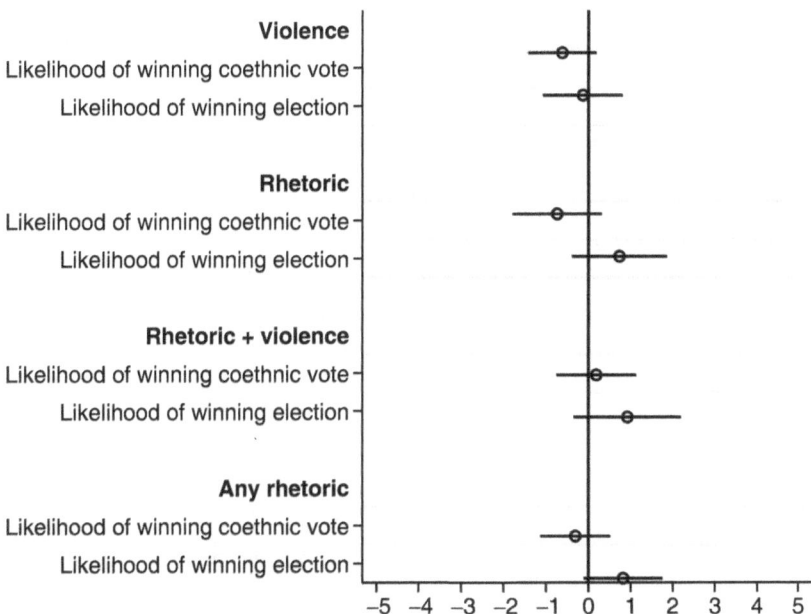

FIGURE 6.1 Politicians' perceptions of the effect of violence and ethnic rhetoric on vote choice

Note: All estimates based on difference in means between treatment and control. The "violence" results are from a comparison between the violence and no violence conditions in the first elite experiment; the "rhetoric," "rhetoric + violence," and "any rhetoric" results are from a comparison of the rhetoric/rhetoric+violence/combination of the two conditions against the control condition in the second elite experiment. The x-axis measures change on a scale from 1 to 10.

likelihood of winning the election overall.³ This is in sharp contrast to the large negative effects of violence on voter support estimated in the voter experiments discussed previously.

Furthermore, qualitative data from interviews with the surveyed politicians demonstrates that they believe violence to be at worst irrelevant – and at best helpful – in their efforts to win office. Strikingly, just seven out of the 35 presented with a description of a violent candidate mentioned the candidate's history of violence as a potential detriment to their ability to win the coethnic vote or the election overall. With respect to their ability to win the support of coethnics, many respondents ignored the candidate's history of violence altogether, apparently deeming it irrelevant in a political context where, they believe, ethnic solidarity trumps all else. A common explanation for why coethnics would vote for the candidate was simply "Because he's [from] their tribe," "Tribe still reigns," or "He's from the same tribe. People will always rally behind their own."⁴ In other words, violence may provide coercive benefits with respect to opposition voters, and when it comes to core, coethnic voters, violence is unlikely to affect their support. Still others cited what they saw as the potential benefits of a violent strategy for consolidating coethnic support. One MCA suggested that coethnic voters would support the violent candidate because "[h]e is considered a fighter for their interests. He cares for them. He's willing to eliminate the intruders as they see them."⁵ Another asserted that coethnics would vote for the candidate because "he can protect them in violence, since he's one of their own," while an MP noted that "he is providing security for his people."⁶ Another MCA said of the candidate's coethnics: "They own him – that's their man. They have a natural bond with him and can trust him more than any other person. They believe he'll see things the same way [as them]."⁷

Similarly, respondents largely failed to mention the candidate's history of violence as a relevant factor in their ability to win office, with ethnic demographics and other factors playing the most important role. For candidates described as running in constituencies in which their tribe

---

[3] Results are based on a t-test of the difference in means between the violence and non-violence conditions. Figure B.7 displays p-values from randomization inference using Fisher's exact test of the sharp null hypothesis. The substantive conclusions are the same.
[4] Interview with Kenyan MCA, 7/1/14; Interview with Kenyan MCA, 5/22/15; Interview with Kenyan MCA, 7/30/14.
[5] Interview with Kenyan MCA, 7/24/14
[6] Interview with Kenyan MCA, 7/30/14; Interview with Kenyan MP, 7/8/14.
[7] Interview with Kenyan MCA, 7/23/14.

dominates, respondents felt they would win because "his tribe is dominant," "he has the numbers [of people from his tribe]," or "he has demonstrated locally that he can deliver. And he's the right tribe."[8] For those running in ethnically mixed constituencies, the outcome would depend "on how predominant Kalenjins [the candidate's coethnics] are in the area," "on turnout from each community [tribe] and the number of candidates from each community [tribe]," or "on how much money he has and the quality of his campaign."[9]

6.1.2 Politicians' Perceptions about the Effect of Ethnic Rhetoric on Vote Choice

What about politicians' perceptions about the efficacy of antagonistic ethnic rhetoric, which the data in Chapter 5 showed can increase the likelihood of violence breaking out? Similar to the role of violence itself, the experimental and qualitative data suggest that elites believe ethnic rhetoric to be at worst irrelevant – or at best an effective tactic – in consolidating coethnic support and winning elections.

As with the results for violence, Figure 6.1 shows that politicians believe heated ethnic rhetoric to have no significant effect, on average, on the likelihood of a candidate winning the coethnic vote or on the likelihood of winning the election overall. Qualitative data from interviews with the politicians who participated in the survey help to clarify the story. A few respondents ignored the candidate's rhetoric when describing their electoral prospects, mentioning tribal solidarity and ethnic demographics as the most relevant factors. Those running in areas dominated by their tribe will win because "the majority of people are from his tribe" or because "There is a high number of Luos; the other tribes are fewer, so their votes won't make a difference,"[10] while victory for those running in more ethnically mixed locales "depends on [which tribe] has the majority."[11] Many politicians, however, mentioned what they saw as the potential benefits of an ethnically charged campaign strategy. On why a candidate that employed ethnic rhetoric would win the coethnic vote, one MP said that "He is talking political language that Kenyans love, which

---

[8] Interview with Kenyan MCA, 7/23/14; Interview with Kenyan MCA, 7/23/14; Interview with Kenyan MP, 7/8/14.
[9] Interview with Kenyan MCA, 7/30/14; Interview with Kenyan MCA, 7/24/14; Interview with Kenyan MCA, 7/17/14.
[10] Interview with Kenyan MCA, 7/17/14; Interview with Kenyan MCA, 3/19/15.
[11] Interview with former Kenyan MP candidate, 11/21/14.

is fighting for the Kikuyu share, fighting for their rights," while another noted that "He's running in an area dominated by his tribe, and he's talking about relevant issues to his constituency."[12] Similarly, an MCA suggested that "He is talking about the rights of his people, protecting what is theirs, protecting the dignity of his tribe" and another that "He's championing their rights and raising their emotions about other communities and promising to get them jobs from others."[13] Tellingly, one MCA argued that by using such rhetoric, the candidate "has shown them [his coethnics] that he cares about them and will fight for them regardless of controversy."[14] A candidate using such rhetoric will win their election because "He will be talking [about] what the community wants to hear and he comes from the dominant tribe" and "he is using the correct strategy, talking about issues at the heart of people."[15]

The mismatch between Kenyan politicians' perceptions about the effects of violence and ethnic rhetoric on voter support and the reality is therefore quite stark.[16] Figure 6.2, which compares the estimates from the politician experiments to estimates from the analogous voter experiments, demonstrates the disconnect clearly. Using 10,000 bootstrapped random samples of 68 voters (the same size as the elite sample) drawn from the larger sample of voters, it shows that the difference between voter preferences over violence and ethnic rhetoric and politicians' perceptions of those preferences is large. Furthermore, a formal test of the differences between the two sets of estimates finds them to be highly statistically significant (Figure 6.3).[17] The mismatch between voter preferences and politicians' perceptions of them is clear, and it suggests that

[12] Interview with Kenyan MP, 7/1/14; Interview with Kenyan MP, 7/3/14.
[13] Interview with Kenyan MCA, 7/23/14; Interview with Kenyan MCA, 7/24/14.
[14] Interview with Kenyan MCA, 5/25/15.
[15] Interview with Kenyan MP, 11/10/14; Interview with former Kenya gubernatorial candidate, 4/9/15.
[16] To be sure, a handful of politicians characterized voter preferences over violence more accurately. One MP suggested that "Luos will generally obviously vote for one of their own, like all other tribes in Kenya, [but] it is not assured here because of his violent ways," while an MCA noted that the "first instinct for them [coethnic voters] will be to vote for him because, like them, he is Kalenjin, [but] the fact that that he is said to be using violence will make him lose reasonable voters from his own tribe." However, such beliefs were clearly the exception rather than the rule.
[17] This analysis pools the sample of politicians and voters and estimates the difference in effects between them by interacting treatment indicators with an indicator for whether the respondent is a politician or voter. Note that the difference between politicians and voters can be statistically significant even if the null results in the politician experiments are attributable to the small sample size.

6.2 Is It Actually "Misperception?" Addressing Alternative 121

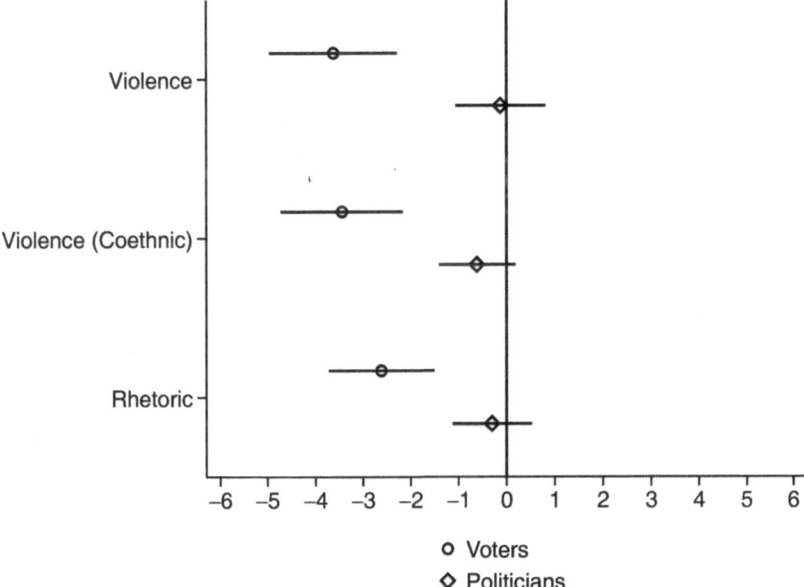

FIGURE 6.2 Politician perceptions vs. voter preferences over violence and ethnic rhetoric
Note: Estimates for politicians are for the violence and any rhetoric treatments, the latter for the "coethnic vote" outcome. Estimates for voters are of the effect of the "attributed violence" and "any rhetoric" treatments based on 10,000 bootstrapped random samples of 68 voters (the same size as the sample of politicians) drawn from the full sample of voters. The *x*-axis measures change on a scale from 1 to 10.

politicians underestimate the size and scope of voter backlash against the use of violence and ethnic rhetoric in electoral competition.

6.2 IS IT ACTUALLY "MISPERCEPTION?" ADDRESSING ALTERNATIVE EXPLANATIONS

While the evidence shows that Kenyan politicians misperceive the effects of violence on voter support, it could still be the case that violence is a useful electoral tactic if the benefits of violent coercion outweigh the loss of voter support associated with such a strategy, especially since those politicians are able to evade – in virtually all circumstances – any legal or professional accountability for their actions. For instance, violence may be used to forcibly prevent people from voting or intimidate them into changing their vote, for example by displacing residents from their homes

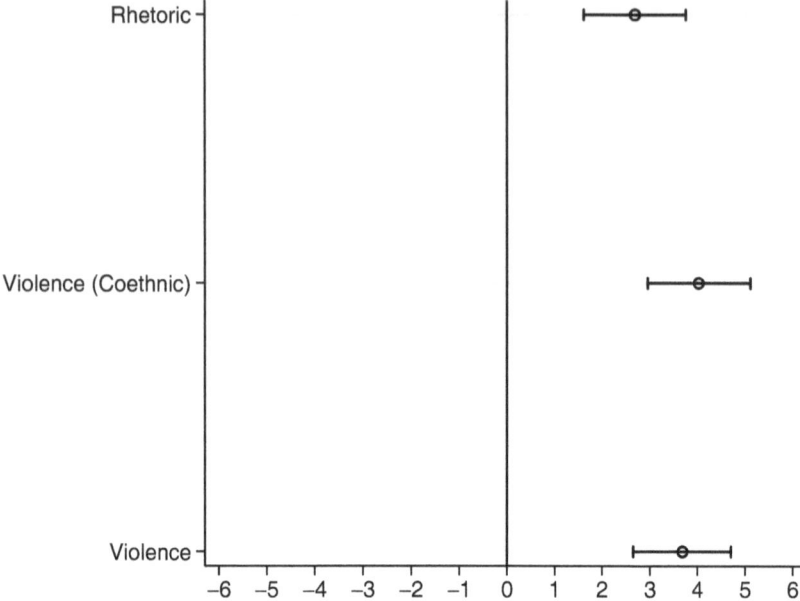

FIGURE 6.3 Difference in politician perceptions vs. voter preferences over violence and ethnic rhetoric

Note: This figure presents estimates of the difference between the effects of violence and ethnic rhetoric on vote choice (estimated from the voter sample) and politician perceptions of these effects (estimated from the politician sample) derived from a pooled sample of voters and politicians, and from a model that interacts treatment with an indicator for whether or not the respondent is a politician. Estimates for politicians are for the violence and any rhetoric treatments, the latter for the "coethnic vote" outcome. Estimates for voters are of the effect of the "attributed violence" and "any rhetoric" treatments.

or threatening violent reprisals should they vote a certain way. If violence can prevent large numbers of opposition supporters from voting or force them to change their vote, might it be a worthwhile strategy, even if it leads to some deterioration in voter support? In particular, might a strategy that targets non-coethnic voters reduce the number of votes for opposing candidates while only minimally affecting support among one's coethnic base? In other words, do the benefits of coercion outweigh the loss of voter support that results from the use of violence?

Certainly, the coercive effects of violence in Kenya are well-documented, resulting at times in significant population displacement, for example in (Harris, 2013). Yet the evidence presented in Chapter 4 – which found no electoral benefit for parties or candidates that employ

6.2 Is It Actually "Misperception?" Addressing Alternative 123

violence – is consistent with the idea that voter backlash against violence may offset whatever electoral benefits coercion may provide. In the elections of 1992 and 1997, thousands of residents were displaced, but the data does not support the idea that the violence was electorally advantageous. Furthermore, the fact that backlash against violence occurs among coethnic voters as well suggests that suppressing non-coethnic votes with violence while maintaining solid support among the coethnic base may not be a viable strategy.

The observational evidence also militates against the alternative explanations discussed in Chapter 3 for why politicians may continue to employ violence even if voters dislike violent politicians and prefer not to see them in office, namely that (1) voters may care more about features of parties and candidates other than their history of violence; (2) voters may not have sufficient information to hold politicians accountable for instigating violence; and (3) voters may engage in motivated reasoning about violent candidates to whom they feel close as a result of social identity or some other subjective criteria, rationalizing their support for them despite their distaste for violence in the abstract. That the observational analysis in Chapter 4 finds that violence does not help – but may hurt – the parties and candidates that use it suggests that politicians are not being savvy by employing violence despite voters' preferences against it, but rather that they underestimate voter backlash against violence and its potential to erode any advantages that violence may provide. Overall, the evidence suggests that violence provokes voter backlash against the candidates that use it and weighs against the idea that the electoral benefits of violence outweigh its costs on balance. While that doesn't imply that violence is *never* an effective strategy, it does suggest that, on the whole, politicians underestimate the breadth and depth of voter backlash against violence and overestimate its efficacy as an electoral tactic.

Finally, even if politicians recognize the possibility of voter backlash against violence, perhaps they lack the requisite level of control over the violent specialists acting on their behalf to determine whether or not violence occurs? In other words, perhaps politicians are not misperceiving voter preferences, but rather failing to act strategically because they as principals cannot ensure that their agents act in their best electoral interests? It is certainly the case that politicians lack perfect control over violent specialists, such as gangs and ethnic militias, acting on their behalf. Yet in Kenya, at least, politicians do appear to have significant control over all but the lowest level electoral violence. The grey literature from government commission and civil society reports on the violence of the 1990s points to the direct organizing role of ruling party politicians and the relative lack of more spontaneous violence (Human Rights Watch, 1995b, 2003; Akiwumi, Bosire, and Ondeyo, 1999a). In addition, the large outbreak of violence in the aftermath of the 2007 election, which was "financed and sustained mainly by local politicians and businesspeople" (KNCHR, 2008), ended abruptly once incumbent and opposition leaders Mwai Kibaki and Raila Odinga agreed to a powersharing agreement and appealed to their supporters to keep the peace. Mutahi and Ruteere (2019) note that the actions of political elites in restraining their followers from engaging in violence – both before and after the highly contested 2017 election – were significant contributors to the relative lack of ethnic and gang-related violence around that election. Data from my interviews with local politicians is consistent with this dynamic, with one county assembly member asserting that "[v]iolence won't happen if the ones at the top don't allow it to happen."[18] Furthermore, research on political violence in contexts beyond Kenya has demonstrated the significant extent to which political elites have the ability to prevent (or not) low-level conflict from spiraling into larger conflagrations (Wilkinson, 2004; Nellis, Weaver, and Rosenzweig, 2016; Nellis and Siddiqui, 2018; Brass, 2003; Human Rights Watch, 1995b).

6.3 ARE POLITICIANS' MISPERCEPTIONS DUE TO LACK OF INFORMATION?

In Chapter 3, I proposed that elite misperception could be due to either a lack of information or cognitive biases that affect politicians' interpretation of the information that they have. Because politicians misperceive voter preferences in high-information environments as well (Hersh, 2015), and because access to information may not correct their false beliefs (Kalla and Porter, 2020), I hypothesized that cognitive biases are more likely to explain misperceptions than lack of information alone. To shed further light on this hypothesis, I conducted a field experiment with Kenyan politicians in the 2017 general elections in which I assess the ability of information about voter backlash against violence to reduce the propensity of politicians to employ violence in their campaigns.

If lack of information about voter preferences over violence explains why politicians overestimate the efficacy of violence as an electoral tactic, then providing them with systematic information about voters' strong

---

[18] Interview with MCA, July 24, 2014.

aversion to violent candidates should lead them to update their beliefs, to see violence as a less effective tactic, and – ultimately – to be less likely to employ violence in their campaigns. To test this, I implemented a field experiment in the run-up to the 2017 elections in Kenya in which I provided MP candidates for the National Assembly in a randomly selected half of constituencies with a memo summarizing the findings about voter backlash against violence described in Chapter 5 and links to the full analysis should they be interested in digging deeper (see Appendix D).[19] The memo explained that academic research on voting in Kenya had found that violence was a losing strategy, and that candidates lose voter support when they employ violence and tribal rhetoric. It provided specific figures from the data, and links to the complete analysis. The idea was that, if politicians overestimate the efficacy of violence as an electoral tactic because of a lack of information about how it undermines support among voters, then being provided with systematic information about voter backlash against violence could mitigate misperceptions and reduce the likelihood of violence being employed in candidates' election campaigns.[20]

To implement the experiment, I first randomly assigned half of constituencies to the treatment (candidates receiving the memo) and half to control, blocking on former province and 2013 ruling party presidential vote share.[21] I then identified all candidates running for MP in Kenya's 290 constituencies – which were listed in a list posted to the Kenya Gazette by the Independent Electoral and Boundaries Commission (IEBC) – and scoured the internet for contact information that might be available for each candidate in the treated constituencies, including on the National Assembly website and Mzalendo for incumbent candidates, as well as on candidates' personal or campaign Facebook pages. I collected as many email addresses, mobile phone numbers, and Facebook accounts

---

[19] The study was deemed exempt from IRB review by the Yale Human Subjects Committee by meeting exemption criteria 45 CFR 46.101(b)(3) under Protocol ID 2000020388.

[20] One concern is that the source of the information (a study conducted by an American researcher) may affect how Kenyan politicians perceive the credibility of the information. This is certainly plausible, though it's not clear which direction (more versus less trustworthy) the effect is likely to go. While a non-Kenyan researcher may be perceived as less knowledgeable about local conditions and therefore less credible, it could also be the case that politicians view an outsider as more objective than a local researcher who they may perceive as potentially politically motivated and therefore biased.

[21] Kenya has eight former provinces, which have become defunct under the 2010 constitution. Ruling party vote share is vote share for the Jubilee Coalition's candidate incumbent Uhuru Kenyatta.

as possible for candidates in the treated constituencies; I was able to find at least one form of contact for 477 candidates in 145 treated constituencies, which resulted in a mean of 3.29, a median of 3, and a mode of 2 candidates contacted per constituency.

Using this information, I then sent the memo via each form of contact I had for a given candidate 7 weeks prior to the election (see Appendix D for the contact scripts). Using publicly available data from ACLED, I analyze the effect of the information treatment on violent incidents and fatalities at the constituency level in the preelection period from the day that the information was sent through the day of the election, controlling for demographic characteristics of the constituencies as well as levels of preelection violence in 2013 and in the 2017 electoral period up to the treatment.[22] I estimate both intent-to-treat effects and two-stage least squares to account for a treatment assignment error that resulted in candidates in some constituencies assigned to the control group receiving the treatment.

The results, summarized in Figure 6.4, show that the information treatment had no effect on the number of violent incidents or fatalities in the posttreatment, preelection period. The treatment effects for both are a rather precisely estimated zero. The results suggest that lack of information alone is not the primary reason why Kenyan politicians overestimate the efficacy of violence as an electoral tactic and underestimate voter backlash against it. Cognitive biases may be more likely to play an important role.

There are several caveats that must be taken into account in interpreting these results, however, most of which have to do with the weakness of the treatment. First, because I was unable to find contact information for all MP candidates in a constituency, there were many candidates that did not receive the information treatment, so the treatment was weaker than if I had been able to send information to all candidates in the constituency. Second, it's not clear that even those candidates for whom I had contact information actually read the information that was sent, or read it closely. Previous studies suggest that politicians' interest in such information is surprisingly low (Kalla and Porter, 2020), so it's possible that

---

[22] Covariates included in the regression model include the geographic size of the constituency, population, poverty level, incumbent Jubilee Coalition 2013 presidential vote share, and whether the constituency is "cosmopolitan" (ethnically diverse) according to the Kenya Election Database. I also include the number of violent incidents/fatalities in the preelection period in 2013 and in the pretreatment election period in 2017.

6.3 Are Politicians' Misperceptions due to Lack 127

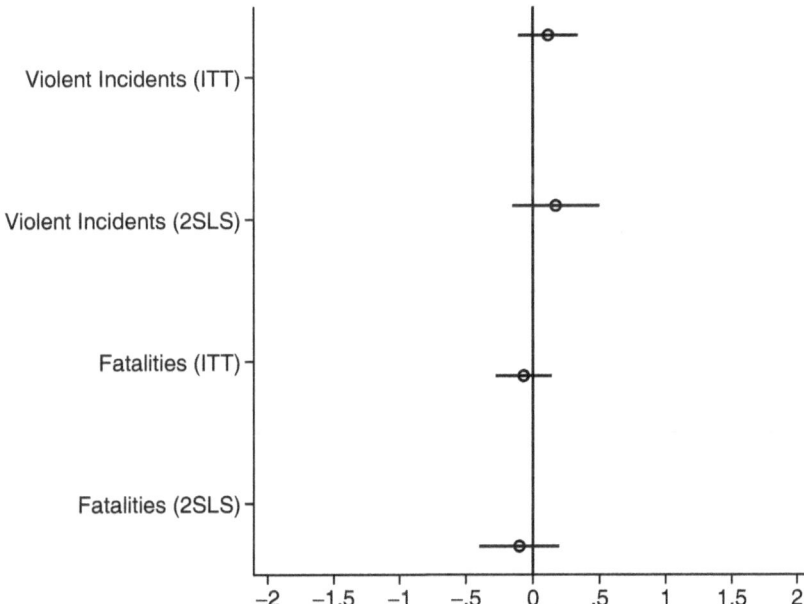

FIGURE 6.4 Effects of providing information to MP candidates on preelection violence
Note: Effect sizes are standardized to facilitate comparison across outcomes. "Violent Incidents" represents the number of violence incidents in the constituency after treatment and until election day. "Fatalities" represents the number of fatalities in violent incidents. Both are estimated as ITT and 2SLS.

only a fraction of the candidates that were contacted actually consumed the information that was sent. In short, the results cast doubt on the idea that a lack of information alone is responsible for politicians' misperceptions about violence because providing such information does not appear to reduce its incidence in the campaign period, but the null effects of the treatment could be due to its weakness in addition to the ineffectiveness of information in correcting politicians' misperceptions.

An additional observable implication of the theory of elite misperception – which holds that politicians employ violence as a result of a conventional wisdom that forms in founding elections that persists due to cognitive biases such as anchoring and confirmation bias – is that outsider candidates should be less likely to employ violence than political insiders. This is because the views and beliefs of insiders are most likely to be in line with the conventional wisdom about how electoral politics is conducted, whereas outsiders are more likely to have fresh ideas about how to run their campaigns. They are also less likely to be subject to anchoring and confirmation bias, having not participated in prior election campaigns that would affect their interpretation of new information in light of previous experience. Importantly, this prediction – that political outsiders are less likely to employ violence – is different from what a number of alternative theories of election-related violence would predict, which is that violence is a tool that less established politicians may resort to in the absence of other options such as clientelism (Collier and Vicente, 2012).

Overall, the evidence appears consistent with the prediction that outsider candidates are less likely than insiders to abide by the conventional wisdom and employ violence. At the macro level, the main presidential campaigns in Kenya associated with violence are those of incumbent president Moi in 1992 and 1997, as well as Mwai Kibaki and Raila Odinga in 2007, all longtime players at the highest levels of Kenyan politics. And as has been emphasized before, the violence of the 1990s was largely organized by ruling party elites, most of whom were sitting elected officials at the time. In addition, of the specific politicians mentioned as alleged participants in the violence of 2007/08 in the leaked, non-public version of the official Waki Report, nearly all (20/26) were sitting elected officials when the violence occurred; others included two former MPs, a previous MP candidate on a major party ticket, and a well-known major party activist. Of course, uneven access to information about violent perpetrators makes any such analysis imperfect, but the fact that the vast majority of politicians said to be involved in election-related violence in Kenya have been political insiders suggests that they may be more likely than outsiders to abide by the conventional wisdom that violent politics works.[23]

6.4 SUMMARY OF FINDINGS

This chapter has presented evidence that politicians underestimate the size and scope of voter backlash against the use of violence and ethnic rhetoric in electoral competition. In particular, politicians believe, despite evidence

---

[23] For sure, whether the Pr(Insider|ViolentCandidate) is greater than Pr(Outsider|ViolentCandidate), which is what is analyzed here, is not the same as the Pr(ViolentCandidate|Insider) being greater than the Pr(ViolentCandidate|Outsider), which is of greatest interest. Yet the near absence of political outsiders in accounts of violent politicians in Kenya suggests that the latter relationship is likely to be true.

to the contrary, that violence and heated ethnic rhetoric are at worst irrelevant – and at best helpful – in their efforts to consolidate coethnic support and win elections. Crucially, they believe that such tactics are viewed by coethnic voters as either irrelevant to their vote choice or, perhaps, as a sign of a candidate's strength and ability to protect their own in times of need, giving them little reason to worry about a loss of support among their core voters. Evaluated in light of the evidence presented in Chapters 4 and 5, these findings suggest that politicians overestimate the benefits – and, more importantly, underestimate the costs – of a violent campaign strategy. Furthermore, access to information about voter backlash against violence does not appear to reduce the propensity to use it. Elite misperception can help explain why violence occurs in the course of electoral competition even where the gains from it are uncertain at best.

7

Voter Backlash, Elite Misperception, and Violence beyond Kenya

While the empirical focus of this book is on Kenya, it is likely to be the case elsewhere in the world that (1) violence is not as effective a tactic as is often assumed and (2) political elites misperceive the effects of violence on voting. On the first point, we saw earlier that the effects of the violent Operation Murambatsvina campaign in Zimbabwe meant to displace opposition supporters in urban areas were surprisingly muted. In particular, the groups targeted in the campaign proved remarkably resilient in the face of violent coercion, with little evidence that they in fact migrated away from the affected areas (Bratton and Masunungure, 2007).

Meanwhile, in a study of political gangsterism in Indonesia (a case we will return to in more detail below), Wilson (2010) provides revealing insight into the costs associated with – and limited returns to – violent electoral tactics in another country that helps place the Kenyan case in broader context. Wilson notes that, in the authoritarian New Order era of Suharto, the ruling party and its military allies used gangs called *preman* to ensure their victory in tightly controlled elections. In the buildup to Indonesia's 1999 elections, the country's first free multiparty elections since 1955, parties copied "the militaristic and thuggish tactics of New Order politics," establishing large paramilitary units known as 'task forces' or '*satgas*' (203). Yet, the decline in the mobilization of *preman* by the subsequent election suggests that "they may have been far less effective than party leaders had originally thought" (204), largely because "voters in most areas could no longer be herded or coerced into voting in particular ways as they once had, and it was clear that to continue to attempt to do so would result in a *voter backlash* [emphasis added]" (207). In fact, for the party most associated with gangs – the

PDIP – its close association with local-level thuggery "ultimately led to a public image problem for the party nationally" (207). Similarly, a party formed by the oldest *preman* group in order to compete for formal political power failed badly at the polls, largely because of "the lingering stigma of New Order thuggery" (209).

This example highlights the central dilemma facing politicians in Kenya and similarly competitive electoral contexts: where politicians and affiliated violent specialists do not have a local monopoly on violence, their ability to directly coerce large numbers of voters is constrained, and they face the prospect of significant voter backlash against them if they employ violence. It also highlights a crucial difference between Kenya and Indonesia, however, that provides additional support for the theory of elite misperception: the relative success of violent parties and candidates in winning power in the first multiparty elections. While the analysis in Chapter 4 casts doubt on the idea that violence actually improved the electoral prospects of Kenya's ruling KANU party, the party *did* manage to win the presidency and a parliamentary majority while employing violent electoral tactics in the country's first multiparty elections.[1] As a result, the conventional wisdom was established in Kenyan politics that violence wins elections, and subsequent elections have frequently been plagued by it. In Indonesia, on the other hand, the parties most associated with violence in the first multiparty elections performed poorly at the polls, leading to a decrease in the use of such tactics in subsequent elections.[2] This difference points, yet again, to the importance of the electoral tactics employed by the *winning* candidate and parties in founding elections, which can lead – rightly or wrongly – to "success contagion" (Boas, 2016).[3]

In the remainder of this chapter, I continue to extend the empirical focus beyond Kenya. In doing so, I explore how well the findings from Kenya travel to other contexts, as well as test additional observable implications of the theory with both cross-national and within-case analysis of

---

[1] Notably, the party managed to win the presidency and a parliamentary majority *without* winning a majority of votes.

[2] Of note is that, unlike Kenya's plurality single member district electoral system and plurality presidential voting which allowed KANU to maintain power nationally despite failing to secure a majority of votes, Indonesia's elections featured a proportional representation system.

[3] Boas also finds that the failure of candidates employing divisive, cleavage-priming tactics in founding elections in Ghana and Nicaragua led candidates in subsequent elections to abandon such appeals, despite their prevalence in similar countries (Boas, 2016, 189–191).

other countries around the world. I begin by analyzing the main observable implications of the theory of elite misperception for cross-national variation in election-related violence, that is, that such violence should most often occur in elections in which the winner of founding elections in the current electoral regime employed violence. Violence should be significantly less common in elections where the winner did not employ violence, even if one or more of the losing candidates or parties *did*. I then delve into an analysis of five case studies of countries with varying levels of election-related violence since their transition to multiparty electoral competition – Indonesia, Pakistan, Ghana, Nigeria, and Brazil – in order to triangulate my data and test the external validity of my argument and the findings from the Kenyan case.

7.1 ELITE MISPERCEPTION, FOUNDING ELECTIONS, AND CROSS-NATIONAL VARIATION IN ELECTION-RELATED VIOLENCE

Beyond a focus on the micro-level decision-making of voters and politicians, the theory of elite misperception yields insights that can help explain variation in the incidence and – in particular – persistence of election-related violence across countries. Specifically, the theory posits that founding elections – the first elections held after the transition to a new multiparty regime – are critical junctures where the electoral tactics of the winning parties and candidates affect how politicians compete in elections for years to come. The theory therefore implies a clear prediction: that countries where the winner of founding elections employs violence are more likely to have violence reoccur in subsequent elections than those where the winner of founding elections does not. Crucially, the theory does *not* predict that violence is more likely in subsequent elections when it is employed by the loser (but not the winner), distinguishing it from other explanations for the persistence of violence over multiple election cycles which argue that violence breeds violence. The logic of the theory of elite misperception homes in on the tactics of the founding election *winner* because it is *their* actions that determine what contestants in future elections seek to emulate.[4]

---

[4] While it does not have any observable implications for the foregoing analysis, it is worth reemphasizing that whether or not violence actually helped the founding election winner electorally does not matter for the logic described here. Politicians simply emulate the tactics of the parties and candidates that succeed because there is usually no more precise information about the efficacy of campaign tactics available to them.

7.1 Elite Misperception, Founding Elections

To test the ability of the theory of elite misperception to explain cross-national variation in election-related violence, I merge data on election winners from the National Elections Across Democracy and Autocracy (NELDA) dataset (Hyde and Marinov, 2012) with data on the incidence and perpetrators of election-related violence in African elections from the African Electoral Violence Database (AEVD) (Straus and Taylor, 2012), estimating the relationship between the incidence of violence in founding elections and the incidence of violence in subsequent elections from 1990 to 2008. I do so by regressing a dummy variable for whether violence occurred in a given national election on (1) a dummy variable for whether violence occurred in the founding election of the multiparty regime ("violent founding election") and (2) a dummy variable for whether the *winner* of the founding election was responsible for violence ("violent winner"), clustering standard errors by country.[5] With this setup, the coefficient on the "violent winner" dummy can be interpreted as the marginal effect of the winner having used violence, assuming violence occurs in the founding election, that is, the effect of the founding election winner using violence relative to the founding election loser use violence. The coefficient on "violent founding election" can be interpreted as the effect of the founding election loser – but not the winner – employing violence. If my theory is correct, then we should observe a positive, significant coefficient on "violent winner" and no significant coefficient (or perhaps, a negative one) on "violent founding election." If standard theories in the vein of "violence breeds violence" are correct, the coefficient on "violent founding election" should be positive and significant, whereas the prediction for "violent winner" is uncertain. If the incidence of violence in founding elections does not matter for whether violence occurs in subsequent elections, both coefficients should be zero.

The results of this analysis, summarized in the first column of Table 7.1, are consistent with what the theory of elite misperception predicts. Multiparty elections held under a regime in which the *winner* of founding elections employed violence are much more likely to be marked by violence, but those where the founding election *loser* but not the winner employed violence are no more likely to be violent (the estimated effect is zero). The results suggest that elections held where the winner of founding elections employed violence are 43.5 percentage points more

---

[5] Note that it is possible for there to be multiple founding elections for a given country in the dataset, for instance if there were multiple transitions to and from multiparty electoral regimes and single-party or military rule in the period under study.

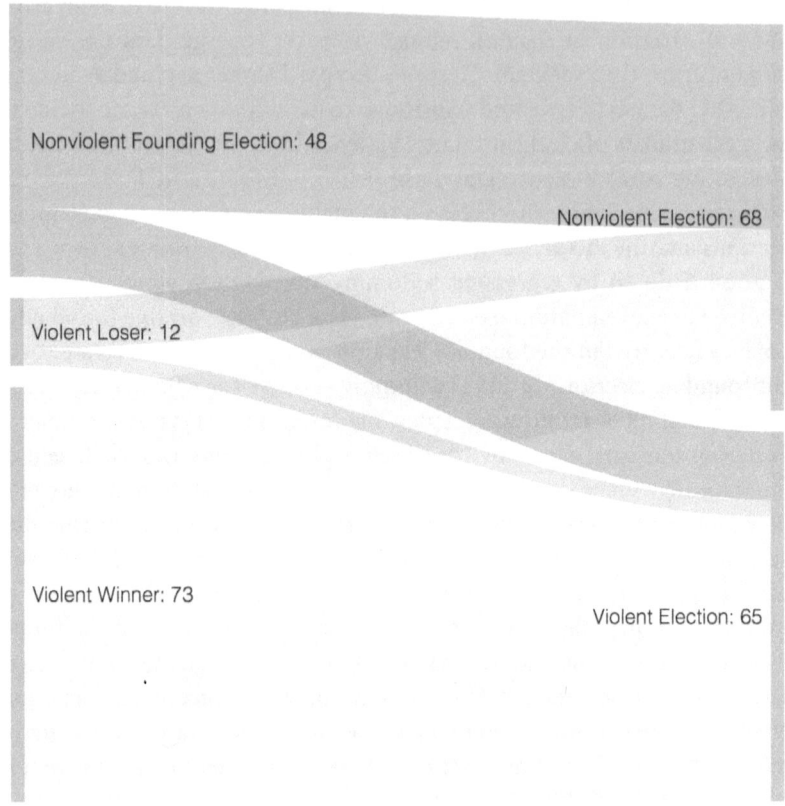

FIGURE 7.1 Sankey diagram of violence in founding and subsequent elections
Note: The diagram demonstrates how the use of violence in founding elections (no violence, violence by the loser, violence by the winner) relates to the incidence of violence in subsequent election cycles. The thickness of the lines connecting founding elections on the left and subsequent elections on the right indicates the number of violent or nonviolent subsequent elections coming after each type of founding election.

likely to experience violence than those where they did not. A Sankey diagram showing visually the proportion of violent and nonviolent elections that occurred after different types of founding elections (nonviolent, violent loser, and violent winner) also clearly demonstrates how the large majority of nonviolent elections – as well as those in which only the loser employs violence – result in nonviolent elections in subsequent cycles (Figure 7.1); the proportion of elections marked by violence is much higher for those that follow a founding election in which violence was employed by the winner.

TABLE 7.1 *Founding election violence and violence in subsequent elections*

	(1) All elections	(2) Second elections only
Violent winner	0.435**	0.433**
	(0.206)	(0.192)
Violent founding election	1.79e−15	−0.300
	(0.200)	(0.193)
Constant	0.250***	0.500***
	(0.0678)	(0.115)
Observations	133	53

Standard errors in parentheses
* $p < 0.10$, ** $p < 0.05$, *** $p < 0.01$

The fact that violence on the part of losers in founding elections does not result in any higher likelihood of violence occurring in subsequent elections militates against the simple version of the "violence breeds violence" thesis. But it is possible that part of what the analysis is picking up is the effect of violence in second elections on violence in third elections, violence in third elections on violence in fourth elections, and so on. In other words, the likelihood of violence in a given election may depend on what happened in the founding election, but also on what happened in previous elections that are more proximate in time, and the analysis described above cannot account for this possibility. To address this concern, I limit the analysis of the effects of violence in founding elections to second elections only (those that take place immediately after founding elections). The results, summarized in Table 7.1, Column 2, are similarly consistent with the theory of elite misperception. The coefficient on "violent winner" is large, positive, and significant, whereas the coefficient on "violent founding election" is insignificant (though negative and somewhat large, suggesting that when the losers but not the winner of founding elections employ violence, it may actually discourage violence in future elections). In short, the logic of the theory of elite misperception appears well suited to not only explaining election-related violence in settings where its efficacy is in doubt, but variation in the incidence and persistence of violence across countries as well.

7.2 CASE STUDIES OF ELECTIONS AND VIOLENCE BEYOND KENYA

In this section, I analyze five case studies of countries with varying levels of election-related violence since their transition to multiparty electoral competition: Indonesia, Pakistan, Ghana, Nigeria, and Brazil.

This within-case analysis of a diverse set of cases allows for triangulation with the quantitative and Kenya-focused data analyzed above, helping me to test the plausibility of the findings from Kenya and how they travel to other contexts, as well as studying whether and how the particular mechanisms underlying the theory of elite misperception may (or may not) explain the incidence (or nonoccurrence) of violence in various contexts. While the survey experiments analyzed in Chapter 5 are characterized by strong internal validity due to randomization mitigating the problem of confounding, and the in-depth quantitative and qualitative analysis of the Kenyan case in Chapters 4–6 provides a rigorous test of the theory in a particular context, the case studies help address concerns about external validity in at least two ways. First, by analyzing the dynamics of election-related violence in a diverse set of countries, we can get a better sense of how well the Kenyan findings travel to other contexts. Second, within-case qualitative analysis of additional cases can help identify whether the mechanisms posited by the theory of elite misperception appear to be at work in shaping electoral violence outcomes in those cases, shedding further light on the plausibility and generalizability of the theory. In short, it provides a useful test of the external validity of my argument and the findings from the Kenyan case.

The cases I analyze were selected for the following reasons. First, they represent contexts of varying levels of violence since transitions to multiparty elections – from relatively low levels (Ghana and Brazil) to high (Pakistan and Nigeria) to somewhere in between (Indonesia). They also represent regional diversity (with two examples from Africa, one from South Asia, one from Southeast Asia, and one from Latin America) and diversity in their political institutions (including both presidential and parliamentary systems, and a range of proportionality versus majoritarianism in their electoral institutions). At the same time, they all fit within the theory's scope conditions outlined in Chapter 3. Specifically, in each case (1) there is genuine multiparty electoral competition and (2) violence is a viable tool in a politicians' toolkit because of weak rule of law, an adequate supply of violent specialists, and/or a low likelihood of facing legal consequences for employing violence.

For each case study, I read accounts of the country's electoral politics and the incidence of election-related violence in academic publications, journalistic outlets, and governmental and nongovernmental reports, with a particular eye toward information about (1) voter responses to violence, (2) the impact of violence on election processes and outcomes, (3) politicians' motivations for employing (or not employing) violence,

(4) their beliefs about the efficacy of violence (and other electoral tactics), and (5) how those beliefs about the efficacy of violence and other tactics appear to have developed over time. These analyses are not meant to be comprehensive; lengthier, more in-depth treatments of each case would be required for a complete understanding of the dynamics of electoral politics and election-related violence in each of them. Rather, the goal of the exercise is to test the plausibility of the theory and the findings from Kenya in other contexts; gather additional evidence on the mechanisms posited by the theory; and generally bolster the external validity of the empirical analysis.

Overall, the evidence from these case studies is consistent with many of the key elements of the theory of elite misperception and the findings from the close analysis of the Kenyan case. I find little to no evidence that violence has helped parties and candidates improve their electoral prospects, instead identifying several instances in which voter backlash appears to have undermined them, especially where viable alternatives exist. Furthermore, I find that the mode of electioneering implemented by the winners of founding elections tends to persist, with contestants in subsequent elections engaging in similar tactics, including whether or not they employ violence. I also find evidence that some of the institutional features of a country's politics emphasized by structural theories of violence – including the competence and independence of election management bodies and the strength of the rule of law – play an important part in determining the prospects for violence, suggesting the joint importance of structural conditions and politicians' individual decision-making logic in determining whether violence occurs.

7.2.1 Indonesia

Indonesia is a country with a reputation for politically motivated ethnic violence, but the reality is rather more complex, with spurts of locally intense violence at times along with significant stretches of peace in most parts of the country. It has also seen a significant decline in such violence since the earliest years of the transition to multiparty politics, and there is reason to believe that this is at least partially due to the poor electoral performance of those parties and candidates who employed violence in the first multiparty elections.

In Indonesia, the last general election held under Soeharto's authoritarian New Order regime in May 1997 was the most violent in the country's history up to that date as the government sought to use all possible means, including force, to maintain its hold on power (Suryadinata, 2002, 32). During the campaign period, "many riots occurred in small towns in both Java and the Outer Islands ... [and] at least 250 people lost their lives" (Suryadinata, 2002, 33). During later elections held in the mid-2000s, violence more commonly occurred in local than national (presidential and parliamentary) elections (Tadjoeddin, 2012, 477), possibly due to their newness; previously (beginning in 1999), direct elections had only taken place for the national legislature. In general, ethnic violence peaked early in the democratic transition and declined rapidly thereafter; whereas ethnic identity was initially mobilized in violent contests for power, such mobilization transitioned to more peaceful contestation via the ballot box (Aspinall, 2011, 295). Furthermore, what violence has occurred has been highly geographically concentrated, with 15 districts and cities constituting just 6.5 percent of the country's population accounting for 85.5 percent of deaths (Varshney, Tadjoeddin, and Panggabean, 2008).

Where ethnic violence has occurred, there is some evidence of what Paul Brass has termed "institutionalized riot systems" in reference to the instigation of Hindu–Muslim riots in India, often in pursuit of electoral gain (Brass, 2003). In the case of the large-scale riots in Ternate in 1999, for example, where local politicians were angling for power in the newly created province of North Maluku, "the violence in the city appears to have been premeditated by a wide section of the political elite and bureaucracy who felt threatened by the growing political and strategic dominance of the sultan [of Ternate, a local traditional leader]" (Wilson, 2008, 131). In addition to targeting particular groups, candidates themselves have been frequent targets of violence in the run-up to elections (Harish and Toha, 2019).

Crucially, the evidence from Indonesia suggests that parties and candidates that employed violence in the earliest competitive multiparty elections fared poorly at the polls, and that this poor performance led parties and candidates to avoid such tactics in subsequent electoral cycles, at least partially accounting for the relative decline in violence over time. As noted above, the ruling Golkar party employed substantial violence in elections held in May 1997, then performed poorly in the first free and fair elections held in 1999. But backlash was not limited to the ruling party and its poor overall performance; in Sampang in Madura, supporters of the opposition PPP (Partai Persatuan Pembangunan) burnt a number of polling stations, which led to the holding of fresh elections where – contrary to its poor overall performance – Golkar won with a convincing majority (Suryadinata, 2002, 35). In addition, gangs known as *preman* that emerged as violent political players around the transition in the late 1990s have become increasingly irrelevant. While their leaders have sought elected office by running on established party tickets or forming parties of their own, their newly created parties have failed, and individual gang leaders have fared poorly in running for office (Wilson, 2010; Aspinall, 2011). Fadloli el-Muhir, for example – leader of a group known as the FBR – ran for a local council seat in Jakarta and finished a distant seventh (Wilson, 2010; Aspinall, 2011). As noted above, *preman* played a much diminished role in parties' campaigns after 1999, suggesting that political elites learned from those first elections that employing violent actors "may have been far less effective than party leaders had originally thought," and that continuing to employ violent coercion "would result in voter backlash" and "a public image problem" for their parties (Wilson, 2010, 204–207).

There is also evidence that the instigation of politically motivated ethnic violence has often failed to achieve its goals. Ethnic riots and cleansing in Central Kalimantan in 2001 (in which ethnic Dayak attacked Madurese migrants) expelled the Madurese population, but did not lead to any pereceivable electoral gain for the group (the LMMDD-KT) associated with it. As van Klinken notes, "Not much has actually changed in Central Kalimantan's political scene [as a result of the violence], ... the whole militant Dayak movement seemed to evaporate," and its politically ambitious leader K.M.A. Usop failed again in his run for governor in 2005 (van Klinken, 2007, 135–136).

Communal riots in Poso district provide another example where violence failed to achieve its instigators' goals (van Klinken, 2007, Chapter 5). The conflict in Poso centered over the selection of a new district chief, who would be appointed by a newly elected district assembly, and where Muslim and Christian factions each sought to install one of their own in the seat. Christians' favored candidate was Yahya Patiro, the serving district secretary (second in command); while he had been a Golkar member, he mobilized support via the PDI-P, an opposition party with ties to the local Protestant church. Muslim elites, meanwhile, backed Damsyik Ladjalani, first assistant to the district secretary. He, too, had been in Golkar, but mobilized support from the Muslim PPP.

As van Klinken (2007, 81) recounts, "On Christmas Eve 1998 a Christian youth – he was the loutish son of a political party leader – stabbed the son of the priest (imam) at a local mosque. He was drunk. Muslims were celebrating the fasting month Ramadan. Outraged Muslim youths attacked Christian Chinese shops for selling alcohol ... The town was in uproar for a week. Christian youths arrived on trucks from the mission heartland of Tentena. Muslim youths arrived from coastal towns of Ampana in the east, Parigi in the north-west and even from Palu ... [and] [t]he elite and largely Christian suburb of Lombogia suffered much damage." Over the course of the violence, attacks were mobilized by politicians and their associates on each side. Yet, at the end of the day, neither candidate favored by the two sides that had instigated the riots prevailed, and the opposition parties that had backed them fared poorly in the elections that followed. The ruling Golkar comfortably won local district assembly elections despite the national mood against it, and the newly elected assembly elected a Muslim district head who was not associated with either of the factions associated with the violence (van Klinken, 2007, 81).

Why has election-related violence not gone away entirely, given its apparent ineffectiveness in Indonesian elections? First, while it has not been eliminated, the sharp reduction in its prevalence should not be overlooked. Collective violence peaked at the outset of the multiparty era, falling consistently and drastically from more than 700 incidents in 1999 to fewer than 300 in 2003, and from more than 3,500 deaths in 1998 to fewer than 100 in 2003 (Varshney, Tadjoeddin, and Panggabean, 2008, 377). Furthermore, what violence occurred in the 2000s was primarily related to local elections (Tadjoeddin, 2012, 477), which were being held for the first time and thus perhaps not subject to the same lessons that had been learned at the national level.

In sum, while Indonesia has seen substantial election-related violence since transitioning to multiparty politics, especially in its early years, it does not appear to have been effective in achieving its electoral goals. Furthermore, after parties and candidates that used violence in the country's founding elections fared poorly, the incidence of violence declined, at least in part because political elites recognized its limited utility and the potential for voter backlash against it. The Indonesian case therefore provides evidence in favor of several of the book's propositions about voter backlash against violence; about the drawbacks of its use as an electoral tactic; and about the long-run impact of the relationship between violence and election outcomes in founding elections on the incidence of violence in subsequent electoral cycles.

7.2.2 Pakistan

Pakistan is another country with a reputation for political violence (Bueno de Mesquita et al., 2015). With respect to election-related violence, specifically, politics in the megacity of Karachi may be most prominent, having seen violence perpetrated by – or on behalf of – the MQM (Muhajir/Muttahida Quami Movement) and the PPP (Pakistan People's Party), two parties that have angled for electoral dominance in different parts of the city. The sharp decline of these violent parties in recent years suggests that violence – rather than bolstering their electoral dominance – may have contributed to their eventual downfall via voter backlash, as viable nonviolent alternatives arose and handily defeated them at the polls.

The MQM has historically operated as a party seeking to exclusively represent the interests of the Muhajir group, which it has cast as oppressed and underrepresented in politics and the economy (Siddiqui, 2022).[6] Its role as an explicitly ethnic party in an ethnically polarized, violent electoral environment has led analysts to suggest that the party could employ violence against its rivals and out-groups without suffering electoral blowback from its core, coethnic voters that make up a plurality in the city (Siddiqui, 2022). In fact, survey experiments conducted in 2015 showed that MQM candidates suffered no electoral penalty among coethnic Muhajirs in Karachi for employing violence, which was not the case among voters outside Karachi (Siddiqui, 2022).

Yet the success of the violent MQM over the years – which, crucially, came to a sudden end in elections held in 2018 – seems to have been strongly reliant on the lack of viable, nonviolent alternatives that weren't themselves aligned with particular ethnic out-groups. The rise of the PTI (Pakistan Tehreek-e-Insaf) party – running on an explicitly non-ethnic, nonviolent platform – created a clear opening for Muhajir voters fed up with the MQM's violent tactics to support another party. Starting by winning 15 percent of the provincial election vote and 18 percent of the vote for the National Assembly in 2013, the PTI dislodged the MQM from power in 2018, when the MQM won just seven seats in the National Assembly as compared to the 19 it had won in 2013 (Siddiqui, 2022). While it's difficult to attribute the MQM's fall to any particular factor – and the party was subject to a military crackdown that weakened its organizational capacity after 2013 – recent developments in Karachi suggest that many voters, including core coethnic ones, were eager to vote against the violent MQM at the polls once a credible challenger emerged. That those voters turned to a non-ethnic, nonviolent alternative suggests that

---

[6] In the late 1990s, the party made a half-hearted attempt to expand its appeal – changing its name from Muhajir Quami Movement to Muttahida (united) Quami Movement, casting itself as a party of all the oppressed, and engaging in less overt violence – but the transformation was slow and incomplete, and did not last (Verkaaik, 2004, 57).

voter backlash against the violent tactics of the MQM may have played a role in its demise, providing another example that voters – even many core, coethnic voters – may be eager to turn against violent politicians when there is a credible challenger to turn to. MQM politicians may have believed their violent tactics were crucial to their dominance when they in fact contributed to their downfall once a viable alternative appeared.

It's also notable that it took a new party – one perhaps more willing to challenge the conventional wisdom about how politics in Karachi works – to provide a nonviolent alternative that could win over the MQM's voters. Chapter 3 noted that one somewhat counterintuitive implication of the idea that founding elections establish the standard model of campaigning in subsequent electoral cycles is that more mainstream/experienced candidates are generally more likely – and political outsiders or newcomers less likely – to follow the conventional wisdom. Thus, outsider/newcomer candidates and parties who are more likely to think outside the box may be more willing to buck the norm and eschew violence when competing in elections. As in Kenya – where the analysis in Chapter 4 showed that most individuals allegedly involved in the 07/08 violence were established politicians – the case of the MQM and PTI in Karachi seems to suggest that in traditionally violent electoral contexts, established parties and politicians are more likely than newcomers to employ violence, and that eschewing violence can give outsiders an advantage when they're seen as a viable alternative. It also provides an example of the sort of shock to the system – in this case, the emergence of a competitive new party – that can help undermine a violent equilibrium established in prior elections.

The PPP, unlike the MQM, competes for power at the national level in Pakistan. But it too has been known to employ violence when contesting elections, including through its alliance with a Karachi-based ethnic militia known as the People's Aman Conference (PAC) in its stronghold of Lyari, a neighborhood in the city considered the birthplace of the party. And like the MQM in the city at large, the PPP has recently lost its grip on its home turf of Lyari. In 2018, Bilawal Bhutto – PPP candidate for the National Assembly in Lyari constituency and the son of former party leader Benazir Bhutto – lost, and by a significant margin: he came in third behind the PTI and a relatively new religious party called the Tehreek-e-Labbaik Pakistan (TLP) (Siddiqui, 2022). The PPP also lost two provincial assembly seats in the neighborhood to religious parties (Siddiqui, 2022).

These examples provide further support for the idea that when a viable alternative exists (i.e., a nonviolent party not considered to be exclusively the party of an out-group), voters will vote for nonviolence over violence, even when least expected. What seemed to be electoral dominance based on violent coercion was in fact ripe for challenge from a nonviolent opposition. The dynamic described here also helps to explain the results I present from Kenya, where most constituencies/counties are dominated by one ethnic group; in such cases, competition within that group and/or the party most identified with that group means that voters don't necessarily even have to make a tradeoff – they can vote for nonviolent members of their group and/or party in a primary that largely determines the outcome of the general election. Yet, the Pakistani case also demonstrates the applicability of the theory beyond Kenya. Whereas voters tend to be the chief victims of violence in Kenya, political assassinations are common in Pakistan (Bueno de Mesquita et al., 2015), demonstrating that voter backlash against violent tactics can occur even when voters are not the primary targets. The case of Karachi, Pakistan is thus consistent with – and helps explain – the findings from Kenya while demonstrating their applicability to other contexts as well. While violent parties and candidates may win elections in many cases, the emergence of a viable alternative poses a severe threat to their continued dominance.

7.2.3 Ghana

Ghana – unlike Indonesia and Pakistan – is a country that has seen relatively little election-related violence since its transition to multiparty politics in the early 1990s. As the theory of elite misperception would predict, the lack of violence employed by the winner of the country's founding elections appears to have established an equilibrium in which violent incidents around elections are rare. In addition, several factors identified by structural theories of election-related violence – such as the strength and independence of electoral institutions and the nature of the party system – appear to have played an important role in limiting the incidence of violence in Ghana's elections.

Ghana – which held its first multiparty elections in decades in 1992 – has two major political parties (the National Democratic Congress or NDC, and the New Patriotic Party or NPP) that compete intensely for control of the national government, and the country has experienced several very close elections and multiple handovers of power.[7]

---

[7] The 1992 elections were held on an electoral playing field heavily tilted toward the ruling party and presidential candidate Jerry Rawlings, but the country was able to hold free and fair elections within two electoral cycles.

While there has been some "localized ethno-political violence in which activists of the main parties have clashed," electoral competition in the country has been "relatively free of the kinds of high-intensity violence that has characterized multi-party elections in some parts of Africa" (Bob-Milliar, 2014, 126). As Boafo-Arthur (2008) remarks, "[t]he common saying in Ghana now is that the power to make and unmake governments no longer resides in the barrel of the gun but with the thumb of individual voters."

Distinct from many party systems in Africa, both major Ghanaian political parties have a national character and draw support from a range of geographic and ethnic groups, even as they tend to be most dominant among particular groups (the Ewe in the Volta Region for the NDC, and the Akan in the Ashanti region for the NPP) (Brierley and Kramon, 2020, 587–588). They're also notable in the region for their mass party networks, which particularly come to life during the campaign period, where "[n]ational and then regional and constituency party offices dispatch resources to polling stations, where party executives draw up and execute local campaign plans" and "[p]olling station executives then canvass voters, organize community meetings and rallies, and distribute election handouts" (Brierley and Kramon, 2020, 588). This level of institutionalization is distinct from the ad hoc, poorly organized structures of parties in Kenya and many other countries on the continent, where there is limited grassroots mobilization and little infrastructure that survives from election to election. Ghanaian party campaigns reach voters at the grassroots, with over 90 percent of party polling station executives canvassing voters in their homes and 30 percent of voters reporting being canvassed by one or both parties in the election campaign of 2012 (Brierley and Nathan, 2020). Furthermore, Ghanaian election campaigns are characterized by meaningful policy debate; in 2012, for example, both parties extensively discussed the NPP's promise to make senior high school free (Brierley and Kramon, 2020, 588).

In addition to its institutionalized parties and party system, Ghana has benefited from the relative independence of its state security forces, which the executive has limited ability to manipulate for partisan ends (Lynch, Cheeseman, and Willis, 2019). Furthermore, its electoral management body – the Electoral Commission of Ghana (ECG) – is widely credited with presiding over a credible electoral process with generally admirable transparency, independence, and professionalism (Gyimah-Boadi, 2009; Zounmenou, 2009; Abdulai and Crawford, 2010; Debrah, 2011). The Commission has encouraged openness in the electoral process, allowing representatives of political parties to observe the registration process and insisting that polling officials count and declare election results at polling stations in the presence of party agents, voters, and independent observers immediately after voting ended, though its management of post-election conflicts has been less effective at times (Debrah, 2011). As noted by Mueller (2008), Kanyinga (2018), Birch (2020), and others, the existence of strong, effective, impartial institutions for managing elections and electoral conflict may be crucial for maintaining confidence in the electoral process and ensuring that election-related disputes are litigated peacefully rather than devolving into violence.

What accounts for the ability of Ghana's electoral commission to act effectively and independently? Debrah (2011) points to several factors. First, the law creating it specifies that members cannot be dismissed by any body except on grounds of incapacitation due to ill health. Second, the president's nominees to the commission are scrutinized by the appointment committee of Parliament, putting a check on the president's ability to simply appoint close allies as commissioners. Third, the commission maintains substantial financial independence because its expenditures are charged to the state's Consolidated Fund, which is less open to control by the elected government than if it were required to appeal for specific funds.

Civil society has also played a role in maintaining the credibility of elections and – relatedly – keeping violence at bay (Gyimah-Boadi, 2009; Abdulai and Crawford, 2010). The Coalition of Domestic Election Observers (CODEO) stands out, in particular; in 2008, for example, they deployed around 5000 observers across the country, conducted civic and voter education, and participated in the counting and tabulation of election results (Gyimah-Boadi, 2009; Zounmenou, 2009).

Finally, political elites themselves have often acted to maintain peace in the face of electoral conflict. While their campaign rhetoric has been heated at times, and they have made claims of fraud against their opponents, the officially declared losers have, in the end, always conceded without encouraging their supporters to take up arms (Gyimah-Boadi, 2009; Abdulai and Crawford, 2010; Sithole, 2012). This may be at least partially due to a history of minimal violence around elections – going back to the first multiparty elections after the transition in 1992 – which serves to limit the amount of coercion the ruling party can claim is necessary in the interest of maintaining stability (Lynch, Cheeseman, and Willis, 2019, 625). In that sense, the role of violence (or its lack thereof) in the country's founding elections may have had the effect in the longer term of limiting the incidence of violence in subsequent electoral cycles.

To be sure, the lack of large-scale violence does not mean that election-related violence never occurs. The voter registration period prior to the 2008 elections, for example, saw a number of attacks on party agents, journalists, and ordinary civilians, as well as clashes between supporters of the two major parties in the Northern, Volta, and Ashanti regions (Danso and Lartey, 2012, 46). What violence occurs is often carried out by so-called "foot soldiers" (youth activists) or "musclemen" (toughs) associated with each party (Okyere, 2016). Known by names such as the Bamba Boys, Gbewaa Youth, Azorka Boys, Invincible Forces, and Bolga Bulldogs, these groups have become "political vigilantes" of a sort employed by parties during election periods (Okyere, 2016). Analysts have attributed the occurrence of election-related violence in Ghana to the perception that elections are winner-take-all, where the winner monopolizes state power and determines the fate of activists for either side, and control of the executive remains by far the top prize, given the concentration of power in the presidency (Gyimah-Boadi, 2009; Bob-Milliar, 2014). Still, even the violence that has occurred around elections in recent electoral cycles seems to be in decline (Bob-Milliar, 2014).

In sum, Ghana has managed to avoid significant election-related violence since its transition to multiparty politics in 1992 due to a combination of effective and independent institutions for managing elections and electoral conflict; strong, well-institutionalized parties and a coherent, stable, nationalized party system; a strong civil society; and responsible behavior by political elites. The latter can be partially attributed to the lack of violence going back to the country's founding elections, which has structured political elites' expectations and beliefs about the viability of violence in subsequent elections, and is consistent with the argument of this book. The analysis also points to the importance of some of the structural factors that scholars have cited as reducing the potential for violence, such as effective, independent institutions for managing elections (Mueller, 2008; Kanyinga, 2018; Birch, 2020) and stronger, more organized parties that appeal to broad constituencies (Fjelde, 2020; Siddiqui, 2022). Thus, the "negative" case of Ghana, with its relatively low levels of election-related violence, highlights how structural factors – and elites' beliefs about violence emphasized in this book – may work together to explain why violence occurs in some contexts and not others.

7.2.4 Nigeria

Nigeria has seen substantial election-related violence since it transitioned to multiparty politics in 1999 after decades of military rule, where the use of violence by the winners of founding elections appears to have established an equilibrium in which politicians frequently employ violence when competing for office. In federal and state elections in 2003, for example, hundreds were killed, with much of the violence perpetrated by members or supporters of the ruling People's Democratic Party (PDP) (Human Rights Watch, 2004). Dozens were killed in local government elections held a year later in 2004, and a minimum of 300 Nigerians were killed in violence linked to the 2007 elections, likely substantially more (Human Rights Watch, 2007). While the PDP was the main driver of violence in the 2003 and 2007 elections, the larger opposition parties used it as well, and violence on the part of one side was often responded to in kind.

Elections in 2019 saw the occurrence of at least 275 violent incidents claiming at least 159 lives, with the pre-election period being the most violent, accounting for 51.3 percent of violent events and 52.2 percent of fatalities (Oyewole and Omotola, 2021). Election day itself was also quite violent, accounting for 25 percent of incidents and 24.5 percent of fatalities (Oyewole and Omotola, 2021).[8] The South-South and South East regions have tended to see the most election violence, with particularly high levels in Rivers, Akwa Ibom, and Delta states (Human Rights Watch, 2007; Oyewole and Omotola, 2021).

Violence is often the result of politicians recruiting and arming criminal gangs, frequently with the assistance of so-called "godfathers," wealthy and influential individuals who sponsor and provide muscle for candidates to finance their campaigns and employ violence in the streets, in return for political influence when they're elected (especially access to government coffers). Gang members are recruited and paid by politicians and party leaders to "attack their sponsors' rivals, intimidate members of the public, rig elections, and protect their patrons from similar attacks" (Human Rights Watch, 2007, 17). Such groups include "cult" organizations (which originated decades ago as campus fraternities) and members of the National Union of Road Transport Workers (Human Rights Watch,

---

[8] This makes the 2019 Nigerian election somewhat of an outlier, in that election day usually does not account for a large proportion of election-related violence overall (Straus and Taylor, 2012; Daxecker and Jung, 2018).

2007). A Human Rights Watch report described the typical manifestation of such violence as follows:

One former cult member told Human Rights Watch that his group was recruited by the PDP in Rivers State to prevent people from voting during the 2003 elections. "My duty was to send you to hell," he said. Members of one Ibadan-based gang acknowledged having ties to Oyo State political godfather Lamidi Adedibu and said that they had been paid to carry out political assassinations. And just ahead of the 2007 elections, one member of the Buccaneers cults in Anambra State told Human Rights Watch matter-of-factly that, "If there is a need to cause commotion during the election, they [local politicians] will call us." In some cases, cult and gang members claimed that they were merely providing "security" for electoral campaigns, but described the work as involving violent clashes with members of communities along the campaign trail. (Human Rights Watch, 2007, 25)

In considering the impact of violence on Nigerian elections, it's important to note that some of the most violent elections have also been marked by massive fraud, such that the results of those elections would be in doubt even independent of the violence that occurred. For instance, the Transition Monitoring Group (TMG), a national coalition of civil society groups that monitored the 2003 elections, described the collation and declaration of results that year as "characterized by monumental fraud" (Human Rights Watch, 2004, 5).

Even the violence itself has often been not just about intimidating voters but disrupting the election entirely, with thugs employed to steal ballots and ballot boxes or prevent voting altogether (not just voting by particular groups of voters). In the 2003 elections in Delta State, for instance, local and international observers agreed that the level of fraud and violence – mostly carried out by PDP supporters – "totally discredited the election process," and that "[i]n some locations, there was not even any pretence [sic] at staging elections … The TMG reported that in Ughelli, angry youths burnt down the INEC office in protest at the postponement of elections. In other locations, armed thugs snatched ballot boxes or vandalized election materials" (Human Rights Watch, 2004, 20). In Kogi State, elections

had to be halted at several polling stations because of violence and intimidation. An independent election observer reported that in one location, the sounds of gunshots initially scattered voters, who then regrouped to vote. However, just an hour later, the voting had to be stopped because ballot boxes were being smashed and armed thugs appeared at the polling site … A different observer reported: "The ANPP supporters attacked other party agents and fired shots in the air. Both ANPP and PDP members were chanting war songs … Eventually some

ANPP supporters stole the ballot box under gunfire." A third observer reported that voting at a polling station had to be stopped after unidentified individuals snatched the ballot box and beat the presiding officer. (Human Rights Watch, 2004, 35–36)

As for the following federal elections, "[m]any seasoned observers stated that the 2007 polls were among the worst they had ever witnessed anywhere in the world" (Human Rights Watch, 2007, 2). In 2007, "armed gangs in the employ of politicians raided polling stations and carried off ballot boxes. Electoral officials reported massive turnout figures in areas where no voting took place at all. In many areas ballot boxes were openly stuffed or results fabricated out of thin air. The final results bore little resemblance to the realities reported by all credible election observers, domestic or foreign ..." (Human Rights Watch, 2007, 15). Assessing the true impact of violence on election outcomes in Nigeria is therefore quite difficult, given the massive fraud that makes reported results poor indicators of parties and candidates true performance in many elections.

Overall, Nigeria's electoral trajectory and history of election-related violence is consistent with this book's argument about the role of founding elections in determining politicians' beliefs about the efficacy of violence and the likelihood that it becomes endemic in a country's electoral politics. The PDP employed violence on its way to winning the (highly flawed) first multiparty elections in 1999, and such tactics have become accepted by politicians in subsequent elections as the way electoral politics in Nigeria is done. A Human Rights Watch report noted that "[v]iolence became such an accepted part of political competition in some areas during the 2003 elections that politicians did not even attempt to conceal it; for example, a PDP ward chairman in the southern city of Port Harcourt told a human rights activist directly how the PDP had distributed guns in the area" (Human Rights Watch, 2004, 4). And in an interview with researchers, the traditional ruler of Awka town in Anambra State said that "[h]ere [in Anambra] elections are connected to how much money you have put into your ability to intimidate others" (Human Rights Watch, 2007, 28). The use of violence by the winners of Nigeria's founding election thus seems to have set the country on a path of persistent violence in its elections as candidates and parties see it as an effective (if not necessary) tool for winning office.

Chapter 3 notes that the theory of elite misperception can help explain not just cross-national, but subnational variation in violence as well, in that election-related violence should be most likely to occur in those subnational units where violence was employed by the winners of founding elections in those particular units, and patterns of violence in Nigeria are highly consistent with what we would expect to see if this were the case. As noted above, violence in Nigerian elections has been particularly concentrated in the South-South and South East regions, especially Rivers, Akwa Ibom, and Delta states (Human Rights Watch, 2007; Oyewole and Omotola, 2021). Crucially, PDP candidates won each of these states' first gubernatorial elections (for the most powerful subnational offices) while running violent campaigns, creating the conditions under the theory of elite misperception for continued violence in their elections for years to come. This is indeed what has occurred, with these states being among the most violent in recent election cycles. Furthermore, while violence was initially primarily the domain of the PDP, opposition parties began employing violence in later election cycles as well (Human Rights Watch, 2004), consistent with the idea that founding elections generate a conventional wisdom about what works and setting the stage for political actors to copy the tactics of founding election winners in subsequent electoral contests.

Also key to understanding the prevalence of election violence in Nigeria is the complete lack of legal accountability for politicians who employ it – an issue raised by structural theories that emphasize weak institutions and rule of law as determinants of violence – ensuring that it remains a viable option for those politicians who may choose to use it. Virtually no politician has been brought to justice in Nigeria for their involvement in violence. In Anambra State, for example,

> police officials told Human Rights Watch that they were helpless to act against powerful PDP gubernatorial candidate Andy Uba, even though they knew him to be mobilizing cult gangs in advance of the elections – Uba was seen as too close to then-President Olusegun Obasanjo and therefore untouchable. Former Rivers State Governor Peter Odili, among others, has not so far faced any formal investigation or sanction for his alleged role in sponsoring armed groups that have plunged Rivers into a lasting state of chaos. (Human Rights Watch, 2007, 3)

In short, high levels of election-related violence in Nigeria since it's transition to multiparty politics in 1999 appears due to a combination of weak rule of law and accountability institutions, which makes violence a viable option for politicians, and the example set by the winning party in the country's founding elections, which set a precedent for the use of violence and generated the conventional wisdom that violence was an effective (and, perhaps, necessary) tactic for winning elections, at least in certain parts of the country where it is particularly endemic. Until one or both of these factors – legal impunity and politicians' beliefs – are addressed, violence seems likely to continue to plague Nigerian elections going forward.

7.2.5 Brazil

Brazil has seen not seen large-scale violence related to its elections since transitioning from authoritarian rule in 1989, though it has occurred at low levels and has increased in recent years along with the rising influence of militias and organized criminal organizations and the election of Jair Bolsonaro as president. The relatively low level of election violence is somewhat surprising, in fact, given the overall high level of violence in the country (with its very high homicide rate) and, relatedly, the prevalence of many of the sorts of violent specialists (gangs and militias) that politicians tend to work with when employing election-related violence in other contexts. Brazil's earliest multiparty elections after the transition to democracy were largely peaceful, however, and analysis of the Brazilian case supports the view of founding elections as setting an important precedent for how campaigns are run (and whether violence becomes common), as well as the idea that violence is of limited electoral utility to the politicians that employ it.

Violence played little role in the electoral tactics of candidates in Brazil's first modern, multiparty election in 1989. Instead, the main candidates ran rather conventional, democratic election campaigns, with the winning candidate, Fernando Collor de Mello, deploying a neopopulist strategy in their successful run. While subsequent candidates did not follow this particular strategy due to its association with what was widely seen as a failed presidency (Collor was impeached and left office with a 9 percent approval rating) (Boas, 2016, 94), Collor's successor, Fernando Henrique Cardoso, pursued a technocratic approach to his election campaign that then became the dominant approach to election campaigns in Brazil due to its association with the perceived political success of the new president. This model of mainly peaceful election campaigns in Brazil created in the early years of its democracy has largely persisted, consistent with the idea that the earliest elections after a transition to multiparty politics are highly influential in shaping how politicians contest elections in the years to come.

What violence does occur in Brazil often involves the assassination of politicians themselves. According to one source, an average of nine elected officials in the country have been killed annually in recent years (Cowie, 2018). In Rio de Janeiro state, specifically, 107 politicians were victims of violent attacks (assassinations or assassination attempts) between 1998 and 2016, with such attacks taking place more often in election years (an average of 7.3 in election years versus 3.8 in non-election years) (Albarracín, 2018, 559). However, many of the killings that occur are "usually because of land, property, or economic interests" (Cowie, 2018), not necessarily politics, per se. They're therefore not election-related violence under the motive-based definition employed here and elsewhere.[9] High levels of violent crime thus do not necessarily translate into the presence of "criminalized electoral politics" (Albarracín, 2018) as they do in other contexts such as Jamaica (see, e.g., Sives, 2010).

One trend in Brazil that appears to contradict the theory put forward in this book is that – despite its relatively peaceful electoral history – election-related violence has increased in recent years, in particular around the 2018 elections in which right-wing populist Jair Bolsonaro was elected president, as well as in the 2020 local elections (Cowie, 2018; Borba et al., 2020; Norris and Dalby, 2020; Paraguassu, 2020). According to Bruno Paes Manso, a researcher at the Center for the Study of Violence at the University of Sao Paulo, whereas "[p]eople didn't kill each other before because of what another demanded from the world politically," more attacks in 2018 were "a result of [the] election ... The fact that immediate interests such as land or property aren't involved is something new" (Cowie, 2018). Violence reached an apogee in the 2020 municipal elections, with politicians (candidates and elected leaders) the primary targets, especially those speaking out against the local government (Borba et al., 2020). The two months of campaigning leading up to the first round of voting saw 200 murders, attempted murders, or otherwise injured candidates as compared to just 46 cases in the previous municipal elections in 2016 (Paraguassu, 2020), with the northeast of the country standing out for its disproportionate share of the violence in the run-up to the elections (Borba et al., 2020).

One explanation for the increase in violence in recent years is the rise to prominence of Bolsonaro, who has often employed violent rhetoric and seemingly encouraged violence among his supporters, in an echo of

---

[9] Rather, politicians and elected officials tend to be local notables, and it's local notables who tend to be targeted in the context of conflict over land and business dealings; the fact that they're politicians or elected officials is somewhat tangential, so what appears to be election-related violence is in fact not.

the rhetoric used by Donald Trump in the US (Cowie, 2018). Another is the increasing influence and consolidation of control of militias and new criminal organizations in cities such as Rio de Janeiro including *milícias*, groups often made up of current and former police officers, prison guards, and firefighters (Albarracín, 2018; Norris and Dalby, 2020). Such groups try to exert influence over local politicians, where "[p]olitical candidates that oppose these paramilitary groups risk a death sentence if they try to campaign in areas under their control" (Bruno Paes Manso, as quoted in Norris and Dalby (2020)).

Still, the record suggests that Bolsonaro and his allies have failed to benefit from the violence – and may have lost popularity over it. Candidates endorsed and supported by Bolsonaro lost badly in the 2020 local elections, two years after the president's election and in a year in which election-related violence surged (Fox, 2020). And while his unpopularity may be attributable to a number of different factors, by late 2021 Bolsonaro held a dismal 24 percent approval rating (52 percent disapproval) and was expected to lose in his bid for reelection (he trailed his main rival, Lula da Silva, by 21 points in the polls) (AFP, 2021). Furthermore, while the coercion by criminal groups in the neighborhoods that they control certainly has an impact on elections in those areas, it generally falls outside my theory's scope conditions as laid out in Chapters 1 and 3, which specify that it is unlikely to apply to violent actors that fully control the local area, thus eliminating any real choice that voters have at the polls. Voter backlash against violence is more likely to be a threat where a violent actor does not maintain complete control over the area.

In sum, the Brazilian case suggests that (1) founding elections set an important precedent for how campaigns are run and (2) violence may backfire against the politicians who instigate it. The campaigns of successful candidates in its earliest multiparty elections set a precedent of nonviolent electioneering and led to mostly peaceful elections in the years that followed. And recent increases in election-related violence have not helped – and may have hurt – the politicians associated with it, at least when voters have a real choice at the polls (i.e., when their neighborhoods are not fully controlled by armed groups). The evidence from Brazil is therefore largely consistent with the argument of this book.

Overall, evidence from the case studies are broadly consistent with the observable implications of the theory put forward in this book, as well as the findings from Kenya. Indonesia has seen substantial election-related ethnic violence since transitioning to multiparty politics, but those who've instigated it do not appear to have achieved their electoral goals. Furthermore, after parties and candidates that employed violence fared poorly in the country's earliest multiparty elections, the incidence of violence in subsequent elections sharply declined, at least in part due to this poor performance. Pakistani elections have also been subject to high levels of violence, most notably in Karachi, yet parties that have employed violence there suffered sharp reversals in their electoral fortunes when viable nonviolent alternatives emerged, suggesting that voters preferred to vote for nonviolent politicians when presented with a real choice. Nigeria, another case of endemic electoral violence, highlights the influence of founding elections on the incidence of violence in the long run, where the use of violence by the winning party of its first multiparty elections established the conventional wisdom that violence is an essential tactic for competing in Nigerian elections, especially in those regions where the winners of its first elections were most violent. It also underscores how structural features of a country's political environment – such as a lack of legal accountability for political elites who employ violence – make violence a viable option in politicians' electoral toolkit.

The "negative" cases of Ghana and Brazil – countries where, for various reasons, violence might be expected but has remained at relatively low levels – also clarify the factors that determine why some countries suffer from endemic election-related violence while others do not. Ghana's effective and independent institutions for managing elections and electoral conflict; its strong, well-institutionalized parties and coherent, nationalized party system; and its vibrant civil society have helped it to avoid high levels of violence and highlight a number of structural features that affect the likelihood that violence occurs. More relevant to the theory put forward in this book, its founding elections were conducted peacefully (if not on a level playing field), establishing a precedent for electoral victory based on nonviolent electoral tactics. As for Brazil, the conventional, nonviolent tactics employed by the winners of its first elections after the transition to multiparty democracy set the standard for elections to come, and there is some evidence that recent increases in election-related violence have not helped – and may have hurt – the electoral prospects of those candidates most associated with it. The case of Brazil will be an important one to follow in coming years to determine how well the theory put forward in this book can explain ongoing developments. On one hand, the recent increase in violence is inconsistent with the theory, given the country's history of successful nonviolent election campaigns; on the other, the momentous developments of the last several years –

including an economic crisis, massive corruption scandals, a presidential impeachment, and the election of right-wing populist Bolsonaro – may be just the sort of shock to the system discussed in Chapter 3 that could shift a country from the equilibrium established during its earliest multiparty elections. Time will tell if recent election cycles constitute a trend or a blip relative to the limited levels of election violence Brazil has seen in the past.

8

Conclusion

This book has presented evidence that the electoral costs of violent campaign tactics are greater than politicians – and the scholars who study them – tend to assume. Specifically, despite Kenyan politicians' beliefs to the contrary, the use of violence and heated ethnic rhetoric reduces support for the candidates that use it, including among the core coethnic voters that make up their primary base of support. Furthermore, analyses of violence and election outcomes in real elections suggest that voter backlash against violence can be large enough to diminish the advantages coercion provides as a tactic for winning competitive elections. Elite misperceptions about the effects of violence on voting can explain the persistence of election-related violence in Kenya. Additional evidence from cross-national quantitative analyses and a handful of qualitative case studies of countries across multiple continents – some with substantial violence like Kenya, others with significantly less – suggest that the findings from Kenya may apply more broadly to countries holding competitive elections in various parts of the world. They also demonstrate how the conduct and outcome of founding elections – in particular, whether or not the winner employs violence, irrespective of its actual effects – sets countries on a track where parties and candidates tend to employ similar tactics for many years to come, even when the efficacy of those tactics may be in doubt.

Chapter 2 summarized the nature and extent of election-related violence globally and in Kenya specifically. It documented the various forms that such violence takes and provided background on the Kenyan case, noting certain key features that make it particularly useful to study. In particular, it established that Kenya is a case where (1) political elites play a primary role in instigating violence and (2) elections are competitive enough that voters have a genuine choice at the polls. It also established it as a "hard" case for testing a theory of elite misperception, as the conventional wisdom holds that violence – working through several of the mechanisms posited in the literature – is an effective tool for winning Kenyan elections.

Chapter 3 summarized existing theories of election-related violence and introduced a theory of violence as a result of elite misperception. It highlighted how structural theories identify the political, social, and economic conditions that make violence a possible and potentially attractive tactic, whereas strategic, micro-level explanations focus on why parties and candidates employ violence when structural conditions make it a viable option. While some existing strategic theories focus on the coercive benefits of violence and others on its potential to persuade, all rely upon the assumption that politicians' choice of violence as an electoral tactic is based on an accurate assessment of its relative costs and benefits. The theory of elite misperception builds on two insights: (1) that voter backlash against violence is substantial and can cost politicians votes and (2) politicians frequently misjudge voter preferences – including with respect to violence – which can lead them to overestimate its benefits as an electoral tactic. The theory points to the difficulties politicians face in accurately assessing the impact of electoral tactics, as well as to the prevalence of cognitive biases that can cause them to misinterpret what information they have. It also highlights the importance of founding elections in determining which electoral tactics – violence included – are considered effective and worthy of emulation. With these insights in mind, the theory explains the incidence and persistence of election-related violence as a result of politicians' misperceptions about voter preferences and the effects of violence on voting rather than the objective electoral benefits that violence provides.

Chapters 4 and 5 analyzed the effect of violence on elections using a range of empirical strategies and sources of data. Chapter 4 evaluated the overall relationship between violence and election outcomes, finding that violence provides no benefit, on average, to the parties that use it. In some cases, it may even undermine the candidacies of the politicians associated with it. In particular, an analysis of the relationship between the incidence of violence prior to elections in Kenya's first two multiparty elections in the 1990s and constituency-level election outcomes for the ruling KANU party (the primary instigator of the violence) found no relationship between the incidence of violence and KANU vote share or the likelihood that their parliamentary candidates won election. Second, an analysis of the subsequent electoral performance of candidates allegedly involved in the large outbreak of violence in 2007/08 found that these candidates lost their reelection bids at a much higher rate than the average incumbent. Several lost in rather unusual ways, including by losing their party primaries, losing to minority ethnic group candidates, or losing the general election after securing the nomination of the locally dominant party.

Chapter 5 explored the particular mechanisms that link violence to electoral outcomes for the candidates that use it. With respect to pure coercion, existing research provides some evidence for the idea that violence can be used to force voters to change their votes in places where the violent actor has a monopoly on the use of violence; it may also be useful for reducing turnout among targeted groups of voters or displacing certain voters to forcefully purge them from the electorate altogether. Yet an analysis of the relationship between violence and turnout in Kenyan elections in the 1990s found no relationship between violence on the one hand, and the aggregate level of voter registration or turnout on the other, suggesting that the relationship between violence, turnout, and long-term electoral geography may be less straightforward than previously thought.

Since direct coercion usually only affects a small portion of the voting population, however, it is crucial to understand how violence affects the voting behavior of the broader electorate, and Chapter 5 explored this question with a variety of survey experiments designed to test how the use of violence and violent ethnic rhetoric shapes vote choice. The results showed that, rather than being a useful tool for persuading voters, violence in fact undermines candidates' support among the voting population, even among their coethnic base. And while antagonistic ethnic rhetoric *does* appear to increase the likelihood of violence breaking out, it is *not* a useful strategy for mobilizing coethnic support. The results help to explain why violence is not associated with better outcomes for candidates in real elections, as any benefits of violent coercion may be diminished by voter backlash against the parties and candidates that use it.

Chapter 6 addressed the puzzle of why politicians employ violence as an electoral tactic in Kenya when the benefits of doing so are uncertain at best. Using survey experiments with politicians that parallel those conducted with voters – as well as evidence from qualitative interviews – I showed that, contrary to what the literature assumes, politicians misperceive the effects of violence and violent ethnic rhetoric on voter preferences over candidates for office, underestimating the size and breadth of voter backlash against the use of these tactics. This misperception explains why election-related violence continues to occur in Kenya despite its questionable efficacy as an electoral tactic. Furthermore, access to information alone does not appear to be enough to correct politicians' misperceptions in this domain.

Finally, Chapter 7 explored whether and how the findings from Kenya travel elsewhere around the world. Cross-national quantitative analyses and case studies of a handful of countries with varying levels of violence demonstrate how the causes and consequences of election-related violence identified in Kenya can help explain violence (or its absence) in other competitive electoral contexts as well. The cross-national quantitative analysis demonstrates the key role that the conduct of founding elections – in particular, the tactics used by the founding election winner – appears to play in whether or not violence becomes commonly employed by parties and candidates in the electoral cycles that follow. The case studies reveal little to no evidence that violence is effective in helping parties and candidates win office but do identify instances in which it may have resulted in voter backlash. And in addition to identifying key structural conditions that make violence a more viable option in some cases than others, the analysis finds evidence consistent with the idea that the conduct of founding elections plays an important role in shaping politicians' beliefs and expectations about the effects of violence on their electoral prospects.

Overall, the findings highlight the role that elite misperception can play in the existence and persistence of violence in electoral competition. Even where violent coercion has its advantages, it can still provoke backlash from voters that diminishes whatever benefits a violent strategy may provide. Yet politicians may fail to perceive this, seeing violence as a more unambiguously effective tactic than it actually is. This misperception can explain why violence may occur even where its objective benefits are limited. To understand why election-related violence occurs, it is therefore crucial to both carefully analyze the effects of violence on election outcomes and directly study elite motivations and beliefs with respect to their choice of campaign tactics.

The findings of this study have a number of important implications for how we understand election-related violence, as well as voting behavior and the decision-making of political elites more generally. For one, they point to a need for research to more carefully evaluate the costs of violent electoral tactics in addition to their apparent benefits. While the literature has done well in identifying the ways in which violence may help candidates at the polls, it has paid far less attention to the potential costs of violence as an electoral tactic, including the possibility of voter backlash among those who turn out to vote.[1] One exception is Collier and Vicente (2012), who posit that weak supporters may abandon their preferred candidate if the candidate employs violence, reducing the candidate's electoral base to their most extreme supporters. Another is Siddiqui (2022), who posits that parties that seek to appeal to voters across groups face a greater threat of voter backlash against violence than those that make exclusionary appeals to in-group members only. To an extent, the results presented here are consistent with these insights; out-group voters are more likely to sanction violent politicians than voters from a candidate's own ethnic group. Yet, the data show that even politicians' core, coethnic voters are willing to punish the use of violence, at least when a viable alternative exists. We therefore need additional careful analyses of the effects of violence on voting in different contexts, with particular attention to whether and how violence provokes voter backlash that may offset the electoral benefits that violent coercion may provide.[2]

In addition, even nuanced models of electoral violence such as Collier and Vicente (2012) and Siddiqui (2022) that consider potential costs assume that politicians accurately assess the relative costs and benefits of violence when deciding whether to employ it as an electoral tactic. The findings of this book suggest that we cannot take this ability for granted; rather, we should ask more explicitly whether and how political elites are able to make this determination. Future research should delve more deeply into the question of when and why politicians fail to accurately infer voter preferences and the effects of violence and other electoral tactics. This book has posited two mechanisms that explain elite misperception – lack of information and cognitive bias – with some evidence that the latter seems to have the greatest explanatory power. But answering this question satisfactorily requires much more research on what drives misperception and the circumstances under which it is more or less likely to occur. To date, the evidence that information alone can correct politicians' misperceptions about voter preferences is mixed, at best (Butler and Nickerson, 2011; Hersh, 2015; Butler and Dynes, 2016; Kalla and Porter, 2020). But research on how cognitive biases affect

---

[1] Hafner-Burton, Hyde, and Jablonski (2018) identify the possibility of provoking post-election protests that threaten the incumbent's hold on power as another potential cost of employing violence.

[2] Malik (2021) suggests one determinant may be voters' experience with past violence and their ability to attribute it to political actors.

politicians' beliefs about public opinion and the efficacy of their campaign tactics – which could shed light on an important alternative mechanism – is lacking.[3]

This book has also argued that the dynamics of founding elections are an important determinant of the electoral tactics that become common in subsequent elections; in particular, that the tactics used by the winner in founding elections are likely to be perceived as effective and therefore emulated by future contenders. While I present evidence consistent with this conjecture, more research is needed to pin down the posited mechanisms and determine when and where they are most likely to apply. Systematic, in-depth analyses of how the tactics used by the winners of founding elections affect the tactics used in subsequent elections – across multiple countries and time periods – would therefore be a highly informative addition to the literature.

The findings of this book are somewhat fatalistic in the sense that, once established, the violent election equilibrium – in which the conventional wisdom holds that violence is effective – is hard to escape. Importantly, however, they also suggest the potential of a different approach to combating election-related violence than what local and international organizations tend to pursue.[4] Many anti-violence initiatives take a normative approach, attempting to convince the relevant actors – such as political elites or violent specialists – not to incite or participate in violence because of its negative externalities, which are many. For instance, in a report on election-related violence in Nigeria, Human Rights Watch argues that "Nigerian politicians must come to recognize that political violence is not about who wins the next election, but that it has important implications for the rights and well-being of all Nigerians that extend far beyond election day" (Human Rights Watch, 2007, 5). Yet the research presented here – by highlighting the existence of voter backlash against violent electoral tactics – suggests the possibility of reducing violence by *appealing to*, rather than *competing against*, political elites' electoral incentives. If violence occurs as a result of misperception due to politicians

---

[3] Sheffer et al. (2018) identify cognitive bias among political elites and how it affects their decision-making about policy, but we have no evidence on how it affects their decisiomaking in other domains such as campaign strategy. Butler and Dynes (2016) identify "disagreement discounting" as an explanation for why American elected officials do not update beliefs about their constituents' opinions, but do not test for the particular mechanism – say, confirmation bias – that explains why it occurs.

[4] See Claes (2016) and Birch and Muchlinski (2018) for discussion of the range of interventions that tend to be implemented and efforts to evaluate their relative effectiveness.

ignoring the potential for costly backlash against it, then correcting those misperceptions can effectively reduce the incidence of violence associated with electoral competition.

Since the theory of elite misperception also implies that new or outsider parties and candidates are more likely than experienced or mainstream politicians to buck the status quo and eschew violence, another potential tactic for combating violence in contexts where it's prevalent may be providing support to new entrants to electoral politics who are committed to nonviolence but that require additional resources and visibility to be viewed as viable alternatives to existing parties and politicians. To that end, weak party systems – that is, those where parties and partisan attachments are constantly changing, and voters' loyalties are primarily to particular politicians or coethnics – are generally viewed as a drag on democratic consolidation; however, they may actually be more conducive to breaking out of a violent electoral equilibrium if they provide more of an opportunity for new parties to emerge or political leaders to shift tactics than those with a more stable status quo.

Finally, it should be noted that elite misperception may help explain the adoption of electoral tactics beyond violence. There is nothing in the theory that limits its applicability to violence alone; scholars and politicians may overestimate the benefits or underestimate the costs of any electoral tactic where sufficient information is lacking or cognitive bias clouds their judgment. As we've noted, politicians misperceive public opinion and pursue ineffective campaign tactics in even the most mature democracies where sophisticated, well-resourced campaigns have access to large amount of information (Miller and Stokes, 1963; Gerber and Green, 2000; Krasno and Green, 2008b; Broockman and Skovron, 2018; Kalla and Broockman, 2018; Hertel-Fernandez, Mildenberger, and Stokes, 2019). Political leaders also miscalculate when attempting to remain in power in competitive authoritarian regimes, resulting in democratization "by mistake" (Treisman, 2020). The possibility that elite misperception explains the existence and persistence of a variety of electoral tactics and political behaviors in various contexts should not be discounted, and future research should further explore whether and when this is the case.

In sum, the electoral costs of violent campaign tactics are greater than politicians – and the scholars who study them – tend to assume. Politicians are only human, and they can err in their judgments as well, even when the stakes are high. Encouragingly, this knowledge supports the notion that violence need not be inherent to hotly contested elections in divided societies. With the general effectiveness of violence in doubt, efforts to reduce election-related violence need not counter but rather *appeal to* politicians' electoral self-interest. Ironically, politicians' desire to win power may be the solution, not the problem, when it comes to promoting peaceful political competition in elections around the world.

Appendix A

Sampling Strategy for the Survey in Nakuru, Kisumu, and Narok

The sample of Kenyan voters was selected as follows. First, three sites were selected for their concentrations of three ethnic groups: Nakuru for the Kikuyu, Kisumu for the Luo, and Narok for the Maasai. These groups were selected since the Kikuyu and Luo are two of the largest and perhaps the most politically salient groups in Kenyan politics, always on opposite sides of the political divide. The Maasai, rather, have tended to a swing voter group in recent years, often splitting their vote between competing electoral coalitions. All three areas were sites of violence in previous election cycles pitting ethnic groups on different sides of the political divide against each other, including during the large outbreak of violence in 2007/08 (see KNCHR (2008) and Akiwumi, Bosire, and Ondeyo (1999*b*) for further details).

Once the sites were selected, a sample of neighborhoods in the urban and peri-urban areas of each town were selected to be included in the sample based on two primary criteria: estimated concentration of the targeted ethnic group and the representativeness of the neighborhood based on the socioeconomic status of its residents and its access to public services. Both dimensions were scored based on the expertise of local research assistants.

Once the sample neighborhoods were selected, a central point in the neighborhood was selected as a starting point using Google Maps, and survey enumerators employed the Afrobarometer random walk method to select households, and then a random adult from within each household, to participate in the survey (see Afrobarometer, 2014). Specifically, the four enumerators would walk in four separate directions from the central starting point and select each fourth household on their path. If someone came to the door, the enumerator would have all adults in the household use numbered cards to randomly select a respondent. If no one answered the door or they were not interested in participating, the enumerator would move on to the fourth household along their path from their last stop. If the path they were on did not continue forward, enumerators were instructed to turn and continue on a path to their right.

As we were only interested in surveying Kikuyu voters in Nakuru, Luo voters in Kisumu, and Maasai voters in Narok (as well as an equal number of female and male, younger and older, and more and less educated voters), a first section of the survey was used to screen respondents to identify whether they met the necessary criteria. Respondents were not told the criteria for participating in the full survey, just that they would be screened based on their demographic information and would receive compensation for the survey regardless of whether they qualified or not. This information was provided in the informed consent script that was read prior to receiving their agreement to participate in the survey.

Respondents had a choice of conducting the survey in English or Kiswahili. All enumerators were also fluent in the respondents' tribal language, so they could translate portions of the survey if needed.

Appendix B

Supplementary Analyses

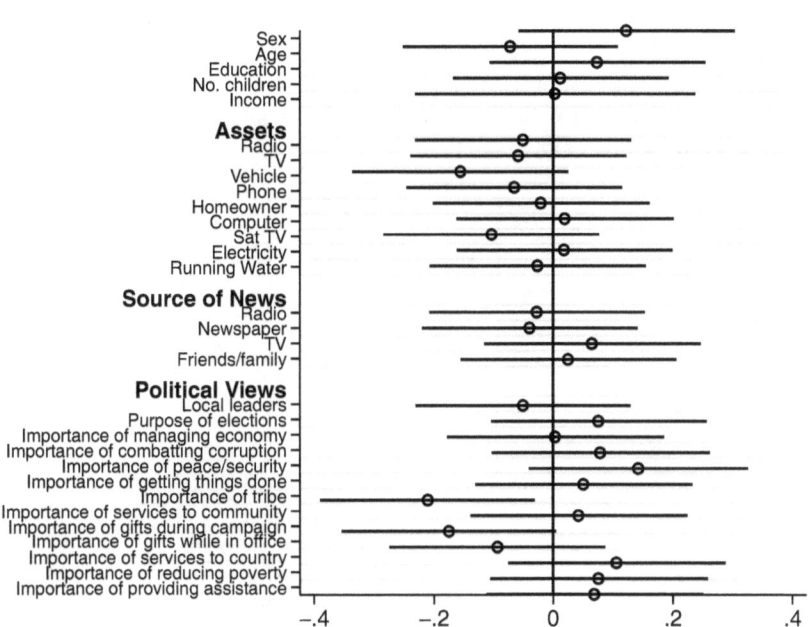

FIGURE B.1 Balance on attributed violence treatment (main voter survey)
Note: Estimates are based on difference in means between treatment and control and are displayed with 95 percent confidence intervals. All variables are standardized for ease of interpretation.

168   Appendix B Supplementary Analyses

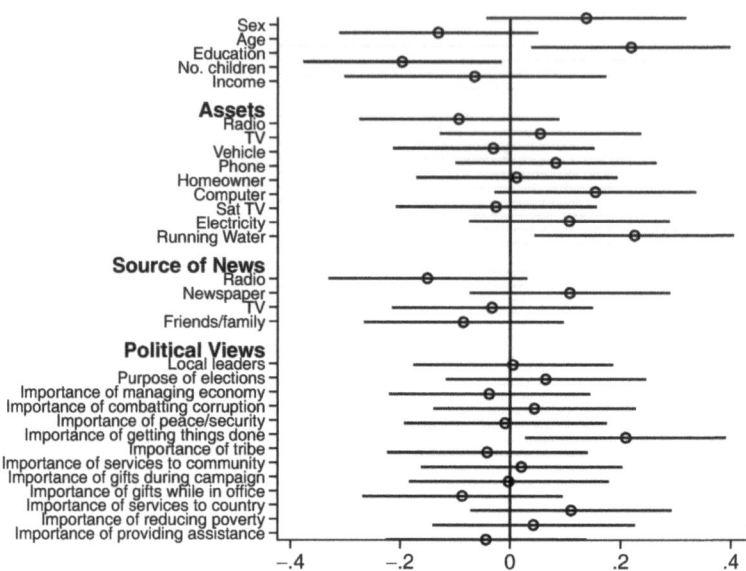

FIGURE B.2 Balance on coethnic vs. non-coethnic treatment (main voter survey)
Note: Estimates are based on difference in means between treatment and control and are displayed with 95 percent confidence intervals. All variables are standardized for ease of interpretation.

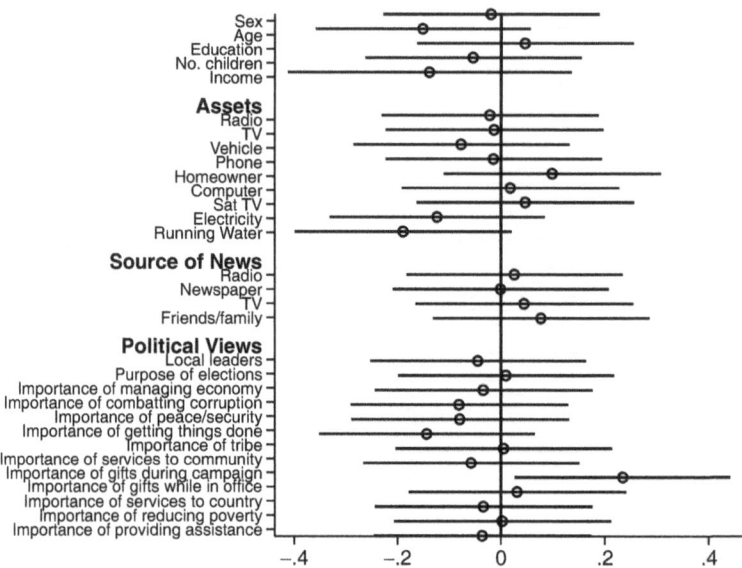

FIGURE B.3 Balance on ethnic rhetoric treatment (main voter survey)
Note: Estimates are based on difference in means between treatment and control and are displayed with 95 percent confidence intervals. All variables are standardized for ease of interpretation.

Balance Tests

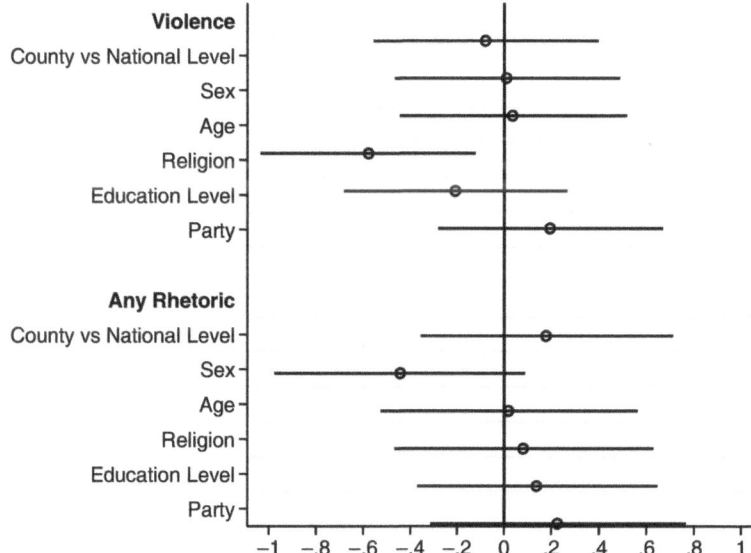

FIGURE B.4 Balance on violence and ethnic rhetoric treatments (politician survey)
Note: Estimates are based on difference in means between treatment and control and are displayed with 95 percent confidence intervals. All variables are standardized for ease of interpretation.

TABLE B.1 *Pretreatment covariate balance for violence and ethnic rhetoric treatments, policy endorsement experiments*

	(1) Violence treatment	(2) Rhetoric treatment
Urban	−0.0179	−0.0850**
	(0.0227)	(0.0362)
Female	−0.00226	0.0357
	(0.0216)	(0.0350)
Age	−0.000248	−0.00141
	(0.000879)	(0.00138)
Level of education	0.0100	0.000297
	(0.00642)	(0.0104)
Household income	−0.00269	−0.0174
	(0.0100)	(0.0170)

TABLE B.1 *(cont.)*

	(1) Violence treatment	(2) Rhetoric treatment
Affected by political violence	0.00673	0.000433
	(0.0308)	(0.0484)
Constant	0.730***	0.589***
	(0.0468)	(0.0751)
Observations	1728	886

Standard errors in parentheses
* $p < 0.10$, ** $p < 0.05$, *** $p < 0.01$
Note: Estimates are based on a regression of treatment on pretreatment covariates.

ADDITIONAL ANALYSES

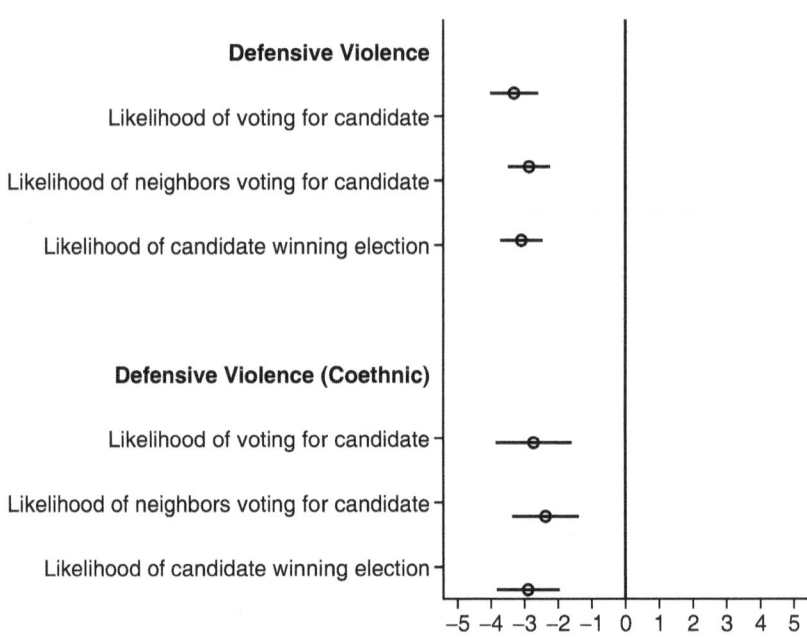

FIGURE B.5 Effect of defensive violence on vote choice

TABLE B.2 *Effect of violence on KANU election outcomes, 1992–1997*

	(1) MP vote share	(2) Likelihood of MP win	(3) Presidential vote share
Violence	0.00245	0.0769	0.00748
	(0.0454)	(0.106)	(0.0376)
Constant	0.435***	0.498***	0.438***
	(0.00746)	(0.0174)	(0.00618)
Constituency fixed effects?	Yes	Yes	Yes
Election-year fixed effects?	No	No	No
Observations	334	334	334

Standard errors in parentheses
* $p < 0.10$, ** $p < 0.05$, *** $p < 0.01$

TABLE B.3 *Effect of any prior violence on KANU election outcomes, 1992–1997*

	(1) MP vote share	(2) Likelihood of MP win	(3) Presidential vote share
Any prior violence	0.0479	0.143	0.0273
	(0.0618)	(0.144)	(0.0512)
Constant	0.430***	0.490***	0.436***
	(0.00905)	(0.0211)	(0.00750)
Constituency fixed effects?	Yes	Yes	Yes
Election-year fixed effects?	Yes	Yes	Yes
Observations	334	334	334

Standard errors in parentheses
* $p < 0.10$, ** $p < 0.05$, *** $p < 0.01$

Appendix B Supplementary Analyses

TABLE B.4 *Effect of any prior violence on voter turnout in Kenyan elections, 1992–1997*

	(1) Votes cast	(2) Voter turnout	(3) Registered voters
Any prior violence	8550.9	0.0213	8367.8
	(5388.6)	(0.0346)	(6531.7)
MP election uncontested	−25739.3***	−0.378***	
	(3878.4)	(0.0249)	
Constant	55631.6***	0.668***	81845.5***
	(915.5)	(0.00589)	(1075.4)
Constituency fixed effects?	Yes	Yes	Yes
Election-year fixed effects?	Yes	Yes	Yes
Observations	334	334	334

Standard errors in parentheses
* $p < 0.10$, ** $p < 0.05$, *** $p < 0.01$

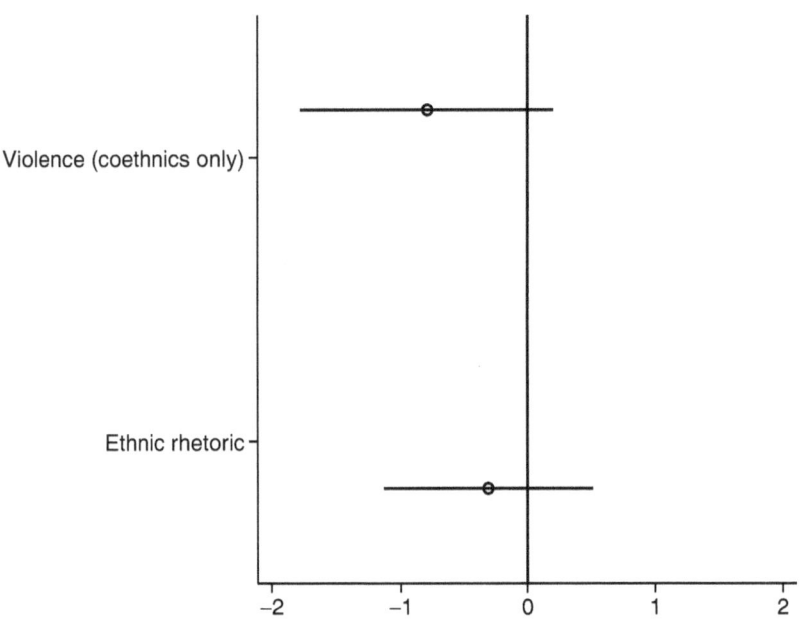

FIGURE B.6 Effect of violence on support for candidate-endorsed policies among young, less educated men
Note: Estimates are based on difference in means between the pooled violence treatments and control and are displayed with 95 percent confidence intervals.

TABLE B.5 *Mean likelihood of supporting candidates across treatment groups, with 95 percent confidence intervals*

	Offensive violence	Defensive violence	Unattributed violence	No violence
Coethnic	3.45 [2.76 – 4.14]	4.58 [3.70 – 5.45]	3.65 [2.85 – 4.45]	7.5 [6.90 – 8.10]
Non-coethnic	2.98 [2.26 – 3.70]	3.10 [2.52 – 3.67]	2.97 [2.39 – 3.55]	6.79 [6.16 – 7.43]

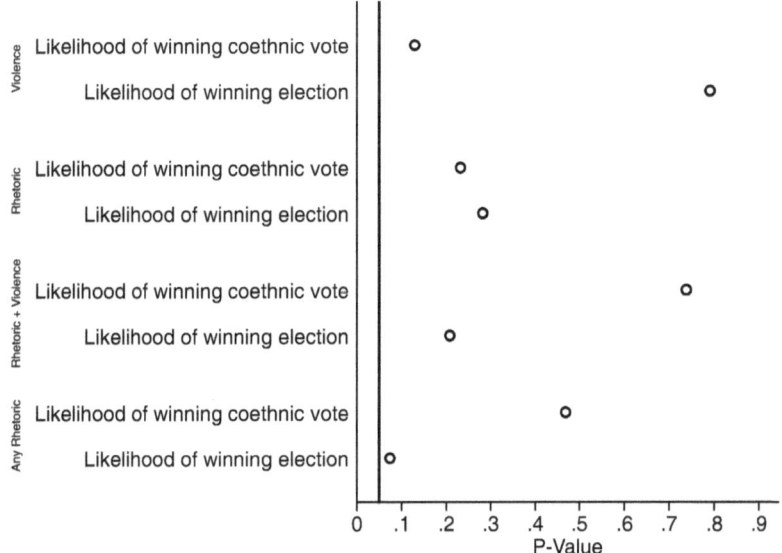

FIGURE B.7 Politicians' perceptions of the effect of violence and ethnic rhetoric on vote choice

Note: This figure reports *p*-values from randomization inference using Fisher's exact test of the sharp null hypothesis. The "violence" results are from a comparison between the violence and no violence conditions in the first elite experiment; the "rhetoric," "rhetoric + violence," and "any rhetoric" results are from a comparison of the rhetoric/rhetoric+violence/combination of the two conditions against the control condition in the second elite experiment. Estimates are based on 1,000 Monte Carlo simulations of the treatment assignment process.

Appendix C

Candidate Vignettes and Outcome Questions

CANDIDATE VIGNETTES

Voter Violence Experiment

[Mr. Peter Chege/Mr. Peter Onyango/Mr. Peter ole Sankale/Mr. Peter Kipkosgei /Mr. Peter Bosire] plans to run for Governor in the next elections in 2017. [Mr. Chege/Mr. Onyango/Mr. ole Sankale/ Mr. Kipkosgei/Mr. Bosire]is 51 years old and a member of the [Kikuyu/Luo/Maasai/Kalenjin/Kisii] tribe. He is currently serving as a County Assembly Member, having previously served one term as a District Councillor. While in office, he focused on issues in the health sector. If elected, he promises to create jobs, reduce corruption, and improve the quality of primary education. [In the last election campaign, [youths in his ward were said to have used pangas to battle members of other tribes] [he was said to have provided youths with pangas to attack members other tribes] [he was said to have provided youths with pangas to defend against attacks from members of other tribes].

Note: Each respondent had a 50 percent chance of seeing a candidate from their own tribe, and a 12.5 percent chance of seeing a candidate from one of four others. For example, a Kikuyu respondent had a 50 percent of seeing a Mr. Chege, and a 50 percent chance of seeing either Mr. Onyango, Mr. ole Sankale, Mr. Kipkosgei, or Mr. Bosire, with an equal chance of seeing each of the latter.

Voter Ethnic Rhetoric Experiment

Mr. Joseph Nderitu/Odhiambo/ole Tonkei plans to run for MP in this constituency in the next elections in 2017. Mr. Nderitu/Odhiambo/ole

176   Appendix C Candidate Vignettes and Outcome Questions

Tonkei is 48 years old and a member of the Kikuyu/Luo/Maasai tribe. He is an advocate of the High Court of Kenya and currently serves as a County Assembly Member. If elected, he promises to improve the quality of the roads in the constituency and help women and the youth to start businesses. [He has also pledged to ensure that Kikuyu/Luo/Maasai people get access to their fair share of the county's land and government jobs, which he says have been stolen by people from other tribes.] [Some observers have suggested that speeches he gave during his last campaign accusing people from other tribes of stealing land and jobs led to violence against those tribes during the campaign.] [Some observers have suggested that speeches he gave during the last campaign led to violence against other tribes.]

Note: Kikuyu respondents only saw Mr. Nderitu, Luo ones only Mr. Odhiambo, and Maasai ones only Mr. ole Tonkei.

Nationally Representative Voter Violence Experiment with Endorsement Experiment

Mr. [Peter Chege/Peter Masinde/Peter Kipkosgei/Peter Onyango/Peter Mutungi/Adan Ibrahim/Peter Bosire/Peter Kazungu/Peter Kithika/Peter Lokwalima/Peter ole Sankale] plans to run for governor in the next elections in 2022. Mr. [Chege / Masinde / Kipkosgei / Onyango / Mutungi / Ibbrahim / Bosire / Kazungu / Kithika / Lokwalima / ole Sankale] is 51 years old and a member of the [Kikuyu / Luhya / Kalenjin / Luo / Kamba / Somali / Kisii / Mijikenda / Meru / Turkana / Maasai] community. He is a prominent businessman who has contributed some of his wealth to sponsor sporting events for county youths. [When he ran for MCA in the last election campaign, [youths in his ward were said to have been involved in clashes with members of other communities] [he was said to have provided youths with pangas to attack members other communities] [he was said to have provided youths with pangas to defend against attacks from members of other communities]. If elected as governor, he promises to create jobs, reduce corruption, and improve the quality of primary education.

Nationally Representative Voter Ethnic Rhetoric Experiment with Endorsement Experiment

Mr. [Joseph Nderitu/Joseph Muhindi/Joseph Chepkwony/Joseph Odhiambo/Joseph Kitonga/Abdi Mohamed/Joseph Nyamongo/Joseph

Ngao/Joseph Mutwiri/Joseph Lokiyoto/Joseph ole Tonkei] plans to run for governor in the next elections in 2017. Mr. [Nderitu / Muhindi / Chepkwony / Odhiambo / Kitonga / Mohamed / Nyamongo / Ngao / Lokiyoto / ole Tonkei] is 48 years old and a member of the [Kikuyu / Luhya / Kalenjin / Luo / Kamba / Kisii / Mijikenda / Meru / Turkana / Maasai] community. He is an advocate of the High Court of Kenya and has been serving as a County Assembly Member (MCA). If elected governor, he promises to improve the quality of the roads in the constituency and help women and the youth to start businesses. [He has also pledged to ensure that Kikuyu / Luhya / Kalenjin / Luo / Kamba / Somali / Kisii / Mijikenda / Meru / Turkana / Maasai people get access to their fair share of the county's land and government jobs, which he says have been stolen by people from other communities.] [Some observers have suggested that speeches he gave during his last campaign accusing people from other communities of stealing land and jobs led to violence against those communities during the campaign.] [Some observers have suggested that speeches he gave during the last campaign led to violence against other communities.]

OUTCOME QUESTIONS

Political Elite Experiments

On a scale from 1 to 10, where 1 indicates that they would never vote for this candidate and 10 indicates that they would definitely vote for this candidate, how likely would voters from the candidate's tribe be to vote for the candidate described above?

On a scale from 1 to 10, 1 indicating very unlikely and 10 indicating very likely, what would you say is the likelihood that this candidate would win the election for MP?

Voter Violence Experiment

Measures of voter support:
On a scale from 1 to 10, where 1 indicates that you would never vote for this candidate and 10 indicates that you would definitely vote for this candidate, how likely would you be to vote for the candidate described above?

On a scale from 1 to 10, where 1 indicates that they would never vote for this candidate and 10 indicates that they would definitely vote for this candidate, what would you say is the likelihood that others in your neighborhood would vote for the candidate described above?

On a scale from 1 to 10, 1 indicating very unlikely and 10 indicating very likely, what would you say is the likelihood that this candidate would win the election for Governor?

Voter Ethnic Rhetoric Experiment

Measures of voter support:
On a scale from 1 to 10, where 1 indicates that you would never vote for this candidate and 10 indicates that you would definitely vote for this candidate, how likely would you be to vote for the candidate described above?

On a scale from 1 to 10, where 1 indicates that they would never vote for this candidate and 10 indicates that they would definitely vote for this candidate, what would you say is the likelihood that others in your neighborhood would vote for the candidate described above?

On a scale from 1 to 10, 1 indicating very unlikely and 10 indicating very likely, what would you say is the likelihood that this candidate would win the election for MP?

Measures of the likelihood of violence:
On a scale from 1 to 10, 1 indicating very unlikely and 10 indicating very likely, what would you say is the likelihood that the next election this candidate runs in would be characterized by violence?

Do you agree or disagree with the following statement: In this country, it is sometimes necessary to use violence in support of a just cause. [Probe for strength of opinion.]

Endorsement Experiments

(Indirect) measures of voter support for the violence experiment:
A recent proposal by Mr. [Chege / Masinde / Kipkosgei / Onyango / Mutungi / Ibrahim / Bosire / Kazungu / Kithika / Lokwalima / ole Sankale] calls for decreasing the share of the budget controlled by the national government and increasing the share controlled by county governments. How do you feel about this proposal?

(a) Strongly agree
(b) Somewhat agree
(c) Indifferent
(d) Somewhat disagree
(e) Strongly disagree

A recent proposal by Mr. [Chege / Masinde / Kipkosgei / Onyango / Mutungi / Ibrahim / Bosire / Kazungu / Kithika / Lokwalima / ole Sankale] calls for creating a county program to provide credit to farmers to buy agricultural inputs. Farmers who fail to repay their loans would have their farms confiscated. How do you feel about this proposal?

(a) Strongly agree
(b) Somewhat agree
(c) Indifferent
(d) Somewhat disagree
(e) Strongly disagree

A recent proposal by Mr. [Chege / Masinde / Kipkosgei / Onyango / Mutungi / Ibrahim / Bosire / Kazungu / Kithika / Lokwalima / ole Sankale] calls for tarmacking 200km of new roads in the county in order to reduce transport times in rural areas. The work would be funded by charging a toll on drivers and passengers for using the new roads. How do you feel about this proposal?

(a) Strongly agree
(b) Somewhat agree
(c) Indifferent
(d) Somewhat disagree
(e) Strongly disagree

(Indirect) measures of voter support for the ethnic rhetoric experiment:
A recent proposal by Mr. [Nderitu / Muhindi / Chepkwony / Odhiambo / Kitonga / Mohamed / Nyamongo / Ngao / Mutwiri / Lokiyoto / ole Tonkei] calls for legislation to shift more responsibility for security from the national to the county level. Observers have suggested that this might help focus efforts on issues of local concern, but it could make it more difficult to fight crime that and banditry that occurs across county lines. How do you feel about this proposal?

(a) Strongly agree
(b) Somewhat agree
(c) Indifferent
(d) Somewhat disagree
(e) Strongly disagree

A recent proposal by Mr. [Nderitu / Muhindi / Chepkwony / Odhiambo / Kitonga / Mohamed / Nyamongo / Ngao / Mutwiri / Lokiyoto / ole Tonkei] calls for closing the worst performing primary schools in the county and transferring students to schools that have been performing better. This would give students in poorly performing schools the opportunity to attend better schools but would require them to travel longer distances to get there, making access more difficult. How do you feel about this proposal?

(a) Strongly agree
(b) Somewhat agree
(c) Indifferent
(d) Somewhat disagree
(e) Strongly disagree

A recent proposal by Mr. [Nderitu / Muhindi / Chepkwony / Odhiambo / Kitonga / Mohamed / Nyamongo / Ngao / Mutwiri / Lokiyoto / ole Tonkei] calls for reallocating funding for the county and sub-county hospitals to local health centers. The proposal seeks to improve the quality of services at local health centers, but could have a detrimental effect on the quality of services at the larger hospitals. How do you feel about this proposal?

(a) Strongly agree
(b) Somewhat agree
(c) Indifferent
(d) Somewhat disagree
(e) Strongly disagree

Appendix D

Politician Information Experiment Memo and Contact Scripts

CONTACT SCRIPTS

Email

Dear Hon. [Name],

My name is Dr. Steven Rosenzweig, a political scientist from Yale University. Linked here, and attached, please find a memo summarizing the results of a study I conducted on the effects of violence on election outcomes in Kenya. The study finds compelling evidence that **violence is a losing electoral strategy for candidates running for office in Kenyan elections.** Specifically, employing violence as a tactic for winning elections costs politicians crucial votes, including from their own communities. In fact, the research suggests that Kenyan voters are up to 50% less likely to vote for candidates that instigate violence in their election campaigns.

Please see the memo for additional information; we hope you will find it useful. If you're interested, the study and its results are described in much greater detail in a working paper (available here) and the complete Ph.D. dissertation (available here).

[I have sent this information to other candidates running for election in your constituency as well.]

Best of luck in your election campaign!

Sincerely,

Steven C. Rosenzweig, Ph.D.
Department of Political Science
Yale University

SMS

Hon [Name]: I am Dr Steven Rosenzweig from Yale University. Linked here (https://tinyurl.com/yc7l9ymn) please find results from my recent study, which finds evidence that violence is a losing strategy for Kenyan politicians. [I have sent this info to other candidates in your constituency as well.]

INFORMATION MEMO

YALE UNIVERSITY STUDY FINDS THAT VIOLENCE IS A LOSING STRATEGY IN KENYAN ELECTIONS

SUMMARY

Research by Yale University political scientist Dr. Steven Rosenzweig (available here and here) has found that **violence is a losing strategy for the politicians that use it.** Specifically, employing violence as a tactic for winning elections costs politicians crucial votes, including from their own communities.

The research finds that **when a politician instigates violence, voters are 50% less likely to vote for that politician, overall.** Even members of the same tribe are 46% less likely to vote for a politician that instigates violence. The results are the same even when it is unclear whether the politician themselves is directly responsible. When given the choice between voting for a violent politician from their tribe and voting for a peaceful politician from another tribe, **80% of voters would vote for a peaceful politician from another tribe over a violent politician from their own tribe.**

Voters also dislike politicians who make statements against other tribes. In fact, **voters are 20% less likely to vote for politicians from their community that use tribal rhetoric.**

Finally, **politicians allegedly involved in the 2007/08 post-election violence were half as likely to win election in 2013 than the average sitting MP.**

In short, the research suggests that violence and tribal rhetoric are *not* effective tactics for politicians seeking elected office in Kenya. In fact, the use of violence and tribal rhetoric reduces voter support, making it difficult for politicians to win their elections. **Based on this evidence, candidates are likely to be most successful if they avoid the use of violence and tribal rhetoric in their campaigns.**

CANDIDATES LOSE VOTES WHEN THEY INSTIGATE VIOLENCE

The researcher conducted household surveys with Kenyan voters to measure their support for different types of candidates for elected office. Specifically, voters were presented with descriptions of candidates for office with different combinations of attributes. They were then asked the likelihood that they would vote for the candidate described.

The data from these surveys demonstrated that the use of violence as an electoral tactic sharply reduces voter support for the candidates that use it, including among voters from their own tribe. Specifically, voters are 50% less likely to vote for a candidate if they instigate violence during the campaign (see Figure 1). Even voters from the same tribe as the candidate are 46% less likely to vote for a candidate that instigates clashes with other tribes (see Figure 1). In addition, when given the choice between voting for a violent politician from their tribe and voting for a peaceful politician from another tribe, 80% of surveyed Kenyans prefer to vote for a peaceful politician from another tribe over a violent politician from their own tribe.

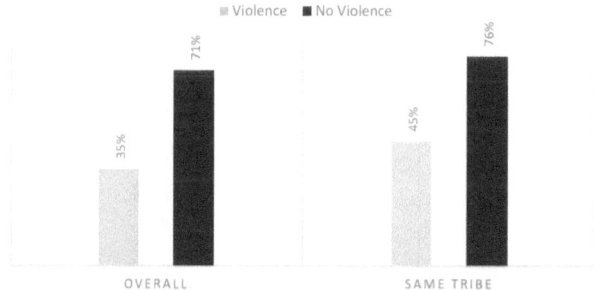

FIGURE 1: VIOLENCE LOSES VOTES
LIKELIHOOD OF VOTING FOR CANDIDATE

Importantly, violence loses votes even when it is organized to defend against perceived threats, for example to defend against attacks from other tribes. The data shows that arming youths to defend against attacks from other tribes reduces the candidate's support among members of the same tribe by 39%. Violence also loses votes even when responsibility for it cannot be directly attributed to the candidate, reducing support for the candidate by more than 50%.

The research also analyzed how politicians accused of instigating violence have fared in their election campaigns. It found that politicians mentioned in the Waki Report as alleged perpetrators of the 2007/08 post-election violence only won election in the next elections in 2013 at a rate of 30%. This is compared to a 60% overall reelection rate for sitting MPs in the same elections. Thus, candidates suspected of instigating violence in 2007/08 fared poorly in the 2013 election campaigns relative to sitting politicians overall.

CANDIDATES LOSE VOTES WHEN THEY USE TRIBAL RHETORIC

Data from the same surveys of Kenyan voters described above shows that, not only does violence lose votes, but using tribal rhetoric loses votes as well. In fact, the study showed that Kenyan voters are 20% less likely to vote for politicians from their own community when the politician makes statements pledging to restore their fair share of land and jobs allegedly stolen by other tribes (see Figure 2). Voters preferred to vote for politicians from their community that did *not* make tribal appeals and instead simply promised to improve the quality of roads and help women and youths start businesses.

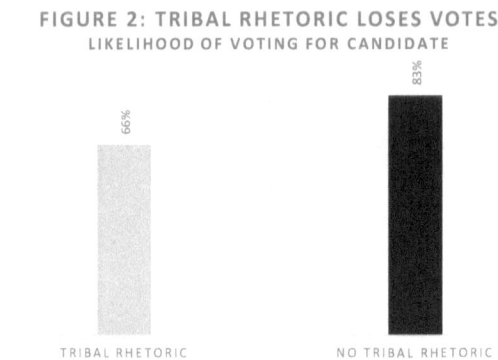

FIGURE 2: TRIBAL RHETORIC LOSES VOTES
LIKELIHOOD OF VOTING FOR CANDIDATE

TRIBAL RHETORIC 66% NO TRIBAL RHETORIC 83%

ADDITIONAL INFORMATION

Additional information about the study, including how it was conducted and more detailed findings, are available from two sources. For a working paper that describes the findings reported here, as well as additional analyses, see "Dangerous Disconnect: Voter Backlash, Elite Misperception, and the Costs of Violence as an Electoral Tactic" by Steven C. Rosenzweig, available here. For the full dissertation, which describes the study in even greater detail, see *Voter Backlash, Elite Misperception, and the Logic of Violence in Electoral Competition* by Steven C. Rosenzweig, available here.

References

Abdulai, Abdul Gafaru and Gordon Crawford. 2010. "Consolidating democracy in Ghana: Progress and prospects?" *Democratization* 17(1):26–67.

Acemoglu, Daron, James A. Robinson and Rafael J. Santos. 2013. "The Monopoly of Violence: Evidence from Colombia." *Journal of the European Economic Association* 11(S1):5–44.

Adida, Claire L., Karen E. Ferree, Daniel N. Posner and Amanda Lea Robinson. 2016. "Who's Asking? Interviewer Coethnicity Effects in African Survey Data." *Comparative Political Studies* 49(12):1630–1660.

AFP. 2021. "Bolsonaro Disapproval Rating Surpasses 50% for First Time." Sao Paulo.

Afrobarometer. 2014. "Round 6 Survey Manual."

Aidt, Toke, Miriam A. Golden and Devesh Tiwari. 2011. "Incumbents and Criminals in the Indian National Legislature." Unpublished manuscript.

Ake, Claude. 1993. "What Is the Problem of Ethnicity in Africa." *Transformation* 22:1–14.

Akiwumi, A. M., S. E. O. Bosire and S. C. Ondeyo. 1999a. Akiwumi Report: Report of the Judicial Commission of Inquiry into Tribal Clashes in Kenya Nairobi.

Akiwumi, A. M., S. E. O. Bosire and S. C. Ondeyo. 1999b. Akiwumi Report: Coast Province. Report of the Judicial Commission of Inquiry into Tribal Clashes in Kenya Nairobi.

Akiwumi, A. M., S. E. O. Bosire and S. C. Ondeyo. 1999c. Akiwumi Report: Introduction. Report of the Judicial Commission of Inquiry into Tribal Clashes in Kenya Nairobi.

Akiwumi, A. M., S. E. O. Bosire and S. C. Ondeyo. 1999d. Akiwumi Report: Rift Valley. Report of the Judicial Commission of Inquiry into Tribal Clashes in Kenya Nairobi.

Albarracín, Juan. 2018. "Criminalized Electoral Politics in Brazilian Urban Peripheries." *Crime, Law and Social Change* 69(4):553–575.

Anderson, David and Emma Lochery. 2008. "Violence and Exodus in Kenya's Rift Valley, 2008: Predictable and Preventable?" *Journal of Eastern African Studies* 2(2):328–343.

Aspinall, Edward. 2011. "Democratization and Ethnic Politics in Indonesia: Nine Theses." *Journal of East Asian Studies* 11(2):289–319.
Balaton-Chrimes, Samantha. 2021. "Who Are Kenya's 42(+) Tribes? The Census and the Political Utility of Magical Uncertainty." *Journal of Eastern African Studies* 15(1):43–62.
Banerjee, Abhijit, Donald P. Green, Jeffery McManus and Rohini Pande. 2014. "Are Poor Voters Indifferent to Whether Elected Leaders Are Criminal or Corrupt? A Vignette Experiment in Rural India." *Political Communication* 31(3):391–407.
Bekoe, Dorina A., ed. 2012. *Voting in Fear: Electoral Violence in Sub-Saharan Africa*. Washington, DC: United States Institute of Peace Press.
Bekoe, Dorina A. and Stephanie M. Burchard. 2017. "The Contradictions of Pre-election Violence: The Effects of Violence on Voter Turnout in Sub-Saharan Africa." *African Studies Review* 60(2):1–20.
Benesch, Susan. 2011. "Election-Related Violence: The Role of Dangerous Speech." *Proceedings of the Annual Meeting (American Society of International Law)* 105:389–391.
Berenschot, Ward. 2012. *Riot Politics: Hindu-Muslim Violence and the Indian State*. New York: Columbia University Press.
Birch, Sarah. 2020. *Electoral Violence, Corruption, and Political Order*. Princeton, NJ: Princeton University Press.
Birch, Sarah and David Muchlinski. 2018. "Electoral Violence Prevention: What Works?" *Democratization* 25(3):385–403.
Birch, Sarah, Ursula Daxecker and Kristine Höglund. 2020. "Electoral Violence: An Introduction." *Journal of Peace Research* 57(1):3–14.
Blair, Graeme, Alexander Coppock and Margaret Moor. 2020. "When to Worry about Sensitivity Bias: A Social Reference Theory and Evidence from 30 Years of List Experiments." *American Political Science Review* 114(4): 1297–1315.
Blakeslee, David S. 2013. "Propaganda and Ethno-Religious Politics in Developing Countries: Evidence from India." Unpublished manuscript.
Bleck, Jaimie and Nicolas van de Walle. 2018. *Electoral Politics in Africa since 1990: Continuity in Change*. Cambridge: Cambridge University Press.
Boafo-Arthur, Kwame. 2008. "Democracy and Stability in West Africa: The Ghanaian Experience." www.pcr.uu.se/digitalAssets/18/18579_CAMP4-Kwame.pdf
Boas, Taylor C. 2010. "Varieties of Electioneering Success Contagion and Presidential Campaigns in Latin America." *World Politics* 62(4):636–675.
Boas, Taylor C. 2016. *Presidential Campaigns in Latin America: Electoral Strategies and Success Contagion*. New York: Cambridge University Press.
Boas, Taylor C., F. Daniel Hidalgo and Marcus André Melo. 2018. "Norms versus Action: Why Voters Fail to Sanction Malfeasance in Brazil." *American Journal of Political Science* 63(2):385–400.
Bob-Milliar, George M. 2014. "Party Youth Activists and Low-intensity Electoral Violence in Ghana: A Qualitative Study of Party Foot Soldiers' Activism." *African Studies Quarterly* 15(1):125–152.

Boone, Catherine. 2011. "Politically Allocated Land Rights and the Geography of Electoral Violence: The Case of Kenya in the 1990s." *Comparative Political Studies* 44(10):1311–1342.

Borba, Felipe, Miguel Carnevale, Livia Brito and Pedro Bahia. 2020. Observatorio da Violencia Política E Eleitoral no Brasil. Grupo de Investigação Eleitoral, Universidade Federal do Estado do Rio de Janeiro Rio de Janeiro.

Branch, Daniel. 2011. *Kenya: Between Hope and Despair, 1963–2010*. New Haven and London: Yale University Press.

Brass, Paul R. 1997. *Theft of an Idol: Text and Context in the Representation of Collective Violence*. Princeton, NJ: Princeton University Press.

Brass, Paul R. 2003. *The Production of Hindu-Muslim Violence in Contemporary India*. Seattle and London: University of Washington.

Bratton, Michael. 2008. "Vote Buying and Violence in Nigerian Election Campaigns." *Electoral Studies* 27(4):621–632.

Bratton, Michael and Eldred Masunungure. 2007. "Popular Reactions to State Repression: Operation Murambatsvina in Zimbabwe." *African Affairs* 106(422):21–45.

Bratton, Michael and Mwangi S. Kimenyi. 2008. "Voting in Kenya: Putting Ethnicity in Perspective." *Journal of Eastern African Studies* 2(2):272–289.

Brierley, Sarah and Eric Kramon. 2020. "Party Campaign Strategies in Ghana: Rallies, Canvassing and Handouts." *African Affairs* 119(477):587–603.

Brierley, Sarah and Noah L. Nathan. 2021. "The Connections of Party Brokers: Which Brokers Do Parties Select?" *Journal of Politics* 83(3):884–901.

Broockman, David E. and Christopher Skovron. 2018. "Bias in Perceptions of Public Opinion among Political Elites." *American Political Science Review* 112(3):542–563.

Brosché, Johan, Hanne Fjelde and Kristine Höglund. 2020. "Electoral Violence and the Legacy of Authoritarian Rule in Kenya and Zambia." *Journal of Peace Research* 57(1):111–125.

Bueno de Mesquita, Ethan, C. Christine Fair, Jenna Jordan, Rasul Bakhsh Rais and Jacob N. Shapiro. 2015. "Measuring Political Violence in Pakistan: Insights from the BFRS Dataset." *Conflict Management and Peace Science* 32(5):536–558.

Burchard, Stephanie M. 2015. *Electoral Violence in Sub-Saharan Africa: Causes and Consequences*. Boulder and London: First Forum Press.

Burchard, Stephanie M. 2020. "Get Out the Vote or Else: The Impact of Fear of Election Violence on Voters." *Democratization* 27(4):588–604.

Butler, Daniel M. and Adam M. Dynes. 2016. "How Politicians Discount the Opinions of Constituents with Whom They Disagree." *American Journal of Political Science* 60(4):975–989.

Butler, Daniel M. and David W. Nickerson. 2011. "Can Learning Constituency Opinion Affect How Legislators Vote? Results from a Field Experiment." *Quarterly Journal of Political Science* 6(1):55–83.

Chaturvedi, Ashish. 2005. "Rigging Elections with Violence." *Public Choice* 125(1/2):189–202.

Cheeseman, Nic. 2008. "The Kenyan Elections of 2007: An Introduction." *Journal of Eastern African Studies* 2(2):166–184.
Claes, Jonas, ed. 2016. *Electing Peace: Violence Prevention and Impact at the Polls.* Washington, DC: United States Institute of Peace Press.
Collier, Paul and Pedro C. Vicente. 2012. "Violence, Bribery, and Fraud: The Political Economy of Elections in Sub-Saharan Africa." *Public Choice* 153(1–2):117–147.
Collier, Paul and Pedro C. Vicente. 2014. "Votes and Violence: Evidence from a Field Experiment in Nigeria." *The Economic Journal* 124(574): 327–355.
Condra, Luke N., James D. Long, Andrew C. Shaver and Austin L. Wright. 2018. "The Logic of Insurgent Electoral Violence." *American Economic Review* 108(11):3199–3231.
Coppedge, Michael, John Gerring, Carl Henrik Knutsen, Staffan I. Lindberg, Jan Teorell, Nazifa Alizada, David Altman, Michael Bernhard, Agnes Cornell, M. Steven Fish, Lisa Gastaldi, Haakon Gjerlow, Adam Glynn, Allen Hicken, Garry Hindle, Nina Ilchenko, Joshua Krusell, Anna Luhrmann, Seraphine F. Maerz, Kyle L. Marquardt, Kelly McMann, Valeriya Mechkova, Juraj Medzihorsky, Pamela Paxton, Daniel Pemstein, Josefine Pernes, Johannes von Romer, Brigitte Seim, Rachel Sigman, Svend-Erik Skaaning, Jeffrey Staton, Aksel Sundstrom, Eitan Tzelgov, Yi-ting Wang, Tore Wig, Steven Wilson and Daniel Ziblatt. 2021. "V-Dem Country-Year Dataset v11.1."
Cowie, Sam. 2018. "Political Violence Surges in Brazil as Far-Right Strongman Bolsonaro Inches Closer to the Presidency." https://theintercept.com/2018/10/16/jair-bolsonaros-brazil-political-violence/
Danso, Kwaku and Ernest Lartey. 2012. Democracy on a Knife Edge: Ghana's Democratization Processes, Institutional Malaise and the Challenge of Electoral Violence. In *Managing Election-Related Violence for Democratic Stability in Ghana*, ed. Kwesi Aning and Kwaku Danso. Accra: Friedrich-Ebert-Stiftung Ghana, Chapter 2.
Datta, Sreeradha. 2004. *Bangladesh: A Fragile Democracy.* Delhi: Shipra Publications.
Daxecker, Ursula. 2020. "Unequal Votes, Unequal Violence: Malapportionment and Election Violence in India." *Journal of Peace Research* 57(1): 156–170.
Daxecker, Ursula and Alexander Jung. 2018. "Mixing Votes with Violence : Election Violence around the World." *SAIS Review of International Affairs* 38(1):53–64.
Daxecker, Ursula E. 2012. "The Cost of Exposing Cheating: International Election Monitoring, Fraud, and Post-election Violence in Africa." *Journal of Peace Research* 49(4):503–516.
Daxecker, Ursula, Elio Amicarelli and Alexander Jung. 2019. "Electoral Contention and Violence (ECAV): A New Dataset." *Journal of Peace Research* 56(5):714–723.
De Quidt, Jonathan, Johannes Haushofer and Christopher Roth. 2018. "Measuring and Bounding Experimenter Demand." *American Economic Review* 108(11):3266–3302.

Debrah, Emmanuel. 2011. "Measuring Governance Institutions' Success in Ghana: The Case of the Electoral Commission, 1993–2008." *African Studies* 70(1):25–45.
Dercon, Stefan and Roxana Gutiérrez-Romero. 2012. "Triggers and Characteristics of the 2007 Kenyan Electoral Violence." *World Development* 40(4):731–744.
Dhattiwala, Raheel and Michael Biggs. 2012. "The Political Logic of Ethnic Violence: The Anti-Muslim Pogrom in Gujarat, 2002." *Politics & Society* 40(4):483–516.
Eck, Kristine 2012. "In Data We Trust? A Comparison of UCDP GED and ACLED Conflict Events Datasets." *Cooperation and Conflict* 47(1):124–141.
Ellman, Matthew and Leonard Wantchekon. 2000. "Electoral Competition Under the Threat of Political Unrest." *Quarterly Journal of Economics* 115(2):499–531.
Eyster, Erik and Matthew Rabin. 2010. "Naïve Herding in Rich-Information Settings." *American Economic Journal: Microeconomics* 2(4):221–243.
Fearon, James D. and David D. Laitin. 1996. "Explaining Interethnic Cooperation." *American Political Science Review* 90(4):715–735.
Fearon, James D. and David D. Laitin. 2000. "Violence and the Social Construction of Ethnic Identity." *International Organization* 54(4):845–877.
Fischer, Jeff. 2002. "Electoral Conflict and Violence. A Strategy for Study and Prevention." *IFES White Papers*. Washington, DC: International Foundation for Electoral Systems.
Fjelde, Hanne. 2020. "Political Party Strength and Electoral Violence." *Journal of Peace Research* 57(1):140–155.
Fjelde, Hanne and Kristine Höglund. 2015. "Electoral Institutions and Electoral Violence in Sub-Saharan Africa." *British Journal of Political Science* 46(2):297–320.
Fox, Michael. 2020. "Bolsonaro Loses Big in Brazil's Local Elections." https://theworld.org/stories/2020-11-16/bolsonaro-loses-big-brazil-s-local-elections
Geer, John G. 1996. *From Tea Leaves to Opinion Polls: A Theory of Democratic Leadership*. New York: Columbia University Press.
Gerber, Alan, Donald P. Green and Edward H. Kaplan. 2004. The Illusion of Learning from Observational Research. In *Problems and Methods in the Study of Politics*, ed. Ian Shapiro, Rogers M. Smith and Tarek E. Masoud. Cambridge: Cambridge University Press, Chapter 12, pp. 251–273.
Gerber, Alan S. and Donald P. Green. 2000. "The Effects of Canvassing, Telephone Calls, and Direct Mail on Voter Turnout: A Field Experiment." *American Political Science Review* 94(3):653–663.
Gibson, Clark C. and James D. Long. 2009. "The presidential and parliamentary elections in Kenya, December 2007." *Electoral Studies* 28(3):497–502.
Gleditsch, Nils Petter, Peter Wallensteen, Mikael Eriksson, Margareta Sollenberg and Håvard Strand. 2002. "Armed Conflict 1946–2001 : A New Dataset *." *Journal of Peace Research* 39(5):615–637.
Goldring, Edward and Michael Wahman. 2018. "Fighting for a Name on the Ballot: Constituency-level Analysis of Nomination Violence in Zambia." *Democratization* 25(6):996–1015.

Greenberg, Jeff, Tom Pyszczynski, Sheldon Solomon, Abram Rosenblatt, Mitchell Veeder and Shari Kirkland. 1990. "Evidence for Terror Management Theory II: The Effects of Mortality Salience on Reactions to Those Who Threaten or Bolster the Cultural Worldview." *Journal of Personality and Social Psychology* 58(2):308–318.

Gutiérrez-Romero, Roxana. 2014. "An Inquiry into the Use of Illegal Electoral Practices and Effects of Political Violence and Vote-Buying." *Journal of Conflict Resolution* 58(8):1500–1527.

Gutiérrez-Romero, Roxana and Adrienne LeBas. 2020. "Does Electoral Violence Affect Vote Choice and Willingness to Vote? Conjoint Analysis of a Vignette Experiment." *Journal of Peace Research* 57(1):77–92.

Gyimah-Boadi, E. 2009. "Another Step Forward for Ghana." *Journal of Democracy* 20(2):138–152.

Hafner-Burton, Emilie M., Susan D. Hyde and Ryan S. Jablonski. 2013. "When Do Governments Resort to Election Violence?" *British Journal of Political Science* 44(1):149–179.

Hafner-Burton, Emilie M., Susan D. Hyde and Ryan S. Jablonski. 2018. "Surviving Elections: Election Violence, Incumbent Victory and Post-Election Repercussions." *British Journal of Political Science* 48(2):459–488.

Hagen, Ryan, Kinga Makovi and Peter Bearman. 2013. "The Influence of Political Dynamics on Southern Lynch Mob Formation and Lethality." *Social Forces* 92(2):757–787.

Hainmueller, Jens, Daniel J. Hopkins and Teppei Yamamoto. 2014. "Causal Inference in Conjoint Analysis: Understanding Multidimensional Choices via Stated Preference Experiments." *Political Analysis* 22(1):1–30.

Hainmueller, Jens, Dominik Hangartner and Teppei Yamamoto. 2015. "Validating Vignette and Conjoint Survey Experiments against Real-world Behavior." *Proceedings of the National Academy of Sciences* 112(8):2395–2400.

Harish, S. P. and Risa Toha. 2019. "A New Typology of Electoral Violence: Insights from Indonesia." *Terrorism and Political Violence* 31(4):687–711.

Harris, J. Andrew. 2013. "'Stain Removal': Measuring the Effect of Violence on Local Ethnic Demography in Kenya." Unpublished manuscript.

Hersh, Eitan D. 2015. *Hacking the Electorate: How Campaigns Perceive Voters.* New York: Cambridge University Press.

Hertel-Fernandez, Alexander, Matto Mildenberger and Leah C. Stokes. 2019. "Legislative Staff and Representation in Congress." *American Political Science Review* 113(1):1–18.

Hoffman, Bruce and Gordon H. McCormick. 2004. "Terrorism, Signaling, and Suicide Attack." *Studies in Conflict & Terrorisim* 27(4):243–281.

Höglund, Kristine. 2009. "Electoral Violence in Conflict-Ridden Societies: Concepts, Causes, and Consequences." *Terrorism and Political Violence* 21(3): 412–427.

Höglund, Kristine and Anton Piyarathne. 2009. "Paying the Price for Patronage: Electoral Violence in Sri Lanka." *Commonwealth & Comparative Politics* 47(3):287–307.

Horiuchi, Yusaku, Zachary Markovich and Teppei Yamamoto. 2022. "Does Conjoint Analysis Mitigate Social Desirability Bias?" *Political Analysis* 30(4): 535–549.

Horowitz, Donald L. 1985. *Ethnic Groups in Conflict.* Berkeley, Los Angeles, and London: University of California Press.
Horowitz, Donald L. 2001. *The Deadly Ethnic Riot.* Berkeley and Los Angeles: University of California Press.
Horowitz, Jeremy. 2016. "The Ethnic Logic of Campaign Strategy in Diverse Societies: Theory and Evidence from Kenya." *Comparative Political Studies* 49(3):324–356.
Horowitz, Jeremy and Kathleen Klaus. 2020. "Can Politicians Exploit Ethnic Grievances? An Experimental Study of Land Appeals in Kenya." *Political Behavior* 42(1):35–58.
Human Rights Watch. 1993. Divide and Rule: State-Sponsored Ethnic Violence in Kenya.
Human Rights Watch. 1995a. Kenya. In *Slaughter Among Neighbors: The Political Origins of Communal Violence.* New Haven & London: Yale University Press, Chapter 7.
Human Rights Watch. 1995b. *Slaughter Among Neighbors: The Political Origins of Communal Violence.* New Haven & London: Yale University Press.
Human Rights Watch. 2002. Playing with Fire: Weapons Proliferation, Political Violence, and Human Rights in Kenya.
Human Rights Watch. 2003. Testing Democracy: Political Violence in Nigeria. New York.
Human Rights Watch. 2004. Nigeria's 2003 Elections: The Unacknowledged Violence.
Human Rights Watch. 2007. Criminal Politics: Violence, "Godfathers" and Corruption in Nigeria.
Human Rights Watch. 2013. High Stakes: Political Violence and the 2013 Elections in Kenya.
Husain, Neila. 2002. "Armed & Dangerous: Small Arms and Explosives Trafficking in Bangladesh." *South Asia Intelligence Review* 1:13–14.
Hyde, Susan D. and Nikolay Marinov. 2012. "Which Elections Can Be Lost?" *Political Analysis* 20(2):191–210.
Iyer, Sriya and Anand Shrivastava. 2018. "Religious Riots and Electoral Politics in India." *Journal of Development Economics* 131:104–122.
Kagwanja, Peter Mwangi. 2003. "Facing Mount Kenya or Facing Mecca? The Mungiki, Ethnic Violence and the Politics of the Moi Succession in Kenya, 1987–2002." *African Affairs* (102):25–49.
Kalla, Joshua L. and David E. Broockman. 2018. "The Minimal Persuasive Effects of Campaign Contact in General Elections: Evidence from 49 Field Experiments." *American Political Science Review* 112(1):148–166.
Kalla, Joshua L. and Ethan Porter. 2021. "Correcting Bias in Perceptions of Public Opinion among American Elected Officials: Results from Two Field Experiments." *British Journal of Political Science* 51(4):1792–1800.
Kalyvas, Stathis N. 2006. *The Logic of Violence in Civil War.* Cambridge: Cambridge University Press.
Kamungi, Prisca Mbura. 2009. "The Politics of Displacement in Multiparty Kenya." *Journal of Contemporary African Studies* 27(3):345–364.

Kanyinga, Karuti. 2009. "The Legacy of the White Highlands: Land Rights, Ethnicity and the Post-2007 Election Violence in Kenya." *Journal of Contemporary African Studies* 27(3):325–344.

Kanyinga, Karuti. 2011. "Stopping a Conflagration: The Response of Kenyan Civil Society to the Post-2007 Election Violence." *Politikon* 38(1):85–109.

Kanyinga, Karuti. 2018. "Elections without Constitutionalism: Votes, Violence, and Democracy Gaps in Africa." *African Journal of Democracy and Governance* 5(4):147–168.

Kapferer, Bruce. 1988. *Legends of People, Myths of State: Violence, Intolerance, and Political Culture in Sri Lanka and Australia*. Washington and London: Smithsonian Institution Press.

Kasara, Kimuli. 2016. "Electoral Geography and Conflict: Examining the Redistricting through Violence in Kenya." Unpublished manuscript.

Katumanga, Musambayi. 2005. "A City under Siege: Banditry & Modes of Accumulation in Nairobi, 1991–2004." *Review of African Political Economy* 32(106):505–520.

Kaufmann, Chaim. 1996. "Possible and Impossible Solutions to Ethnic Civil Wars." *International Security* 20(4):136–175.

Kearney, Robert N. 1985. "Ethnic Conflict and the Tamil Separatist Movement in Sri Lanka." *Asian Survey* 25(9):898–917.

Kenya National Bureau of Statistics. 2019. 2019 Kenya Population and Housing Census, Volume IV: Distribution of Population by Socio-Economic Characteristics. Government of the Republic of Kenya Nairobi: www.knbs.or.ke/down load/2019-kenya-population-and-housing-census-volume-iv-distribution-of-po pulation-by-socio-economic-characteristics/.

Kenya Truth Justice and Reconciliation Commission. 2013. Report of the Truth, Justice and Reconciliation Commission: Abridged Version.

Kimenyi, Mwangi S. and Njuguna S. Ndung'u. 2005. Sporadic Ethnic Violence: Why Has Kenya Not Experienced a Full-Blown Civil War? In *Understanding Civil War: Evidence and Analysis, Volume 1: Africa*, ed. Paul Collier and Nicholas Sambanis. Washington, DC: The World Bank Chapter 5.

Kishi, Roudabeh, Hampton Stall and Sam Jones. 2020. The Future of 'Stop the Steal': Post-Election Trajectories for Right-Wing Mobilization in the US. ACLED.

Klaus, Kathleen. 2020. *Political Violence in Kenya: Land, Elections, and Claim-Making*. Cambridge: Cambridge University Press.

Klaus, Kathleen and Matthew I. Mitchell. 2015. "Land Grievances and the Mobilization of Electoral Violence: Evidence from côte d'ivoire and Kenya." *Journal of Peace Research* 52(5):622–635.

Klopp, Jacqueline M. 2001. "'Ethnic Clashes' and Winning Elections: The Case of Kenya's Electoral Despotism." *Canadian Journal of African Studies* 35(3):463–517.

Klopp, Jacqueline and Prisca Kamungi. 2008. "Violence and Elections: Will Kenya Collapse?" *World Policy Journal* 24(4):11–18.

KNCHR. 2008. On the Brink of the Precipice: A Human Rights Account of Kenya's Post-2007 Election Violence – Final Report. Kenya National Commission on Human Rights.

KNCHR. 2017*a*. Mirage at Dusk: A Human Rights Account of the 2017 General Election. Nairobi.
KNCHR. 2017*b*. Still a Mirage at Dusk: A Human Rights Account of the 2017 Fresh Presidential Elections.
Koch, Michael T. and Stephen P. Nicholson. 2016. "Death and Turnout: The Human Costs of War and Voter Participation in Democracies." *American Journal of Political Science* 60(4):932–946.
Kramon, Eric. 2016. "Electoral Handouts as Information: Explaining Unmonitored Vote Buying." *World Politics* 68(3):454–498.
Krasno, Jonathan S. and Donald P. Green. 2008*a*. "Do Televised Presidential Ads Increase Voter Turnout? Evidence from a Natural Experiment." *Journal of Politics* 70(1):245–261.
Krasno, Jonathan S. and Donald P. Green. 2008*b*. "Do Televised Presidential Ads Increase Voter Turnout? Evidence from a Natural Experiment." *Journal of Politics* 70(1):245–261.
Laakso, Liisa. 2007. Insights into Electoral Violence in Africa. In *Votes, Money and Violence*, ed. Matthias Basedau, Gero Erdmann and Andreas Mehler. Pietermaritzburg: University of KwaZulu-Natal Press, pp. 224–252.
Lau, Richard R. and Gerald M. Pomper. 2002. "Effectiveness of Negative Campaigning in U. S. Senate Elections." *American Journal of Political Science* 46(1):47–66.
Lau, Richard R., Lee Sigelman and Ivy Brown Rovner. 2007. "The Effects of Negative Political Campaigns: A Meta-Analytic Reassessment." *Journal of Politics* 69(4):1176–1209.
LeBas, Adrienne. 2010. "Ethnicity and the Willingness to Sanction Violent Politicians: Evidence from Kenya." Unpublished manuscript.
LeBas, Adrienne. 2013. "Violence and Urban Order in Nairobi, Kenya and Lagos, Nigeria." *Studies in Comparative International Development* 48(3): 240–262.
Linantud, John L. 1998. "Whither Guns, Goons, and Gold? The Decline of Factional Election Violence in the Philippines." *Contemporary Southeast Asia* 20(3):298–318.
Lindberg, Staffan I. 2004. "The Democratic Qualities of Competitive Elections: Participation, Competition and Legitimacy in Africa." *Commonwealth & Comparative Politics* 41(1):61–105.
Lupu, Noam and Rachel Beatty Riedl. 2013. "Political Parties and Uncertainty in Developing Democracies." *Comparative Political Studies* 46(11): 1339–1365.
Lynch, Gabrielle. 2009. "Durable Solution, Help or Hindrance? The Failings and Unintended Implications of Relief and Recovery Efforts for Kenya's Post-election IDPs." *Review of African Political Economy* 36(122): 604–610.
Lynch, Gabrielle. 2014. "Electing the 'Alliance of the Accused': The Success of the Jubilee Alliance in Kenya's Rift Valley." *Journal of Eastern African Studies* 8(1):93–114.
Lynch, Gabrielle, Nic Cheeseman and Justin Willis. 2019. "From Peace Campaigns to Peaceocracy: Elections, Order and Authority in Africa." *African Affairs* 118(473):603–627.

Mac Giollabhui, Shane. 2018. "Battleground: Candidate Selection and Violence in Africa's Dominant Political Parties." *Democratization* 25(6): 978–995.

Malik, Aditi. 2018. "Constitutional Reform and New Patterns of Electoral Violence: Evidence from Kenya's 2013 Elections." *Commonwealth and Comparative Politics* 56(3):340–359.

Malik, Aditi. 2021. "Hindu–Muslim Violence in Unexpected Places: Theory and Evidence from Rural India." *Politics, Groups, and Identities* 9(1):40–58.

Miller, Warren E. and Donald E. Stokes. 1963. "Constituency Influence in Congress." *American Political Science Review* 57(1):45–56.

Moniruzzaman, M. 2009. "Party Politics and Political Violence in Bangladesh: Issues, Manifestation and Consequences." *South Asian Survey* 16(1): 81–99.

Muchlinski, David, Xiao Yang, Sarah Birch, Craig MacDonald and Iadh Ounis. 2021. "We Need to Go Deeper: Measuring Electoral Violence Using Convolutional Neural Networks and Social Media." *Political Science Research and Methods* 9(1):122–139.

Mueller, Susanne D. 2008. "The Political Economy of Kenya's Crisis." *Journal of Eastern African Studies* 2(2):185–210.

Mueller, Susanne D. 2011. "Dying to Win: Elections, Political Violence, and Institutional Decay in Kenya." *Journal of Contemporary African Studies* 29(1):99–117.

Mummolo, Jonathan and Erik Peterson. 2019. "Demand Effects in Survey Experiments: An Empirical Assessment." *American Political Science Review* 113(2):517–529.

Mutahi, Patrick and Mutuma Ruteere. 2019. "Violence, Security and the Policing of Kenya's 2017 Elections." *Journal of Eastern African Studies* 13(2): 253–271.

Mutiga, Murithi. 2017. Violence, Land, and the Upcoming Vote in Kenya's Laikipia Region. Crisis Group.

Mutui, David Mutemi. 2011. Violence in Kenya: An Analysis of the Dimensions of Ethnic Violence Associated with Elites, 1991–2008. MA Thesis. University of Nairobi.

Nellis, Gareth, Michael Weaver and Steven C. Rosenzweig. 2016. "Do Parties Matter for Ethnic Violence? Evidence from India." *Quarterly Journal of Political Science* 11(2):249–277.

Nellis, Gareth and Niloufer Siddiqui. 2018. "Secular Party Rule and Religious Violence in Pakistan." *American Political Science Review* 112(1):49–67.

Nemeth, Stephen C. and Holley E. Hansen. 2022. "Political Competition and Right-Wing Terrorism: A County-Level Analysis of the United States." *Political Research Quarterly* 75(2):338–352.

Norris, Isaac and Chris Dalby. 2020. "Why Have Political Assassinations More Than Doubled in Brazil?". https://insightcrime.org/news/analysis/political-assassinations-doubled-in-brazil/

Oberschall, Anthony. 2000. "The Manipulation of Ethnicity: From Ethnic Cooperation to Violence and War in Yugoslavia." *Ethnic and Racial Studies* 23(6):982–1001.

Okoth-Ogendo, H. W. O. 1991. *Tenants of the Crown: Evolution of Agrarian Law and Institutions in Kenya*. Nairobi: African Centre for Technology Studies Press.

Okyere, Frank. 2016. Electoral Violence and Mass Atrocity Prevention in Ghana: Contextualizing the Atrocity Prevention Framework. In *Managing Election-Related Conflict and Violence for Democratic Stability in Ghana II*, ed. Kwesi Aning, Kwaku Danso and Naila Salihu. Accra: Kofi Annan International Peacekeeping Training Centre, Chapter 3.

Ortoleva, Pietro and Erik Snowberg. 2015. "Overconfidence in Political Behavior." *American Economic Review* 105(2):504–535.

Oyewole, Samuel and J. Shola Omotola. 2022. "Violence in Nigeria's 2019 General Elections: Trend and Geospatial Dimensions." *GeoJournal* 87:2393–2403.

Paraguassu, Lisandra. 2020. "Brazilian Politics Hit by Wave of Violence Ahead of Sunday Vote." www.reuters.com/article/brazil-politics-violence/brazilian-politics-hit-by-wave-of-violence-ahead-of-sunday-vote-idUSKBN2872A0

Petersen, Roger B. 2002. *Understanding Ethnic Violence: Fear, Hatred, and Resentment in Twentieth-Century Eastern Europe*. Cambridge: Cambridge University Press.

Rabushka, Alvin and Kenneth A. Shepsle. 1972. *Politics in Plural Societies: A Theory of Democratic Instability*. Columbus, OH: Charles E. Merrill Publishing Company.

Rauschenbach, Mascha and Katrin Paula. 2019. "Intimidating Voters with Violence and Mobilizing Them with Clientelism." *Journal of Peace Research* 56(5):682–696.

Reeder, Bryce W. and Merete Bech Seeberg. 2018. "Fighting Your Friends? A Study of Intra-party Violence in Sub-Saharan Africa." *Democratization* 25(6):1033–1051.

Reno, William. 2011. *Warfare in Independent Africa*. New York: Cambridge University Press.

Riedl, Rachel Beatty. 2014. *Authoritarian Origins of Democratic Party Systems in Africa*. Cambridge: Cambridge University Press.

Robbins, Joseph, Lance Hunter and Gregg R. Murray. 2013. "Voters versus Terrorists: Analyzing the Effect of Terrorist Events on Voter Turnout." *Journal of Peace Research* 50(4):495–508.

Robinson, James A. and Ragnar Torvik. 2009. "The Real Swing Voter's Curse." *American Economic Review: Papers & Proceedings* 99(2):310–315.

Rosenfeld, Bryn, Kosuke Imai and Jacob N. Shapiro. 2016. "An Empirical Validation Study of Popular Survey Methodologies for Sensitive Questions." *American Journal of Political Science* 60(3):783–802.

Rosenzweig, Steven C. 2020. "Group Norms, Social Pressure, and Ethnic Voting." Unpublished manuscript.

Rosenzweig, Steven C. 2021. "Dangerous Disconnect: Voter Backlash, Elite Misperception, and the Costs of Violence as an Electoral Tactic." *Political Behavior* 43(4):1731–1754.

Seeberg, Merete Bech, Michael Wahman and Svend Erik Skaaning. 2018. "Candidate Nomination, Intra-party Democracy, and Election Violence in Africa." *Democratization* 25(6):959–977.

Sheffer, Lior, Peter John Loewen, Stuart Soroka, Stefaan Walgrave and Tamir Sheafer. 2018. "Nonrepresentative Representatives: An Experimental Study of the Decision Making of Elected Politicians." *American Political Science Review* 112(2):302–321.

Siddiqui, Niloufer A. 2022. *Under the Gun: Political Parties and Violence in Pakistan*. Cambridge: Cambridge University Press.

Sithole, Anyway. 2012. Ghana: A Beacon of Hope in Africa. The African Centre for the Constructive Resolution of Disputes.

Sives, Amanda. 2010. *Elections, Violence and the Democratic Process in Jamaica: 1944–2007*. Kingston and Miami: Ian Randle Publishers.

Smidt, Hannah. 2016. "From a Perpetrator's Perspective: International Election Observers and Post-electoral Violence." *Journal of Peace Research* 53(2): 226–241.

Smidt, Hannah. 2020. "Mitigating Election Violence Locally: UN Peacekeepers' Election-Education Campaigns in Côte d'Ivoire." *Journal of Peace Research* 57(1):199–216.

Söderberg Kovacs, Mimmi. 2018. Introduction: The Everyday Politics of Electoral Violence in Africa. In *Violence in African Elections: Between Democracy and Big Man Politics*, ed. Mimmi Söderberg Kovacs and Jesper Bjarnesen. Uppsala and London: Nordic Africa Institute and Zed Books, pp. 1–26.

Sorrensen, M. P. K. 1968. *Origins of European Settlement in Kenya*. Nairobi: Oxford University Press.

Stall, Hampton, Roudabeh Kishi and Clionadh Raleigh. 2020. Standing By: Right-Wing Militia Groups and the US Election. ACLED.

Staniland, Paul. 2014. "Violence and Democracy." *Comparative Politics* 47(1):99–118.

Steele, Abbey. 2011. "Electing Displacement: Political Cleansing in Apartado, Colombia." *Journal of Conflict Resolution* 55(3):423–445.

Straus, Scott and Charlie Taylor. 2012. Democratization and Electoral Violence in Sub-Saharan Africa, 1990–2008. In *Voting in Fear: Electoral Violence in Sub-Saharan Africa*, ed. Dorina A. Bekoe. Washington, DC: United States Institute of Peace Press, Chapter 2, pp. 15–38.

Suryadinata, Leo. 2002. *Elections and Politics in Indonesia*. Singapore: Institute of Southeast Asian Studies.

Tadjoeddin, Mohammad Zulfan. 2012. "Electoral Conflict and the Maturity of Local Democracy in Indonesia: Testing the Modernisation hypothesis." *Journal of the Asia Pacific Economy* 17(3):476–497.

Tadjoeddin, Mohammad Zulfan. 2014. *Explaining Collective Violence in Contemporary Indonesia: From Conflict to Cooperation*. London: Palgrave Macmillan.

Tolnay, Stewart E. and E. M. Beck. 1995. Southern Politics and Lynching, 1880–1900. In *A Festival of Violence: An Analysis of Southern Lynchings, 1882–1930*. Vol. 2 Urbana and Chicago: University of Illinois Press, Chapter 6, pp. 167–201.

Traviglianti, Manuela. 2014. "Coercing the Co-Ethnic Vote: Violence against Co-Ethnics in Burundi's 2010 Elections." Unpublished manuscript.

Treisman, Daniel. 2020. "Democracy by Mistake: How the Errors of Autocrats Trigger Transitions to Freer Government." *American Political Science Review* 114(3):792–810.
Turnbull, Megan. 2021. "Elite Competition, Social Movements, and Election Violence in Nigeria." *International Security* 45(3):40–78.
Vaishnav, Milan. 2017. *When Crime Pays: Money and Muscle in Indian Politics*. New Haven & London: Yale University Press.
van Klinken, Gerry. 2007. *Communal Violence and Democratization in Indonesia: Small Town Wars*. New York: Routledge.
Varshney, Ashutosh, Mohammad Zulfan Tadjoeddin and Rizal Panggabean. 2008. "Creating Datasets in Information-Poor Environments: Patterns of Collective Violence in Indonesia, 1990–2003." *Journal of East Asian Studies* 8(3):361–394.
Verkaaik, Oskar. 2004. *Migrants and Militants: Fun and Urban Violence in Pakistan*. Princeton: Princeton University Press.
von Borzyskowski, Inken. 2019. *The Credibility Challenge: How Democracy Aid Influences Election Violence*. Ithaca: Cornell University Press.
von Borzyskowski, Inken, Ursula Daxecker and Patrick M. Kuhn. 2021. "Fear of Campaign Violence and Support for Democracy and Autocracy." *Conflict Management and Peace Science* 39(5):073889422110263.
Wahman, Michael and Edward Goldring. 2020. "Pre-election Violence and Territorial Control: Political Dominance and Subnational Election Violence in Polarized African Electoral Systems." *Journal of Peace Research* 57(1):93–110.
Waki Commission. 2008. Waki Report. Commission of Inquiry on Post Election Violence.
Wantchekon, Leonard. 1999. "On the Nature of First Democratic Elections." *Journal of Conflict Resolution* 43(2):245–258.
Wanyama, Fredrick O. and Jørgen Elklit. 2018. "Electoral violence during party primaries in Kenya." *Democratization* 25(6):1016–1032.
Wasserman, Justin and Edwin Jaggard. 2007. "Electoral Violence in Mid Nineteenth-Century England and Wales." *Historical Research* 80(207):124–155.
Weidmann, Nils B. 2015. "On the Accuracy of Media-Based Conflict Event Data." *Journal of Conflict Resolution* 59(6):1129–1149.
Weidmann, Nils B. 2016. "A Closer Look at Reporting Bias in Conflict Data." *American Journal of Political Science* 60(1):206–218.
Wilkinson, Steven I. 2004. *Votes and Violence: Electoral Competition and Ethnic Riots in India*. Cambridge: Cambridge University Press.
Wilkinson, Steven I. 2012. A Constructivist Model of Ethnic Riots. In *Constructivist Theories of Ethnic Politics*, ed. Kanchan Chandra. New York: Oxford University Press, pp. 359–386.
Wilkinson, Steven I. and Christopher J. Haid. 2009. "Ethnic Violence as Campaign Expenditure: Riots, Competition, and Vote Swings in India." Unpublished manuscript.
Wilson, Chris. 2008. Political Exploitation: the Putih-Kuning. In *Ethnoreligious Violence in Indonesia: From Soil to God*. London and New York: Routledge.

Wilson, Ian. 2010. The Rise and Fall of Political Gangsters in Indonesian Democracy. In *Problems of Democratization in Indonesia: Elections, Institutions and Society*, ed. Edward Aspinall and Marcus Mietzner. Singapore: Institute of Southeast Asian Studies, pp. 130–146.

Young, Lauren E. 2019. "The Psychology of State Repression: Fear and Dissent Decisions in Zimbabwe." *American Political Science Review* 113(1):140–155.

Zounmenou, David. 2009. Ghana's 2008 Election: Towards a Consolidated Democracy? Institute for Security Studies.

Index

Acemoglu, Daron, 26, 51, 52, 60, 87
Afrobarometer, 11, 53, 61, 87, 95, 103, 165
Akiwumi report, 31–32, 38, 77, 165
anchoring, 12–13, 65, 66, 69–70, 127, see also cognitive bias

Bangladesh, 6, 22, 25, 26
Birch, Sarah, 4, 8, 46, 145, 161
Boas, Taylor, 12, 62, 63, 67–71, 131, 151
Bolsonaro, Jair, 151–153, 155
Boone, Catherine, 8, 36, 49, 79, 110
Brass, Paul, 10, 22, 26, 29, 57, 59, 124, 138
Bratton, Michael, 9, 53, 55, 60, 97, 130
Brazil, 136, 151–155
Broockman, David, 12, 63, 64, 162
Burchard, Stephanie, 8, 46–47, 53
Burundi, 22, 24–25, 28–29, 52
Butler, Daniel, 64–65, 69, 160

Coast (region of Kenya), 31, 34, 35, 38, 68, 76, 79
cognitive bias, 12–14, 65–66, 69–72, 124, 126, 127, 160, see also anchoring, confirmation bias, overconfidence, status quo bias
Collier, Paul, 9, 11, 27, 52–53, 58, 60–61, 105, 128, 160
Colombia, 6, 26, 28, 51–52, 55, 60
communal riots, see ethnic riots
confirmation bias, 13, 65, 66, 69–71, 127, see also cognitive bias

core voters, 11, 35, 41, 52, 61, 98, 105, 118, 129, 141, 156, 160
criminal gangs, see gangs
criminal organizations, see gangs

Daxecker, Ursula, 3–5, 8, 27, 47, 50, 147
displacement, 6, 9, 31–33, 35, 37, 41, 53–55, 87–90, 114, 121–123, 130

El Salvador, 51
electoral commissions, see electoral institutions
electoral fraud, see fraud
electoral institutions, 8, 46–47, 50, 137, 143–146
electoral rules, see electoral institutions
elite misperception, see misperception
ethnic riots, 22, 26, 29, 59, 138–140, see also riots

founding elections, 2, 13–14, 44, 66–72, 127, 131–135, 140, 142, 143, 146, 147, 149–151, 153–154, 159, 161
fraud, 49, 51, 148–149

gangs, 6, 7, 24–26, 28, 32, 36, 39, 51, 130, 138, 147–148, 150, 151, 153
Ghana, 131, 136, 143–146, 154
Golkar, 138–140
Gutiérrez-Romero, Roxana, 27, 61, 62, 91, 103

Hafner-Burton, Emilie, 8, 46–47, 52, 160

Harish, S.P., 4, 27, 45
Harris, J. Andrew, 5, 9, 32, 54, 88, 90
Höglund, Kristine, 4–5, 25
Horowitz, Donald, 4, 10, 29, 41–43, 56–58
Horowitz, Jeremy, 30, 105, 112
Hyde, Susan, 8, 46–47, 52, 133, 160

ICC, see International Criminal Court (ICC)
India, 6, 22, 26, 29, 57, 59, 138
Indonesia, 6, 22, 25–26, 29, 130–131, 136–140, 153
  New Order, 25, 130
internal displacement, see displacement
International Criminal Court (ICC), 37, 40, 81, 83

Jablonski, Ryan, 8, 46–47, 52, 160
Jamaica, 6, 22, 25, 28, 51

KADU, see Kenya African Democratic Union (KADU)
Kalenjin (ethnic group), 30–31, 34–40, 55, 84, 88
Kalla, Joshua, 12, 64, 65, 69, 124, 126, 160, 162
Kamba (ethnic group), 30
KANU, see Kenya African National Union (KANU)
Kanyinga, Karuti, 8, 33–37, 47–49, 110, 145
Karachi, 25, 62, 72, 140–143
Kasara, Kimuli, 5, 9, 54, 88
Kenya
  1990s election violence, see 1990s tribal clashes
  1990s tribal clashes, 6, 7, 31–32, 35–38, 68, 76–80, 89–90
  2007/08 election violence, 5, 7, 32–33, 36–55, 80–84, 103, 124, 128
  colonial era, 33–34, 49
  ethnicity in, 30–38, 40, 105, 110, see also Kalenjin (ethnic group), Kamba (ethnic group), Kikuyu (ethnic group), Luhya (ethnic group), Luo (ethnic group), Maasai (ethnic group)
  land conflict, 31, 35, 37, 49, 110, see also land distribution, land politics
  land distribution, 33–34, 49, 110, see also land conflict, land politics

land politics, 33–36, 49, 110, 111, see also land conflict, land distribution
tribes, see ethnicity in
Kenya African Democratic Union (KADU), 34
Kenya African National Union (KANU), 7, 31–32, 34–36, 38, 68, 71, 75–79, 88–90, 103, 131, 157
Kenyatta, Jomo, 34, 36
Kenyatta, Uhuru, 36, 37, 40, 83–125
Kibaki, Mwai, 36–37, 124, 128
Kikuyu (ethnic group), 30, 34–37, 39–40, 54, 83–84, 88, 94
Kimenyi, Mwangi, 33, 34, 41
Kisumu, 94, 116
Klaus, Kathleen, 8, 49, 110, 112
Klopp, Jacqueline, 1, 7, 10, 32, 35, 38, 57

LeBas, Adrienne, 32, 61, 62, 91
Luhya (ethnic group), 30, 35, 36
Luo (ethnic group), 30, 34–36, 83–84, 94

Maasai (ethnic group), 34–36, 38, 83, 94
majimbo, 34, 36, 68
Malik, Aditi, 11, 58, 160
militias, 6, 7, 21, 23–25, 37–39, 84, 88, 142, 151, 153
misperception, 2, 10–15, 63–66, 68–72, 115–129, 160, 162
Moi, Daniel arap, 31, 34–36, 68, 71, 77, 128
MQM (Muttahida Qaumi Movement), 25, 62, 72, 141–142
Mueller, Susanne D., 8, 37, 46, 145
Muhajir Qaumi Movement, see MQM (Muttahida Qaumi Movement)
Muttahida Qaumi Movement, see MQM (Muttahida Qaumi Movement)
Mutui, David Mutemi, 7, 33–35, 38

Nakuru, 31, 35, 94, 116
NARC, see National Rainbow Coalition (NARC)
Narok, 27, 31, 94, 116
National Rainbow Coalition (NARC), 32
Ndung'u, Njuguna, 33, 34, 41
NELDA (National Elections Across Democracy and Autocracy dataset), 133
Nickerson, David, 64–65, 69, 160
Nigeria, 6, 9, 22, 25, 28, 53–54, 60–61, 86, 136, 147–151, 154, 161

Odinga, Oginga, 34, 36
Odinga, Raila, 36–37, 83–128
ODM, *see* Orange Democratic Movement (ODM)
Orange Democratic Movement (ODM), 36, 40, 55
overconfidence, 12–13, 65, 66, 70, 71, *see also* cognitive bias

Pakistan, 6, 25, 62, 72, 136, 140–143, 154
Pakistan People's Party (PPP), 141, 142
paramilitaries, 6, 24–26, 28, 51–52, 60, 130, 153
Party of National Unity, *see* PNU (Party of National Unity)
PDP, *see* People's Democratic Party (PDP)
People's Democratic Party (PDP), 147–150
PNU (Party of National Unity), 33, 36, 55
politician misperception, *see* misperception
Porter, Ethan, 65, 69, 124, 126, 160

Rift Valley (region of Kenya), 31–32, 34–36, 38, 39, 54, 55, 68, 76, 79
right-wing militias, 21, 23, 26, 28, 51, 60
riots, 6, 22, 24, 26, 29, 36, 59, 138–140, *see also* ethnic riots
Robinson, James, 26, 51, 52, 60, 87
Ruto, William, 31, 40, 83–84

Santos, Rafael, 26, 51, 52, 60, 87
Siddiqui, Niloufer, 11–12, 24, 48, 58, 62, 91, 98, 105, 141, 160
Skovron, Christopher, 12, 63, 162
Söderberg Kovacs, Mimmi, 3, 5
Sri Lanka, 6, 22, 25, 26, 29, 56
Staniland, Paul, 1, 4, 9, 23, 24, 59

status quo bias, 12, 66, *see also* cognitive bias
Steele, Abbey, 5, 9, 55
Straus, Scott, 5, 27, 133, 147
Suharto, 25, 130
swing voters, 27, 52

Taylor, Charlie, 5, 27, 133, 147
TNA (The National Alliance), 83, 84
Toha, Risa, 4, 27, 45
Travaglianti, Manuela, 27, 29, 52, 87

United States of America (U.S.), 12, 21, 22, 63–65

van Klinken, Gerry, 29, 139–140
Vicente, Pedro, 9, 11, 27, 52–53, 58, 60–61, 105, 128, 160
vigilante groups, 24, 25, 32
violent displacement, *see* displacement
von Borzyskowski, Inken, 8, 9, 49, 50
voter backlash, 2, 6, 10–12, 44, 48, 58, 61–63, 66, 97, 99–101, 105, 113, 123, 125, 130–131, 138–139, 141–142, 158–160
against violence, *see* voter backlash
voter turnout, 9, 43, 52–54, 58, 60, 64, 87–91, 113–114

Wahman, Michael, 28, 48
Waki commission, 32, 37, 39, 76, 81, 128
Wilkinson, Steven, 1, 6, 10, 14, 22, 26, 29, 43, 48, 57, 59, 124
Wilson, Ian, 25, 130, 139

Zimbabwe, 55, 130

For EU product safety concerns, contact us at Calle de José Abascal, 56–1°, 28003 Madrid, Spain or eugpsr@cambridge.org.

www.ingramcontent.com/pod-product-compliance
Lightning Source LLC
LaVergne TN
LVHW041631060526
838200LV00040B/1529